SECRETS

OF YOUR

FAMILY

TREE

About the Authors

Dave Carder (B.A., M.A., Calvary Bible College; M.A., Wayne State University) serves as assistant pastor for counseling ministries at the First Evangelical Free Church of Fullerton, California. Together with his wife, Ronnie, Pastor Carder conducts marriage and family seminars. They are the parents of four children. Dave is the author or co-author of *Promises from Proverbs, Steps to a New Beginning,* and *Torn Asunder.*

As a licensed marriage, family, and child psychologist, **Earl R. Henslin** (Psy.D., Biola University) is in practice at the Harbor Family Practice in Fullerton, California. Dr. Henslin and his wife, Karen, have three children.

In addition to being co-director of the Minirth-Meier Clinic West, **John Townsend** (B.A., North Carolina State University; Th.M., Dallas Theological Seminary; M.A., Ph.D., Rosemead Graduate School of Psychology) has a private practice in Newport Beach, California. Dr. Townsend lives in Southern California with his wife, Barbi, and their son, Ricky.

Henry Cloud (B.S., Southern Methodist University; M.A., Ph.D., Rosemead Graduate School of Psychology) is co-director of the Minirth-Meier Clinic West, a Christian inpatient treatment program. He also has a private practice in Newport Beach, California. Dr. Cloud is the author of *When Your World Makes No Sense.*

Alice Brawand (B.A., Mars Hill College; M.A., Azusa Pacific University) has served for thirty-one years with Wycliffe Bible Translators, eleven of them in counseling missionaries and pastors from Wycliffe's International Headquarters in Dallas, Texas. Alice and her husband, John, have three children, all of whom were reared in Guatemala, where the Brawands served.

SECRETS

OF YOUR

FAMILY

TREE

*Healing for adult children
of dysfunctional families*

DAVE CARDER, M.A.
DR. EARL HENSLIN
DR. JOHN TOWNSEND
DR. HENRY CLOUD
ALICE BRAWAND, M.A.

Foreword by Charles R. Swindoll

MOODY PRESS
CHICAGO

To our fellow travelers,
who have taught us these concepts
in the various support groups
and therapy programs
with which we work

Contents

Foreword

How times have changed!

Back in the forties when I was a boy, the church and Christian circles had neither time nor tolerance for life's raw realities. Words such as rape and incest, homosexuality and child molestation were never heard from the pulpit and seldom, if ever, discussed in small groups. Those who were the involuntary victims of divorce or the objects of brutality were left to suffer in silence, feeling alienated and ashamed.

By the time I entered the ministry in the early sixties, the evangelical Christian community was a bit more open and realistic but still guarded and certainly reluctant to get involved. Families who struggled could find perhaps a caring pastor or a compassionate counselor, but the hope of receiving help from support groups in the church was virtually nonexistent. Those in the church who wrestled with an addiction were more often than not told to confess their sins and get a grip on themselves. And it wasn't uncommon for preachers to use the Bible as the basis for such exhortations. If they didn't "snap out of it," they were labeled as "sick" or, worse, "rebellious."

As we find ourselves in the last decade of the twentieth century, the painful truth has finally been allowed to come out of the closet. At long last, pastors and congregations alike have stopped whispering and started addressing the secret struggles that plague many, if not most, families. Rather than pounding pulpits and demanding instant change, we have discovered that dysfunctional families are often in the church, and that recovery takes time and is a painful process, and, in fact, that the process cannot be accelerated by cramming more and more convicting Scriptures down the throat of the abandoned or the abused. Guilt and shame are not friends of grace that prompt inner healing.

One of the benefits emerging from the long-awaited and much-needed change is a growing number of books that are designed to help those who hurt find healing. Unfortunately, many of these books are long on psychology and short on theology. The timeless principles of God's Word are eclipsed by human reasoning and man-made techniques and conclusions. They may sound plausible and make good sense, but they lack the power to effect lasting recovery. Frequently, these books reflect the bias of one author's pet hobbyhorse.

The book you hold in your hand is different. It is the result of five authors' work, not one. It has been written by those who are regularly in touch with reality, not dreamers dabbling in theory. Furthermore, it is based on the rock-hard truths of Scripture, not the sandy soil of nice-sounding ideas and suggestions dredged up from a collection of academic textbooks. Again and again you will find biblical examples and scriptural references, but they fit; they aren't forced. This balanced approach reassures the reader that he is not being led astray.

But don't think this is just another book on dysfunctional families. As I mentioned earlier, this one is different. It is hard-hitting, insightful, unpredictable, direct, and refreshingly candid. Best of all, it is realistic. The book promises no superquick fixes, no surefire guarantees, and no airtight solutions. It does, however, confront the issues that must be addressed, and it does ask the questions that need to be answered in order to find recovery.

I am encouraged that you are about to discover some essential *Secrets of Your Family Tree* and that in doing so, the all-important process of inner healing will soon be underway. Consider yourself fortunate to be living in this decade. It is doubtful that a book this straightforward would have even been published fifty years ago. If it had been, most in the church would never have read it.

I'm glad times have changed!

CHUCK SWINDOLL
Pastor, Author, Radio Bible Teacher

Acknowledgments

Collectively we are indebted to our spiritual mentor, Chuck Swindoll, who not only models an open family system but exemplifies in all his personal relationships the healthy patterns of emotional intimacy. Thanks too, Chuck, for making "church" a family worship time that is healing and biblical.

To Duncan Jaenicke, Acquisitions Editor at Moody Press, we say, *"We can't believe it!"* You win. You made us do it on time, in tune with each other, all the while staying in touch with our dreams, our desires, and our demands. Your way with words, your editorial expertise, and the energy you invested in this project are all unbelievable. Dunk, you're awesome!

Dave also wishes to thank Annie Husman, late night typist, after-hours editor, and behind-the-scenes computer expert, who translated all the wiggly lines, red arrows, and scratch marks into English.

Thanks go as well to Pat Lampman, Ph.D., Dave's friend and critic, who, after reading the entire manuscript and Dave's portion several times, asked all of the right questions to help make this book what it is.

John and Henry want to thank each other for the other's contribution to their thinking. Seriously, they have had a great impact on each other for the good of the kingdom.

Alice appreciates the encouragement she has received from Grace Watkins, Dr. John Powell of Michigan State University, Dave Pollock of Interaction, and Dr. Ted Dowell of Southwestern Baptist Seminary.

A special note of thanks:

from Dave to Buck Buchanan of First Evangelical Free Church
from Alice to Dr. Laura Mae Gardner of Wycliffe Bible Translators
from Earl to Willard Hawkins, M.D., of Harbor Family Practice
from John and Henry to Laura, Lisa, Rebecca, Carolina, and
Corienne from the Minirth-Meier West office.

Finally, and especially, a word of thanks to our spouses and our children, who sacrificed time with us, overlooked our grumpy words as we worked to reach the deadlines required for this project, and refined most of what we know.

John	*Dave*	*Alice*	*Earl*
Barbie	Ronnie	John W.	Karen
Rickie	Jeanna	David	Ben
	Christie	John E.	Rachel
	Jon	Bonnie	Amy
	Aimee		

Introduction

By Dave Carder

Even at twenty-nine, Julie vividly remembered the countless Thursdays at school when she realized with horror that she had forgotten to do her early morning chore at home. Thursday was "vacuuming day" for her mother, and Julie's job before she left for school was to put on top of her bed everything usually stored underneath it. With overwhelming sickness and fear she knew what lay in store for her when she came home.

How could I have forgotten again? she agonized. And if her mind was so forgetful, why couldn't she ever forget the look on Dad's face when he found out? Why did Mom always have to tell Dad when he got home that she had forgotten?

And why did it seem that everything went in slow motion when Dad began to punish her? Even as he was pulling his belt out of his pants' belt loops, it seemed to take forever. It was like a horror movie in painful freeze-frame.

And why, dear God, why did she have to totally disrobe, especially as a fourteen-year-old girl?

Even now she could see the pattern on the old linoleum floor. It was only inches from her face as she lay over that cold kitchen chair. At times she remembered begging for mercy and promising to reform in the same breath, but it was always hopeless.

Julie's lying across the chair was the signal for her two older brothers to enter the kitchen and watch the macabre family ritual. Her father said that having them see what happened to her would help them not to make the same mistake themselves.

Then the blows would start. The abuse was almost incomprehensible in its horror and duration. It often ended with her either vomiting or urinating on the floor. Then everybody walked out. When she had finished her soul-rending sobs, she was expected to clean herself up, along with her mess. Shortly thereafter, it was back to business as usual, with Dad often returning to his office at the church that evening.

Left alone with her pain into adulthood, Julie became consumed with finding ways to sedate it. She had to numb it at all cost. A sense of rage lurked constantly just beneath the surface of her emotions and occasionally flared up if she didn't keep it stifled. On other occasions the pain would leave her so depressed she could hardly function.

It wasn't long until she got the nickname "Wild One." She drank to excess and slept around. As a nursing student, she found access to pharmaceuticals that helped temporarily. She figured out ways to get them on the sly, even if that meant keeping them from patients who desperately needed their pain-killing properties. She started racing four-wheel-drive vehicles on weekends, and the rowdy relationships that spun out of that crowd eventually destroyed her marriage.

Desperate for a new relationship to ease the pain, she remarried with hardly a thought about the consequences. She bore a child, which resulted in extra responsibilities. The religious training she had received in her youth began to appeal to her as a source of relief from her pain, but her new husband had no interest in such matters. In yet another attempt to reach out for help in her prolonged agony, she decided to attend church by herself. Fortunately, she chose a church that was open to and understanding of the process of recovery.

Julie is known as an *ACDF,* an *Adult Child of a Dysfunctional Family.* Although it is obvious that a parent should not beat a child over failure to clear things out from under a bed, Julie's situation is, tragically, not uncommon, even among Christian families. Her dad's overreaction, her mother's inability to confront her daughter directly about a household chore, the terrible shaming effect of being nude as a young teen in front of her brothers, the fact that nobody ever talked about the beatings, that everybody learned to shut down his feelings, and that everyone left the family to enter into troubled and broken marriages all describe the characteristic patterns of a dysfunctional family.

Those patterns are often easier to see in other families than in your own; that is exactly what chapters 1 and 2 are about. Most of you reading this book will be familiar with the biblical families we discuss, so it makes sense that we look at them first. Besides, most Christians tend to over-sanctify the families described in the Bible, so there is new ground to cover in terms of seeing them in a different, more realistic light. God's Word has some helpful things to say regarding their behavior and its consequences in their family tree.

Throughout this book, you may find yourself resisting and even denying the dysfunctionality described. That is not surprising, since this is painful material to cover, especially if your family of origin (or present family) is dysfunctional to one degree or another. But don't succumb to the temptation of letting that discomfort serve as an excuse to stop the journey of discovery. Healthy, God-honoring behavior and relationships are too important.

You may feel that your family of origin wasn't dysfunctional since your father wasn't an alcoholic, or even a "rage-aholic," as Julie's father was. The truth is, however, that, due to the fallen nature of all parents (and children), all families are flawed and therefore dysfunctional to a certain degree. Addictive and compulsive behaviors (addictions to food, sex, work, and so on) are extremely common in even "the best of families," and such behavior is almost always linked to some form of dysfunctional family background. We believe that the vast majority of readers will benefit from studying the concepts presented in this book, whether for help in their own lives or for the sake of ministering to friends, business associates, or loved ones.

Remember, too, that it is common for multiple siblings raised in the same family system to perceive that family very differently. Your brother or sister might have such a different view of your family that you wonder if he or she is remembering the same group of people you do! Chapters 3 and 4 will look at what happens within families that causes children to see their family of origin so differently.

Everyone outside Julie's family saw it as a normal family, but Julie's family had a secret. That secret was made more powerful by the realization that if word of the beatings got out, her dad could lose his place of leadership in the church. Worse yet, the ultimate humiliation for a Christian family, he might go to jail. The unique stresses and tensions within the families of vocational Christian workers (pastors, missionaries, parachurch workers, and so on) are the focus of chapter 5. Almost every moral failure in the ministry has a family history to it that few are aware of. Even observers within the family that produced the Christian worker would not link family patterns with individual sins, but chapter 5 shows otherwise.

Julie's mother is known as the "enabler." She did exactly what the term says: she enabled the family system to function the way it did. If she had not reported Julie's failures to her father, little would have happened. In addition, by not holding her husband accountable for his cruel behavior, she gave tacit approval to the physical and sexual abuse. If she did protest and he refused to listen, she should have sought outside help for the family. Yet, for systemic reasons, she could not or would not. In any case, she did not.

Strange as it may sound, the cycle of forgetting, with its punishment, served Julie in a needs-based way. She suffered from an extreme lack of attention and love from her parents, and this punishment, though it was excessive and abusive, served as a form of attention from her parents. An unwritten rule in a dysfunctional family is that if attention is lacking it is always better to be picked on than it is to be ignored. By way of the abuse, at least everybody knew Julie existed.

Things actually came to the point where the pattern of abuse became predictable in Julie's family. As bizarre as it might sound, everybody in the family needed to have Julie forget to put her stuff on top of the bed. Dad needed to release his rage, Mom needed to be in control of the family, Julie needed to know that she was important in this otherwise emotionally sterile family, and her brothers needed someone to bear the family anger and shame, someone to be the "family scapegoat," so that they could feel safe and unafraid that Dad might blow up at them. This pattern is typical of dysfunctional family systems, and it is one with which ACDFs are all too familiar.

Julie's mother's own pain grew so intense that she took a job as far away from home as she could commute in one day. That job served as a haven for her; it became her "other world." For her, going to work spelled *freedom*. Julie's mom's separation from the pain-filled family contributed also to the emotional alienation that existed at home. As is often the case, the family's general emotional void led to inappropriate sexual relationships between Julie and her brothers. Sadly and shockingly, it even led to one incestual experience with her mom.

As we examine Julie's family of origin, the list of "family secrets" grows and an interesting phenomenon emerges. Julie, who felt like the least important member of the family, who served as the "identified patient" (a term explored more fully in chapter 3), who felt so victimized and helpless, was actually the most powerful figure in the family system. She knew enough about everyone in the family to destroy each of them, should the information leak. But because she felt so helpless and so responsible, she couldn't perceive herself as having any power. The pain and hurt had "gone underground" in Julie and had become what counselors call "unfinished business." It was impossible for her actually to leave home. Oh, she could leave physically, and she did so as soon as it was legal, but when she left she took all the family's secrets with her and their unfinished business, which contributed to the agony in adulthood.

It was exhausting for Julie to carry her family's secrets and unfinished business inside her heart. A pattern of depression, alcoholism, wild partying, and even abortions followed. Instead of finding relief, she only compounded the pain. This rage of no relief had to be tranquilized. Any solution, no matter how temporary or unhealthy, was acceptable.

Only in desperation, when God appeared to be the last of what had been a number of hopes, did she come back to faith. Yet that salvation experience in adulthood did not by itself do away with the unfinished business in Julie's life, as so many modern-day critics of Christian counseling mistakenly believe it should have.

It did not and it could not. It is Christianized wishful thinking for people who have never experienced serious emotional damage, or recovery, to assert that therapy for persons who have been damaged isn't necessary, that all they need is Jesus. Now it is true that sometimes God does deliver an individual in one moment from vast amounts of pain accumulated in the past, but that is not the norm. Instead, He more usually allows a certain amount of damage from the past to carry over into the present, even after the person receives Christ. The Lord wants us to dig out the sinful thinking and behaviors of the past and put on godliness in the present. We will look at this matter more fully later, principally in chapter 3. Suffice it to say for now that Julie's step back toward God was a critical first step.

Julie's salvation experience initially increased the load she bore. She had a great deal of unfinished business to do with God first. After all, her biological father was one of God's representatives on earth. How and why he went into the ministry, the kind of church he chose, the kind of people who chose the church he pastored—all those are the focus of chapter 6. Since churches are made up of families, it only makes sense that they often operate exactly like the family-of-origin pattern of the dominant leader and/or the congregants. Many of us select the church system we do because of the unfinished business we carry from our family of origin.

The family today faces challenges and threats unlike those any previous generation experienced. Shocking divorce statistics, rising numbers of incest victims, surging increases in incidents of abuse, and the presence of multitudes of single adults afraid to marry (or remarry) after observing the pain around them—all are symptomatic of a society responding to, and inundated with, trauma.

Is this book just another depressing review of the downward trend of the family? Absolutely not! As Christian ministers and counselors we are wholeheartedly committed to recovery, to healing, and to restoration of relationships—all of which can lead to healthy new patterns for the future. We dare to think it is possible for the next generation to have a better family environment than the current generation. That is why a major thrust of this book is looking at healthy —godly—family living.

Is this just another book on codependence? Yes, and no. Yes in that it is about codependence and other similar patterns, but no in the sense that it is not a general look at codependence. It focuses instead on the roots of dysfunctional and codependent behavior and relationships by examining family systems first in the light of Scripture and then in the light of family systems and recovery theory and experience.

This book is not based on untested theory. All five authors are daily in the trenches of full-time ministry to hurting people. In addition, we reflect a variety of stages in the family life cycle. At the time of publication, Henry is single, having yet to be married; John is newly married to Barbara and has an infant child; Earl and his wife, Karen, enjoy a sixteen-year marriage and have three elementary school-age children; my wife, Ronnie, and I have just celebrated twenty-four years together and are the parents of three adolescents and a fourth-grader; and Alice and her husband, John, have completed almost forty years together and have three grown children who are starting the family life cycle with their own families! As a result of this breadth of experience and ministry, you will find chapters 7 through 13 practical, biblical, and capable of delivering exactly what the section title says about developing family health: how to do it right when you learned it wrong.

Throughout, you will find thought-provoking, challenging input from the Bible. At the end of each chapter we have provided review questions and exercises that you will find a benefit whether you do them by yourself or in a group setting. We are praying that many groups will study this book and use the study questions to spark discussion. We urge you to personalize the study questions by writing down on the page (yes, we're giving you permission to write in this book) any insights the Lord may give you as you prayerfully consider the concepts discussed. We hope that while you process the concepts in this book you will feel an inner urge to explore your own family tree and that you will develop insight into your present family system.

One final caution before I set you free to explore the pages of this book. This is not a book that explores only highly abusive families. Though Julie's story starts us on our journey, it is important to remember that *this is a book about ordinary families in ordinary, everyday struggles.* Family secrets don't have to be extraordinary to be powerful. They only have to remain secret. Family secrets can be simple, but they are always significant. Such "secrets" are the things, events, or people that are "off limits" to family discussion or discussion with outsiders. They are the things strictly subject to the official "party line" of the family—that family system's interpretation of behavior and relationships.

Many times family secrets are common everyday occurrences that are painful and shameful (and unchangeable) for the child who experiences them: a mother who goes to work and a child who feels abandoned; parents who get divorced and the child who as a consequence feels torn; a father who is physically or emotionally absent and the child who as a result feels ignored.

Often these circumstances (and many others like them) are inescapable, so please keep in mind that we are not trying to make anyone feel guilty. We want to encourage those of you who hurt, who wonder if there is any relief available for the pain, who desire to do family things less painfully, to step out and start the journey of understanding your past so that you can choose to live the present differently. Our hope is that you will find our combined efforts in this book helpful and health-giving and, as a consequence, glorifying to our heavenly Father, who wants to heal our hurts.

Jesus said, "You shall know the truth, and the truth shall set you free" (John 8:32), and it is for this reason that we have put this book together. He is the Truth, and He wants us to deal in truth with ourselves and our loved ones. We want the truth about you and your family to flood into and overrun the secrets that keep you in bondage to dysfunctional behavior and relationships.

May God bless you as you read these pages. One thing we are all sure of: the pain of discovery, and recovery, will be worth it.

Part 1

Dysfunctional Families of the Bible

1

David and His Family Tree

By Earl Henslin, PsyD.

For two months Ron found himself obsessed with his sister, Marita. Every time he watched her walk through the house his desire for her grew. She was agonizingly beautiful, with long dark hair, and always so nicely dressed.

Ron was confused and ashamed. How could he desire and even lust for his own sister? Then he began to rationalize. After all, she wasn't his full-blooded sister. When his dad married a second time he could remember when their new little baby was brought home. It was so exciting to have a little sister. Even though she was only a half sister, she had always felt like a full sister to him. Yet now she was becoming more than a sister; she was a beautiful young woman about whom he thought day and night. He fantasized unceasingly about being with her, being close to her.

One morning Ron woke up too depressed to move. His dilemma had finally caught up with him. He just didn't want to get out of bed. His cousin Mike stopped by and asked him to go to the health club to work out, but Ron's ailment soon became apparent. Ron decided to dump his dilemma on Mike and get some advice. From fleeting thoughts of desire for his lovely sister it had now grown into a full-blown obsession. He wanted her just like any other woman, yet he felt tremendous guilt, too. Half sister or full sister, either way he knew in the pit of his stomach that such a desire was wrong. Yet the aching desire persisted.

At first Mike couldn't believe what he was hearing. Yet deep inside he, too, had similar thoughts about Marita and had felt the same attraction. But when he had reminded himself that she was his cousin, he had stopped thinking of her in that way. Hearing Ron talk about her now, though, he found himself helping Ron devise a plan for being with her.

Ron at first rejected Mike's plan. *Ask his dad to send Marita to take care of him?* Yet the more he thought about it, the more he felt justified. Dad had never been faithful to Mom: it wasn't too many years ago that he had had an affair with the wife of one of his most treasured employees. Dad's pattern was direct and forthright: he saw a beautiful woman and went out and got her. Right to the point, just the way he had built his business. What he wanted, he got. He never denied himself anything. He never saw any roadblock as too big. No matter how gigantic the problem, Dad always conquered it.

Later that day Ron's dad stopped in to see if he was feeling any better. He didn't hesitate to agree to send Marita to take care of Ron. Ron was a bit surprised at how easily his dad granted the request. Secretly he had hoped his dad would say no, or at least ask him why it was his sister whose help he requested. For once, maybe his dad would take a deeper interest in him and be there to help him understand this agonizing problem.

Yet the whole encounter was typical of what he had seen his father do over and over: listen to the employee's request and make a decision quickly, yes or no. His dad was great at making quick decisions and then moving on to the next item. But what Ron needed was a father who would take the time to talk with him and understand his emotional struggles.

Events moved quickly after his dad left. Marita didn't suspect a thing and was genuinely concerned for Ron. She hadn't even questioned her dad's instructions, even though lately she had been uncomfortable with the way her brother had been looking at her. Yet she would never disobey her dad and was always there to help if someone needed her.

Though his father hadn't meant it that way, Ron felt as though his dad's "yes" to his basic request was tacit approval for all that he wanted to do. He watched Marita walk through the bedroom door carrying a frozen lunch she had heated in the microwave for him. The steam from it swirled among her dark locks of hair, which fell bountifully on her shoulders.

As she walked through the door, something in Ron's face made Marita feel uneasy about being alone with him, but she dismissed it. She felt ashamed to be attributing evil motives to her brother. Probably she was just imagining things in his glance. He was sick, after all, and probably not in his right mind.

But when she went to Ron's bedside to serve him the food, he grabbed her. Before she knew it, he was pressing his body against hers, kissing and touching her in ways that should only be between husband and wife, not a brother and sister. She cried out, but the building was empty, since it was midday. She tried to fight him off, but he was stronger than she, and he prevailed. Ron thus forcefully and brutally raped his sister.

Afterward, Ron felt nauseated. He looked at Marita with a mixture of guilt and growing disgust. For some reason he couldn't bear to look at her anymore, which was strange, for he had been daydreaming about her for months. But his contempt for her grew. He hurriedly dressed in some trousers and practically threw her out of the apartment door. He locked the door and sighed heavily.

Outside, Marita was crying and screaming and tearing her clothes. She felt as though her very soul had been torn apart, felt violated and ashamed, so ashamed and used that she would never be worthy of a relationship again.

Her assault was avenged, however. When word got out about what had happened, Marita's brother Andrew decided to get even. He waited for two full years in the hope that their father would discipline Ron, but when he did nothing Andrew tracked Ron down and viciously murdered him for having violated Marita.

This story did not come out of my counseling experiences, nor did it come from the pages of a supermarket tabloid. It is the shocking but true story of King David's family, right out of God's holy Book, the Bible. Ron, Mike, Marita, and Andrew are actually David's eldest son Amnon, his nephew Jonadab, his daughter Tamar, and a younger son, Absalom (2 Samuel 13).

The foundation for Amnon's behavior was laid earlier in David's affair with Bathsheba. The story is familiar to most Christians. David sees Bathsheba bathing on the roof of her home, has her brought to the palace, and sleeps with her. She becomes pregnant, and David, to cover up, secretly orders that her husband, Uriah, be sent to the most dangerous part of the battlefield, where he is killed. Bathsheba then comes into David's household as his wife. The baby she is carrying is born and dies, as a discipline from God. We see David mourning and expressing deep grief over the loss of his son (2 Samuel 12:14-23).

Amnon, Tamar, and Absalom were teenagers when this happened. They saw their father (and uncle) model behavior that was manipulative and treacherous: covering up his sin with Bathsheba by secretly giving the orders that led to Uriah's death. What those teenagers learned was how to cover up, how to not face issues, and how to ignore the hurt that grew out of one's actions. The stage was set for a thoroughly dysfunctional family history to unfold.

Part of the tragedy of David's family is that it never truly dealt with the incest between Amnon and Tamar. Time went by after the attack, two years in fact, and David still had taken no disciplinary action against Amnon. But Absalom did take action. He invited his father and the family to his house for a party; the sheep shearing was over and a celebration was in order. David declined the invitation, saying that it would be too much of a burden on Absalom to have the whole family over to his home. Absalom pleaded, and David relented; Amnon and his brothers would be allowed to attend. Amnon went to his brother's house for the party—and, after he had been drinking heavily, was slain by Absalom and his servants. Absalom took full responsibility for the murder, for he had thus avenged his sister's rape. He fled and was in exile from his family for three years (2 Samuel 13:23-38).

CONCEPTS THAT CAN LEAD TO HEALING

Stop and think about it. What did you learn about Absalom in Sunday school when you were growing up? Probably that Absalom was the "bad guy." He is usually seen as the scapegoat, supposedly the only one in David's family who had problems. It is easy to dump all the problems and responsibilities of a family on a single one of its members. Yet when we look at David's family we can see that the whole family needed to deal with a number of issues and to apply key principles of healthy family functioning. Those key concepts are today helping ACDFs (Adult Children of Dysfunctional Families) begin the understanding process that can lead to recovery. Let's look at them.

1. *Each member of the family has hurt. Each member of the family needs help. There is no such thing as a scapegoat.* It is easy for a family to designate one of its members the family scapegoat. In the story just told, Absalom, the brother who avenged the rape of

Tamar, is the obvious one. After all, it was he who plotted to kill his brother Amnon, even though it was revenge. Later on, it was he who set a wheat field on fire and led a revolution against his own father, eventually winding up dead (2 Samuel 14-18). Surely it is not difficult to single Absalom out as the only one in his family who had problems.

But in reality Absalom was not the only one in the family who needed help. There was something broken in David himself that prevented him from taking appropriate steps to deal with Amnon or to fully address the damage done to Tamar when Amnon raped her. And that damage was very great. After the molestation she lived the rest of her life in desolation (2 Samuel 13:20). She never married or had children, in her culture the ultimate defeat and disgrace. She seems never to have recovered. The pain of Amnon's violation impacted her whole life.

I hurt for Tamar. She needed help after that incident. She needed counseling and the compassion of a group of women who had experienced the same hurt. She needed to have people around her with whom she could share her hurt so that some of the trauma of the incident could dissipate. But she never got that help. She lived the rest of her life in "desolation" (2 Samuel 13:20). What happened to her was a tragedy of the first order.

In a dysfunctional family each member of the family has hurt; each member of the family needs help. That help can take the form of the loving understanding of another family member, or the loving confrontation of a Christian brother, a support group, a sensitive pastor, a physician, or a therapist. Though we may consider some members of the family the scapegoats or label them the "bad guys," in reality all members of the family share the pain and, to varying degrees, the responsibility.

This principle was first applied in the treatment of alcohol and drug addiction. It was easy at first to treat the alcoholic/addict, but therapists began to see that if you only treated the alcoholic it was likely that the marriage would still fall apart because the spouse of the alcoholic no longer had any one to take care of. We know that children of alcoholic parents have higher rates of drug and alcohol abuse, experience problems in school more frequently, and often exhibit higher incidences of stress illness than do children who are not from alcoholic families. If only the alcoholic is treated and no one else in the family gets help, there is a higher rate of relapse than is the case if the whole family is involved in treatment. This is the basis

for the family systems treatment approach, one of the most successful approaches to date in healing hurting families.

It takes tough work to help family members see that scapegoat-
ing is counter-productive and that all share the pain. Take Mark. He
was eight years old when he was brought into counseling. He was
failing academically in school and was constantly fighting with the
other boys on the playground. The boys teased him because he was
small for his age. At that time the movie *Karate Kid* was popular.
During recess Mark turned into his version of the karate kid and beat
up the boys on the playground. When he got angry no one could
control him. He just wanted to destroy whoever was in his path.

His school counselor referred him to me for counseling. I met
with the whole family (except the [divorced] father and the grandparents, who refused to come). It turned out that Mark had an older
brother who was "just perfect." He made straight A's and was well
liked by students and teachers alike. This older brother was the sort
of kid who ought to be knighted, or at least declared a saint. His
"goodness" was so pronounced he held himself aloof from his little
brother, whom he saw as "just a troublemaker."

Mark was a sad, lonely boy who didn't have any friends. But in
family sessions it became apparent that he was not the only one in
this family with pain. Whenever I asked Mark what he was feeling, his
mother began to cry and his "perfect" brother would make some disparaging remark about his brother.

As the sessions progressed, Mark was able to bring words to his
hurt. It made him angry and sad that his dad never showed up when
he said he would. His dad had promised to be there for his birthday
but was too drunk to make it to the party. On the weekends when it
was Dad's turn to have him and his brother over, his father would
rent the boys some videos and then head for the bar, not returning
until very late.

As Mark began to feel his hurt and cry more in the sessions, his
mother began to share her hurt, too. Her father was an alcoholic, and
she had been through the same thing as her sons. Down deep, she
knew all too well the hurt that they were going through, but she had
tried to pretend her children did not have it as bad as she had had it
as a youngster. As long as she did not feel their pain, then her own
hurt would remain underground.

I mentioned to Mark's mother that her "perfect" son might not
stay perfect for long. Sure enough, as he began to feel his own hurt
and anger, his perfectionism shifted and he became more genuine

and more normal. As a family they were able to heal and to accept the fact that their father was not going to "be there" for them, not because he did not care, but because he had a chronic illness that put his life out of control. That is the nature of alcoholism. It is a usually fatal disease that is pervasive: it affects the spiritual, emotional, and physical aspects of your life. (For a comment on the use of the term *disease* in connection with alcoholism, see note 1, chapter 4.)

During the course of family therapy, Mark changed from the scapegoat in the family to a normal eight-year-old boy who got into normal trouble. With this new self-concept, he began to do better in school.

The sad truth is that the father did not make it into treatment for his addiction, and at the time they discontinued family therapy, he was still drinking. If he continued unabated, he is probably dead today.

2. *As parents we do the best we know how to do.* David was furious at what Amnon did to Tamar (2 Samuel 13:21), but the Scripture does not indicate that he did anything about it. The custom in those days was to stone or exile the perpetrator of such a crime (see Leviticus 18:9, 11; 20:17; Deuteronomy 27:22 for the laws Amnon violated), but David did not do either. Too bad, for either option would have helped all parties concerned.

In order for Tamar to have regained her self-respect, her father needed to have taken her violation and hurt seriously. David was a godly man, as shown in the book of Psalms, where the depth of his spirituality shines forth. Yet though he was deeply spiritual, he did not know how to face pain in his family directly and deal with it in a healthy way.

When David's son Absalom fled after killing Amnon (2 Samuel 13:38), David remained passive in addressing hurts in his family until the woman from Tekoa (2 Samuel 14:1-24) confronted David and challenged him to bring Absalom home. Absalom returned to Jerusalem, but he remained isolated from David for two full years. Moreover, the eventual contact between Absalom and his father was not initiated by David. That contact was initiated by Absalom, who created a crisis by setting Joab's field on fire as a means of getting an audience with Joab, who could arrange a meeting with his father.

Absalom seems to have wanted to meet his father face to face so that the issue could be brought to an end. Father and son did finally connect in a warm embrace (2 Samuel 14:33), but Absalom ended up actually leading a revolution against his own father. What took place between David and Absalom did not bring about a change in the father-son relationship.

Why didn't David do something to resolve the family sickness? He was a great warrior and leader, adored by his people. He was talented, gifted in music and poetry. He had been successful in defending his nation. As a teenager he had kept his country safe by killing the giant warrior Goliath. Yet the truth is that with all of his confidence and spirituality, he did not know how to deal with the conflict among his children. He did not know how to handle pain in any other way than by avoidance and passivity. What we need to learn here is that even though David failed his family in this way, that doesn't mean he wanted to fail them: *he was doing the best he knew how to do.*

The parenting style I practice today is different from the style I practiced fourteen years ago, when our first child was born. Today I am at a whole different level of experience and expression of feelings. Even I, a family therapist, painfully but realistically recognize that someday I will probably need to make amends and ask forgiveness of my children for the lacks in my parenting behavior toward them. On that day I will have to reassure myself that I did the best I knew how to do then. Each day, as I try to deal with my own issues from the past, I can take encouragement in the fact that "the best I can do" is getting better, bit by bit, day by day.

As parents we cannot be and do toward our spouses and/or children what we have not experienced ourselves. In other words, our natural tendency is to repeat with our kids what we experienced as kids (examined in detail in chapter 3). That truth can give us comfort, for example, in helping us understand why our parents behaved dysfunctionally toward us (they were simply "passing it on"), and it can cause us alarm, in that it suggests that we will repeat dysfunctional patterns if no intervention in the cycle happens. If we have only experienced a family that keeps everything secret, that is how we will naturally conduct our own family. If communication has been indirect in the family, that is the way our relationships will be, unless we take steps to improve it.

In many families all kinds of decisions and assumptions are made on the basis of a mere look and a glance. A child enters the room hurting and wanting to tell his father about his predicament but sees a look in his father's face that he interprets as anger and rejection. The child has nowhere to go with that feeling but inward. No words were exchanged, yet hurt that could have been resolved was quietly shoved deep down inside, to remain smoldering, doing its "dirty work" on the child's self-concept until dealt with properly.

David probably was passing on to his own kids the dysfunction he had "inherited" from his family of origin (chapter 2 will look at some of David's ancestors in that light). The tragedy is that some of us as well will not change until we experience massive pain, or until our children begin to feel pain and act it out through destructive behavior. The human and familial carnage can be devastating.

3. *Time does* not *"heal all wounds" when it comes to family issues.* Years can go by and nothing changes in the family. I know one family where unresolved wounds still fester even though the older generation has now died. Only two brothers in their early sixties are left. They worked together faithfully for many years in the family business, meeting the financial needs of their parents when they grew too old to work. When their mother needed extensive medical care and a supervised living situation the two brothers even split those expenses.

Their father died, and a few years later their mother followed him in death. Then the will was read. To their shock, the father had left all the assets of the business to the older brother. The younger brother received nothing.

The younger brother bitterly felt the hurt of his father's not leaving him anything. For him it was a statement of his father's lack of love toward him. For the older brother, it was quite different: he saw the father's decision to leave everything to him as a wise choice. The brothers argued ferociously over the outcome of the will, but the older brother refused to share the assets. They were more important to him than his relationship with his brother.

That caused a bitter canyon to open up between the brothers. Though their parents have now been dead a number of years, the brothers do not talk with one another except for a cursory hello when they are unavoidably in the same place. I doubt their relationship will ever change until they take active steps to reconcile. They need to find a way that both can understand the issues of the other.

Now the two brothers have children who are middle-aged. Those cousins share the family bitterness. No one talks about the problem. If anyone tries to talk about it, anger erupts. The family has never learned to solve a conflict without anger and defensiveness.

No one knows how to compromise or say, "I'm sorry." Sad, isn't it, when money becomes more crucial than relationships?

Such behavior promotes divisions and long-held anger and disappointment. That must have been what Absalom experienced during the seven years it took before he finally had the chance to hug his father, King David, again. He had tried in many destructive ways to get the message across, as for example in burning Joab's field, but no one picked up the message or detected his need. As time progressed, his anger and hurt must have turned into a well of rage that overflowed in the revolution he led against his father. The decisions Absalom made led to a grisly death: Joab took three spears and thrust them through his heart (2 Samuel 18:14). In dying he probably never knew what his father felt about him.

Even seven years after his estrangement from Absalom, David grieved over the loss of his son. In his grief it is apparent that he loved his son deeply:

> And the king was deeply moved and went up to the chamber over the gate and wept. And thus he said as he walked, "O my son Absalom, my son, my son Absalom! Would I had died instead of you, O Absalom, my son, my son!" (2 Samuel 18:33)

The pain and the frustration of never having experienced a warm relationship with his son must have been excruciating; it must have been a deep hurt that only intensified with time. The adage "Time heals all wounds" was not true in this case, as it is rarely true in life today.

While David was wailing for Absalom on the parapet, I wonder if he was also grieving over the death at childbirth of his first son by Bathsheba, his son Amnon's violent death by Absalom's hand, and his daughter Tamar's living her life broken and in desolation. The King of Israel was experiencing deep grief. The sad truth is that time in itself does not heal. If it is not accompanied by active, purposeful steps toward healing, it will only allow family hurts to grow deeper. Then, when the pain finally does erupt into the open, it will be even more destructive than it might have been before.

4. *Change that happens within the parent needs to translate into change in family relationships.* David is known as a "man after [God's own] heart" (Acts 13:22; see also 2 Samuel 13:14). His writings in the book of Psalms indicate that he was capable of deep feelings and emotions, at least when it came to his relationship to God.

Moving expressions of the depth of his hurt, the grief and shame of his sin, and other emotions come leaping out of those pages.

Take Psalm 69. At the beginning of that psalm, David is a broken man. He feels guilt, shame, and even abandonment by his brothers:

> I am a stranger to my brothers,
>   an alien to my own mother's sons;
> for zeal for your house consumes me,
>   and the insults of those who insult you fall on me. . . .
>   People make sport of me.
> Those who sit at the gate mock me. . . .
> Rescue me from the mire,
>   do not let me sink; . . .
> You know how I am scorned, disgraced and shamed;
>   all my enemies are before you.
> Scorn has broken my heart
>   and left me helpless.
>   (Psalm 69:8-9,11b-12a, 14a, 19-20a, NIV*)

Yet at the end of the psalm he is experiencing God's closeness and the resolution to his pain. He has bared his soul and his feelings deeply and honestly before God, and he is able to say near the end of the psalm:

> May your salvation, O God, protect me.
> I will praise God's name in song,
>   and glorify him with thanksgiving. . . .
> Let heaven and earth praise him. . .
>   (Psalm 69:29b-30, 34a)

So we see David as one who can work out emotionally difficult situations with God. Yet did that translate into improved relationships with his children? We have no evidence that his children knew or experienced the sensitive side of their father. Through his emotion-laden writings, we likely know more about David's vulnerable side than Amnon, Tamar, or Absalom did three thousand years ago.

David seems to have had a different kind of relationship with his son Solomon, for there seems to have been a stronger emotional connection between Solomon and David than between David and his other children. Sad, isn't it? Solomon experienced emotional closeness with his father, yet that was lost on the other children in the

*New International Version.

family. Take a look at Proverbs 4. The entire chapter can be viewed as an example of the caring Solomon experienced in his relationship with his parents, David and Bathsheba.[1] Listen to the wording:

> When I was a son to my father,
> Tender and the only son in the
>   sight of my mother,
> Then he taught me and said to me,
> "Let your heart hold fast my words;
> Keep my commandments and live. . . ."
> Hear, my son, and accept my sayings,
> And the years of your life will be many.
> I have directed you in the way of wisdom;
> I have led you in upright paths. . . .
> Take hold of instruction; do not let go.
> Guard her, for she is your life.
>   (Proverbs 4:3-4, 10-11, 13)

In reflecting on this relationship, I wonder if David didn't somehow grow closer to the boy Solomon as a result of his estrangement from his other children. It was good that David and Solomon were close, but it is a pity that the relationship had to come at the cost of emotional connection with Amnon, Tamar, and Absalom. David seemed to have "moved in" close to Solomon, yet he lived at the emotional fringe with the others.

One family I have known had a family relationship similar to the one David and his estranged children had. The father—I'll call him Charles—was a well-respected physician. His practice was intense and busy, and he was rarely home. When he *was* home, he was exhausted and withdrawn. As a result, over the years his wife and children developed their own lives.

Charles's wife poured herself into the children, and although the family did well in a material sense, the kids grew up never experiencing anything from their father. He in turn lived on the fringe of the family emotionally, maintaining one life at work and another at home. At work he was the caring, perceptive, and sensitive doctor. At home he was bland, aloof, and emotionally detached. Sadly, Charles made no effort to connect at a feelings level with his wife and children, though at work people saw him as a warm and thoughtful person. The family longed for the man they saw at work, but the man at work never translated into a close, interested, initiating father and husband at home.

The children are now adults and carry in themselves what I call a "father wound," an aching emptiness that was never filled by a father's love and feeling during their formative years. The wife and mother has a deep void in her life, too, with an accompanying grief and longing for the love and intimacy that never took place. It is sad that the Dr. Jekyl-Mr. Hyde life-style Charles maintained was never addressed.

Powerful forces in our culture work against healthy family life, especially for men. In our culture, for example, sharing feelings is considered wimpy, or soft. It is hard for a man to share with his wife the deep pain or struggle going on inside. After all, if you are soft, someone might take advantage of you. And what woman would respect you if she knew you cried?

What Does It Take for a Family to Recover?

A six-step equation for family recovery can be expressed "mathematically" (table 1.1). Let's take a brief look at those steps.

ALL FAMILY MEMBERS INVOLVED

Families are systems. They are *complex living organisms* made up of *interdependent individuals.* When problems need to be resolved in a family, all family members need to be involved in the process, not just the designated scapegoat. It is not only the teen taking drugs who needs help—we need to look at the entire family and see *why* that teen is abusing drugs. We need to look into the teen's relationship with his or her father, mother, and siblings to get at the root cause of the symptom.

If counseling would help, each member of the family needs to come in when the therapist requests it. I cannot count the times in counseling when we were seriously hindered by the refusal of one or more family members to participate. It is hard to understand the lack of cooperation—if their teen needed blood donated because of an auto accident, the members of the family would line up at the blood center immediately! But when it comes to injured relationships, that is a different story.

It needn't be. Family members can contribute to and stimulate recovery in many ways: attending family seminars together, reading and discussing books that deal with an issue the family struggles with, even holding a weekly family council. That family council can be a place where members pray for one another and share feelings

Table 1.1
Steps for Family Recovery

All Family Members Involved

plus

Each Family Member Taking Responsibility for Working on His/Her Own Issues

plus

Time

plus

New Information and Learning

plus

Doing What It Takes

minus

Shame

plus

A Committed and Genuine Spirituality

Yields

Healing and Recovery

and problems. Each member of the family needs to have a time to share openly without judgment or recrimination—a time to talk about happy and joyful stuff, and yet to share what hurts, too.

Of course there are boundaries and limits that should be observed in sharing family issues at family councils. Exclusively marital issues need to be kept between the husband and wife. To draw the children into marital issues will give them a malignant burden they probably will not be able to let go of until adult life. It is a form of emotional abuse for a parent to share with a child a dissatisfaction, anger, or hurt he has in relation to his spouse. The child will no longer be able to look at the criticized father or mother in the way he once did. He will begin to see his father or mother through the lens of the complaining parent's anger and hurt. Then, years later, when he is faced with resolving issues from his childhood, he will have to learn to give that lens back to the complaining parent, so that he can once again regain his own perspective of the other parent.

EACH FAMILY MEMBER TAKING RESPONSIBILITY
FOR WORKING ON HIS OR HER OWN ISSUES

Although ideally the whole family needs to be involved in the healing process, and although it is beautiful to see Mom and Dad and all the children willing to work on issues, it often does not work out that way. That reality, however, needn't stymie your progress. Begin with yourself and seek the help of a pastor, family physician, or therapist to involve the entire family. After all, every individual is only responsible for himself or herself (see the discussion in chapter 8), so that's a good place to start.

Unfortunately, it is common for family members to identify an issue and then pull back, become passive, bury their feelings, and avoid facing the issue in any number of ways—witness King David's passivity in dealing with hard issues. Yet change does not occur without action, without doing what needs to be done to bring about change. That's where you come in.

Take action. Take a step. Get into a support group where you can gather with other people who are dealing with similar issues. Read books that have to do with recovery issues. Form a small group where you can be with other people who are committed to share honestly and openly, who are willing to be there to support you when help is needed, and who are committed to pray for you—as you are for them. Be active, not passive.

If you elect passivity in the face of difficult problems, what will be the fruit? Consider Bill. No matter what Bill did, his wife got angry at him. He never could do enough to please her. Her moodiness was like a dark cloud over the whole family. Bill and the kids lived in a state of chronic tension, never knowing when a thunderbolt was going to strike or the next tornado whirl through the family, leaving in its path destruction and wreckage of hearts and feelings.

When Bill began to realize that he could change only himself, he gave up trying to pacify his stormy wife. His men's support group gave him a place where he could share and be open about his hurt and frustration. When his wife was depressed and moody, he didn't try to "fix" her. He and the kids just left to go do fun things while she napped at home, depressed and angry.

Eventually, she realized that the family was going to go on without her and began to focus more on resolving her own issues. She saw the wisdom in facing the storm within her rather than allowing that depression and anger to spill out over the whole family. Thankfully, today the family no longer lives in a continuous rainy season— there are times of sunlight, soft clouds, and deep blue skies.

TIME

A sign of being an ACDF is wanting everything to happen yesterday. The belief that everything can be instantly accomplished is a common myth in our culture. People meet, fall in love, get married, and live happily ever after in a thirty-minute prime-time TV show, so why can't I? (If it takes longer than sixty minutes, call it a movie!)

The Huxtables of "The Cosby Show" are able to solve major conflicts and life crises in thirty minutes—and have fun as they do it. Two other popular family programs—"Roseanne" and "The Simpsons"—find in thirty minutes a way to make their family dysfunction move into even deeper family pathology, and we know that in the next show they will find yet more ways to sink to new lows! Maybe you have seen the cartoon of the Simpson family staring in a daze at the TV, the caption reading, "Family Bonding." Yet it is no joke that millions of Americans find time to watch thirty to sixty minutes of family craziness on TV and yet cannot find the time to be with their own families in a meaningful way.

Time is one of the most precious commodities we have, so using it wisely with regard to our families is important. As ACDFs, we need to remember that dealing with dysfunctional family issues will take time—time with God, time for yourself, time with your spouse, time for the children, and time for support groups or supportive relationships. Time to be together.

Time takes on another dimension when we are dealing with issues we must face personally. Some hurts, angers, and traumas will not go away immediately. A woman or man who was the victim of incest as a child must deal not only with the hurt, anger, and betrayal connected with the molestation but must also totally restructure the image he has of himself as a person. He or she needs to resolve issues of sexuality, trust, and shame—in short, he must relearn how to deal with life in general. Likewise, grief over the loss of a parent or child—or of anyone close to you—will not go away in twenty-four hours. The stages of grief a person must experience will take time to resolve.

As Christians it is easy to shame ourselves for taking too much time to get over things. After all, isn't it a lack of faith on my part if I am not able to give my grief to God and be healed? No, healing deep hurt takes time. It is not something that can be rushed, no matter how hard we push ourselves. Not even our well-meaning Christian friends who chide us for taking a healthy amount of time to be OK can shorten that duration.

NEW INFORMATION AND LEARNING

It is hard to know what "normal" is when you come from a dysfunctional family. All you have known as you were growing up may have been abuse or the alcoholism and fighting of your parents. Finding your way after such an upbringing is like trying to land a space shuttle without the owner's manual. It is easy to crash and burn on the landing.

Crashing and burning on the landing is not too far off as a description of marriage and family life for an ACDF. If all you saw as you were growing up was fighting and chaos, how are you to know how to resolve a conflict? How do you work through your anger? After Tamar was raped by Amnon, Absalom did not know how to comfort her (2 Samuel 13:20). As a father how do you emotionally connect with your wife and children if you never had a feelings-level relationship with your own father? If all you knew as a child was sexual abuse, how can you make a positive sexual adjustment in marriage? If you have never seen good communication modeled, how are you supposed to model good communication with your own children and spouse?

Parenting classes, books, call-in talk radio shows, TV specials, and, too infrequently, the Scriptures, are some of the sources people turn to when they are beginning to learn how to deal with some of these issues. Try some of these things yourself, and as you do so, try some other things as well. For starters, read some of the books listed at the end of this book, give this book to friends, and start a discussion group using this book or others. However you do it, get some new information on the problems you face. That may be obvious advice, but it is a critical step in recovery.

You need new information, not just to help you understand your children but also to help you understand the gaps in your own personality development as you were growing up. Find an older man or woman in your church whose life and family you admire. When you feel uncertain, go to that person and ask for help. There is a fountain of untapped wisdom and experience in people in their sixties, seventies, and eighties. An older Christian who has been through it—who has learned to rely on God through the best and worst of times, who knows what it is like to have nothing, to work hard, to sacrifice, and then to build something worthwhile—will be a great resource for you.

There are other resources all around you. Ask for help. Don't pretend to know everything. We have all learned to fake confidence, even when deep down we are scared and uncertain. Yet most times help is available for the asking.

DOING WHAT IT TAKES

People in Alcoholics Anonymous learn how important it is to be willing to do whatever it takes to conquer a problem. Spiritual, emotional, and relational growth will happen when that attitude is yours. If what you must overcome is a mountain, develop the attitude that you will make a way to do it: climbing over the mountain, tunneling though it, walking around it, or hiring a hot air balloon to float your way over it. That's the attitude our parents and grandparents had as they faced life, but somehow today we have lost the basic value of and belief in hard work. There is no easy way out—no magic fix.

The task of healing is one of great faith. Sometimes it is hard to take that step of faith, trusting that the Holy Spirit will lead you as you actively search for the help you need. But in the end it will be worth it.

We live in a throw-away world. Married couples want to divorce if they are merely angry at one another. Couples come into my office for counseling and want to separate because they do not feel "love" toward one another. They either do not know or do not believe that love can return in a marriage. True, it takes long, hard, and sometimes painful work. But the alternative is to let the marriage become a statistic and to let your children join the growing ranks of kids who have not experienced being raised by the same parents who gave them birth.

Such a choice on your part has its own price. In today's world it is becoming the norm to grow up in a blended family—to have at least one set of step-parents and/or step-grandparents. I say this not to shame the people who are already in blended family situations. I am simply saying that it takes a great deal of hard work to make a blended family/marriage work, as you well know if you are already in one. There are no quick fixes.

Doing what it takes means abandoning the excuses you've been using for not getting better. You can't let excuses confine you in your pain. You may need to join a support group or find a 12-step program like A.A. (Alcoholics Anonymous) or Alanon (support group for relatives of substance abusers), groups that will be discussed more fully in chapter 13.

If you have the attitude that you are going to do whatever it takes to recover, that may well make the difference in your progress. Passivity and inactivity will only bring you more trouble, usually in the form of prolonged agony.

SHAME

At the outset of this section, let me stress that this element of the formula is a subtracted item! We need to shed the shame that has been built into our lives. That is why an entire chapter of this book (chapter 4) is devoted to shame. But the subject bears brief mention here, too.

Family shame and religious shame, which is the specific focus of chapter 4, are deadly aspects of family and religious dysfunction. Put briefly, shame is false guilt. It is the pervasive sense that "I am defective, inadequate, and worthless as a person." It is typically piled on us by others, not by God or the Holy Spirit. Shame is something that as Christians we have only begun to understand. We're just now learning to identify it, deal with it, and let it go. It takes work to move from a shame-based family system to one that is respectful and honoring to the people in the family.

The route out of shame is honor, respect, and affirmation of the family members. For example, in many families and churches the only time women are honored and respected is on Mother's Day. The rest of the year, women are relegated to back-of-the-bus status in terms of honor and respect. If a child grows up seeing his father not respect, affirm, and value his mother (or vice versa), he too will devalue the other sex.

It often takes a great deal of new information and learning before a person can get hold of the shaming experiences in his family (or church) of origin and can begin to treat himself and the people around him differently. I can't over-emphasize it: read everything you can find on shame. Learn to deal with it within yourself, and you will be able to change your response to yourself and to the family members around you.

At the time of writing this book, I have just begun to deal with the shame in my life. One of the hardest things for me to share with my wife and children has been how shame-based a person I am. My "shame tanks" are definitely full—inner tanks filled with feelings of never having been quite good enough or achieving enough, of never being spiritually adequate because my life never measured up to the rules set by my family and church.

What in my life caused an orientation toward shame powerful enough that even as a Christian psychologist I struggle with it? Many experiences, but they had a common denominator: that feeling of not being good enough. Words were said and actions taken that communicated to me the idea that I was a bad person. In my youth I was disciplined for feelings, not for behavior. Those experiences of shame left me a shame-bound person, a condition I am now responsible to deal with and not let spill over into my relationship with my wife and children.

Shame-based behavior can be destructive in family life. In a tense situation, shame will come out in a withering look or glance that will leave a child sad and broken. A look or an attitude can bruise a child's soul. I have seen myself do that. I do so less often, now that I realize the effect shame has had on my life, yet my children still carry hurt built up in the past when I shamed them and made them feel like bad, worthless people.

My overabundant defensiveness and the times I overreact to little things are mainly due to shame. If a family member tells me I could do something differently or better, I get defensive because I feel they are telling me I am not good enough or didn't try hard enough. In reality they didn't mean that at all. They were simply making a suggestion—and I make a federal case out of it. A "shame button" in me got pushed, and in turn my defensive reaction shames them! Then I have to apologize for overreacting. There are days when it feels as though I'm saying "I'm sorry" all day!

Shame runs in families (the multigenerational transmission process will be examined in detail in chapter 3). The look of shame I am capable of giving if I'm not careful goes back generations in my family. It comes from something my father and mother experienced, and their parents before them, and so on. It is a river of shame flowing uninterrupted for generations. It is my responsibility to understand the roots of that shame, to experience my own hurt, and to make different choices in the present. It does no good to blame, but it does good to seek understanding and face the issues involved. It is up to me (with the enablement of the Holy Spirit) to stop the cycle of pain.

A COMMITTED AND GENUINE SPIRITUALITY

No authentic and long-lasting change occurs without God's help and the work of the Holy Spirit in a person's life. A committed and genuine spirituality is an essential foundation for recovery. By *genuine* I mean spirituality that is biblically-based and authentic—a real experience with God, not simply going through the motions. By *committed* I mean a relationship with God in which you dedicate yourself to godly living as far as it lies in your power.

Let's face it, most real change in our attitudes is the result of God's grace in our lives. But we have a responsibility to be sold out to following Him, and that comes into focus in a powerful way in recovery. When the heat is on, as it often is when you are trying to forsake old patterns and adopt new ones, your commitment to godly living will be truly tested. No formula for recovery is complete without this element. I saved it for last in the formula precisely because it is the most crucial link in the chain. Jesus said it succinctly: "I am the vine, you are the branches; he who abides in Me, and I in him, he bears much fruit; for apart from Me you can do nothing" (John 15:5).

Now please don't misinterpret my remarks here. By *committed* and *genuine* I do not mean a perfect spirituality (whatever that is). God begins with us where we are. We do not need to climb a ladder or tower to get to where He is. We do not have to have all our problems solved before we are worthy of calling on Him. If we have anger toward God, it probably has more to do with unresolved family-of-origin issues than with our relationship to our heavenly Father. He understands and is willing to work with us if we will only seek Him.

We can be honest with God, no matter how messed up our life is. Read the psalms, and see the honesty of the emotions expressed there. Read the gospels, and see Jesus' honest reactions to emotionally-charged situations. Notice the way He responded to the hurt people felt and the way He expressed compassion for their need. He will deal with you in a similar manner if you seek His help in resolving your issues.

It's hard for us ACDFs to believe that God will treat us fairly and with compassion, because we often had little emotional honesty in our family of origin. Often a complete lack of compassion was what we experienced there. Little wonder that it is difficult to feel consistency in our relationship with God.

HEALING AND RECOVERY

There is great hope: God desires our healing, and He is able to bring it about. That is the strong foundation upon which this book—and the Christian recovery movement—is built.

As time goes by and I see God bringing about profound changes in people's lives as they work through a recovery program, I am more and more convinced that God makes powerful use of the 12-step programs, as they are called. At first when people attend such meetings, they may be unimpressed, since the meetings are often relatively unstructured and not exactly glitzy productions. But as they stay and listen they begin to marvel at the honesty and the lack of judgment apparent in the meetings. They wind up being impressed with the healing that is going on.

Many people first experience the power of God's love and caring through the acceptance and honesty that occurs in a 12-step meeting. Tim was one such young man. His mother tried her best to get him to go to church with her, but the harder she tried, the more he resisted. Sound familiar? If you are the parent of an unsaved teen, it surely does.

Tim finally hit rock bottom. It dawned on him that drug use was ruining his life. It had caused him to drop out of high school and would soon make college out of the question if he didn't make a change. He began attending a 12-step group and for the first time experienced God's giving him the strength to stay sober one day at a time. Amazed, Tim found himself praying and wanting to read the

Bible. His sobriety was allowing him to think clearly—literally for the first time since he was ten.

He decided to attend a church service with his mother. During the service the pastor gave the opportunity for people to accept Christ, and Tim walked down the aisle, making the commitment to ask Christ to be his Lord and Savior. Tim first began to experience God's love and strength through the 12-step program. Now God was using that program to help him find a Savior. Today Tim has a deeply-rooted, genuine, and committed spirituality that continues to help bring about significant changes in his life.

So hope is appropriate, for emotional and relational healing is indeed available. But we may not be healed perfectly. The apostle Paul had to live with a "thorn in the flesh" that was never healed. Yet he still managed to be used mightily of God when the infant church was born some two thousand years ago.

In the book of Romans we see Paul struggling with living a godly life. The lament he makes is one we know well.

> For I know that nothing good dwells in me, that is, in my flesh, for the wishing is present in me, but the doing of the good is not. For the good that I wish, I do not do; but I practice the very evil that I do not wish. (Romans 7:18-19)

Paul was no different from the rest of us in needing to learn how to rely on God's strength one day at a time. As you read through the pages of this book, let Paul's struggles comfort you and reassure you that you are indeed normal. There is hope for healthy and godly living. As you make the insights in this book your own, God will provide you information, circumstances, and motivation from other sources as you continue the recovery process. God is faithful, and He will help you.

Let me close this chapter with the story of George Wedemeyer. George is a former all-American athlete and high school football coach who today has Lou Gehrig's disease. Twenty-four hours a day he needs the help of a breathing machine, his wife, and a nurse by his side. As the disease progresses, muscle control deteriorates, and his airways continuously need to be suctioned out so that he can breathe. He can barely mumble words. Yet in spite of all this, he and his wife have a tremendous ministry to tens of thousands of people. She speaks for him, interpreting his mumblings to her.

At our church he talked about how he had been healed of his need to be healed, and how he was now being used by God in ways that would have been impossible if he had been healed physically. George's life is a beautiful example of emotional and spiritual healing. He has more personal peace and contentment than those of us who can walk, talk, and breathe without mechanical assistance or round-the-clock care.

Ours is a great God. He will be with us as we walk through whatever we must to bring recovery to our inner life and to the significant relationships around us. God will be with us, if we let Him into whatever darkness we need to face in ourselves and in our relationships.

Questions for Reflection

Ask yourself the following questions, and make personal notes in the space provided.

1. As we can see in the lives of David's adult children, time by itself does not heal all wounds. What issues have you put off, hoping that time would change them? What relationships have you been avoiding taking steps to improve? Make a short list below of the issues you might address with God's help.

_____

_____

_____

2. David was honest in his relationship with God, yet he had trouble allowing those relationship skills to translate into improvements in his dealings with his children. What are some risks and steps you can take in your relationships with your young children and/or your adult children?

_____

_____

_____

3. David did not take active steps to deal with the trauma between Amnon and Tamar. The result was destructive. Take a moment and reflect on those issues or events in your family that you do not want to face. Write some of the issues down, and share them with a

support group, your pastor, or someone whose recovery program you respect.

_____

_____

_____

4. Recovery from family-of-origin issues and from compulsive disease takes time and a significant commitment. Write a "recovery commitment letter"—a letter written to God and your family, committing yourself to take whatever steps you need to begin a process of recovery.

_____

_____

_____

Note

1. Charles F. Pfeiffer and Everett F. Harrison, eds., *The Wycliffe Bible Commentary* (Chicago: Moody, 1962), s.v. Proverbs 4:3, 4.

2

Isaac and His Family Tree

By Dave Carder, M.A.

What comes to mind when you read the following description: an only child born late in life to wealthy parents who had an overwhelming need for a male heir? Likely the word *spoiled.*

Isaac was his name. His birth was remarkable. Over many years and on multiple occasions God had given His word to Abraham, Isaac's father, that he should have descendants (Genesis 12:2, 7; 15:1-21), but decades went by and Abraham's wife, Sarah, was still barren. Then, when Sarah was eighty-nine and Abraham ninety-nine, there came a more specific word: "My covenant I will establish with Isaac, whom Sarah will bear to you at this season next year" (17:21; see also 18:14). So when Isaac was born he was more than just the long-awaited fulfillment of a promise: he was a miracle child.

But he also represented a problem. Many years earlier, out of desperation for an heir, Sarah, apparently following a cultural pattern, had offered her personal servant, Hagar, to Abraham as surrogate to bear a son in her name. From that union had come Ishmael (16:1-16). Hagar's pregnancy created severe dissension in Abraham's household (16:1-16), and only the Lord's direct intervention made it possible for Hagar to remain (16:7-12).

Now Isaac's birth kindled anew old animosities. "Drive out this maid and her son," Sarah had raged at Abraham, "for the son of this maid shall not be an heir with my son Isaac" (21:10). Isaac's birth had created what we today would call a blended family: Hagar, Ishmael, Abraham, Sarah, and Isaac; and there could be no family peace unless someone gave way.

The dynamics already present in Isaac's family when he was born and incidents that occurred along the way as he was growing up had a profound impact on his life and are part of the reason why a chapter in this book is devoted to him. For though Isaac was a link in a chain of descendants that would reach all the way to the Lord Jesus Christ, he was not immune from dysfunctional influences brought to bear by his family of origin and family tree. Just as they would for you or me, those influences helped make Isaac what he became.

As we examine the emotional dynamics that impacted Isaac's life, let me emphasize that the goal of this chapter is not to criticize Isaac. Throughout the Old Testament Jehovah cited His special love for His people by describing Himself as "the God of Abraham, Isaac, and Jacob," and Jesus Himself used the expression (Matthew 22:32; Mark 12:26; Luke 12:27). Abraham's trust in God is referred to in Romans 4, Hebrews 11, and James 2 as the epitome of faith, and all of the patriarchs are cited in the roll call of saints found in Hebrews 11 (vv. 17, 20-21).

Moreover, all three of the patriarchs were the special objects of God's love. In Genesis 22:16-18 God says to Abraham, "Because you have . . . not withheld your son, your only son, indeed I will greatly bless you. . . . And in your seed all the nations of the earth shall be blessed, because you have obeyed My voice." The Lord gave similar blessings to Isaac and Jacob years later in separate incidents:

> I am the God of your father Abraham; Do not fear, for I am with you. I will bless you, and multiply your descendants, for the sake of My servant Abraham. (26:24)

> I am the Lord, the God of your father Abraham and the God of Isaac; the land on which you lie, I will give it to you and your descendants . . . . And behold, I am with you, and will keep you wherever you go, and will bring you back to this land; for I will not leave you until I have done what I have promised you. (28:13-15)

So Isaac, his father, and his son Jacob had a special, unique relationship to God. But there are two sides to Isaac's life. One side reflects his walk with and obedience to God. The other side, the one on which this chapter will focus, reflects the sometimes dysfunctional interpersonal relationships that existed among the members of Isaac's family. Again, this is not to suggest that the patriarchs were afflicted by some sort of Jekyll-Hyde personality or that they habitually said one thing while doing the other. Quite to the contrary; each truly had a heart for God. It is simply to say that, like you and me, the patriarchs were humanly flawed and that we can learn something from those flaws.

The patriarchs were the products of their own families of origin and of the everyday situations they encountered. They struggled regularly with their emotions and in their personal relationships. Real life, both then and now, is difficult. On this planet it has always been that way and will continue to be so until Jesus establishes the new heaven and new earth (see Genesis 3:17-19).

If any of the material in this chapter sounds far-fetched or too strongly steeped in twentieth-century thinking, remember that the goal here is to understand the emotional dynamics at work at an important juncture in Isaac's life. If you can take away the "spiritualizing" about the patriarchs you have heard for years and put yourself in Isaac's state of mind, you will begin to understand at a personal level some of the remarkable events chronicled in the book of Genesis.

Being Special
Often Makes Being "Real" Very Difficult

The biographer of the patriarchs does not always tell his story from exactly the same perspective. Sometimes he gives an inside look at the personal struggles the patriarchs experienced. At other times he steps back and allows the reader to draw his own conclusions from the circumstances he presents. Yet always he presents the patriarchs as real people pursuing their walk with God with admirable wholeheartedness. Keep that in mind as you read the discussion in this chapter of the personal side of the relationships and family styles of the patriarchs.

We will examine in detail later the influences crisscrossing the family life of the patriarchs, but for now let's run briefly though a checklist of what the family had to deal with. There was a *father,* Abraham, who was desperate for an heir; a *mother,* Sarah, whose identity was wrapped up in the cultural purpose of producing a male child; a *half-brother,* Ishmael, who was despised; a *blended family* where Isaac was the favored child; an *overly close (fused) relationship* between Sarah and Isaac that produced dependency; a *traumatic* experience between Isaac and his father, Abraham, at the altar of sacrifice at Mt. Moriah; and an *immense inheritance* that Isaac had no part in developing. If one looks at just the basic facts, it is apparent that Isaac grew up in a family that experienced the same sort of negative influences that affect many of our own families. That circumstance should not be surprising. Families are complex systems, whether set in the twentieth century or millennia before the time of Christ.

ISAAC'S NEAR-DEATH EXPERIENCE

To better understand the family system of which Isaac was a part, let's look at the patriarchal family tree from Abraham to Jacob. As we do so, keep in mind that just as it is difficult for us to sort out all the influences that have shaped our development, so also it is difficult to identify all the factors that shaped Isaac's personal history. Assessing Isaac's case is made even more difficult by the cultural difference we need to bridge in reading about him, the lapse in time from his to ours, and the sketchiness of the Genesis history. Many details of the story we would like to know about are not addressed. Nevertheless, one event stands out as overwhelmingly influential in Isaac's formative years: his near-sacrifice on Mt. Moriah at the hands of his father, Abraham.

That experience must have been a turning point in Isaac's life, the kind of experience a person never forgets and from which point his life is forever different. The background we have already mentioned: Isaac is the favorite child in the family; he has virtually no sibling competition; he alone will inherit his father's wealth; he has been trained all of his life to care for his father's business. In short, he has been prepared for life as an "only son of royalty."

As one reads the Mt. Moriah passage in Genesis 22, Isaac's growing apprehension of what is to come stands out. He asks his father, "My father! . . . Behold, the fire and the wood, but where is the lamb for the burnt offering?" (22:7). He must have been puzzled by Abraham's vague answer ("God will provide"), but nevertheless he continued with his father up the mountain. He further submitted to his father amidst mounting fears as his father bound him and laid him upon the altar. Isaac by this time surely would have been strong enough to resist, so his cooperation in being bound demonstrates great respect for his father. Still, it is safe to say that as he lay down upon the altar he experienced mixed emotions about what was taking place.

While bound and lying upon the altar, he must have felt overwhelming confusion as he realized that *he* was the sacrifice. Just as we would, he surely must have struggled with terror at the sight of his father raising a knife above his chest, preparing to plunge it into his throat.

What trauma! Put yourself in Isaac's place: feel the wood on *your* back, the cords on your wrists. In your mind's eye, have *your* father stand in the place of Abraham, and think about the knife entering *your* body. Your thoughts and feelings would have to be magnified one hundred fold for you to truly understand what Isaac went through there.

Trauma reshapes a person's life. People are thoroughly different afterward. Survivors become more cautious, often less trusting, and at the very least more aware of their immediate environment. Recovering victims of trauma, especially where loved ones were involved, will tell you that values such as security, safety, attachment, and predictability become all-important to them. Being human, Isaac would have shared that normal response to trauma.

Possibly you are struggling with the question, Why did this have to happen to Isaac? It seems unfair that Isaac had to experience so traumatic an event. Thinking people through the centuries have wrestled with this Old Testament story, and those of us who hold to the inerrancy of Scripture still need to exercise faith as we cling to Hebrews 11:17: "By faith Abraham, when he was tested, offered up Isaac . . ."

But the question under discussion in this section of the chapter has not to do with *why* but rather with *how.* It is not *why* God set up this test of faith for Abraham but rather *how* that test of faith affected Issac. Don't mix the two. The event on Mt. Moriah was Abraham's great test of faith, and his faithful follow-through placed him in faith's hall of fame (Hebrews 11). The fallout in Isaac's life, however, was somewhat different, and that is the subject of this chapter.

This discussion could be had regarding nearly all of the Christian martyrs throughout Christian history, as well as virtually all the survivors of any modern-day trauma: though we think first of the martyrs themselves, the ones left alive often suffer the most.

THE TRAUMA REPEATED

In counseling victims of sexual and physical abuse, one result that often emerges is their post-trauma struggle to trust others because of the fear they have that they could again be taken advantage of. It is the consequence of the normal human questions: Why would you do this to me? What did I do to deserve this?

Since Isaac was fully human, given the Mt. Moriah experience he naturally would struggle more than most with the concepts of faith and trust. It would be very difficult for him to find himself in a place of risk that exposed him to the danger that others might take advantage of him. He would be especially sensitive to the feeling of being deceived or tricked. People who have been abandoned often fear abandonment when none is intended, and Isaac's response to the event on Mt. Moriah would have led to a similar hypersensitivity regarding issues of deception.

To be sure, Abraham on Mt. Moriah didn't intend to deceive his son. He was simply "following orders" from on high. But it is reasonable to suggest that Isaac, while under the knife, may have felt as though he had been deceived. After all, on the way up the mountain he had specifically asked his father about the missing sacrificial lamb and had received an answer, albeit a puzzling one. It was not until later, on the way down the mountain, that his father would have filled him in on all the details of the episode, including the fact that God had directly set into motion this test of faith.

Isaac's sensitivity to deceit, experienced early in life, probably formed the basis many years later for Isaac's intense emotional reaction (trembling) to his son Jacob's trickery in obtaining the birthright (Genesis 27:33). The conditions of the earlier event on Mt. Moriah have an ironic relationship to the conditions in place when Jacob seeks his father's blessing. In the experience at Moriah, Isaac could see what was happening ("Father, where's the lamb?"), but his innocent heart could not envision that he would be the sacrifice. Now he is old and wise with experience (Genesis 27:21-29), but he is blind and cannot see what is occurring. Earlier, with his father Abraham, Isaac could see what was happening but could not comprehend it. Now, with his son Jacob, he can comprehend that things are not right but cannot see to verify it. The second experience calls forth the pain of the first experience, and Isaac "trembled greatly" (Genesis 27:33), experiencing the combined pain of both deeply felt experiences.

EMOTIONALLY SEPARATED FROM HIS FATHER ABRAHAM

Many years earlier, Abraham had shown genuine concern for Hagar and Ishmael when Sarah had demanded that he banish them to the desert (21:9-13). So intense were Abraham's feelings of divided loyalty that God Himself had to comfort him. Most of us as parents can relate to Abraham's experience of feeling torn apart trying to keep estranged individuals (in this case, Hagar and Sarah) happy with us and with each other. Abraham's response to the tension between Hagar and Sarah, the heartfelt hospitality he showed to strangers (Genesis 18), and his burdened intercession for Lot and his family in Sodom and Gomorrah give us a picture of a man who is self-sacrificing, compassionate, and extremely loyal.

But when it came to his daily relationships with those one might think would matter most, the people in his immediate family, a different picture emerges. Just like us, Abraham had a dark side to his relationships with those in his family tree. For much of his life he was physically and emotionally separated from his kin. Called of God, he left his family of origin in Haran with no biblical record of his ever returning (12:1), even though it was only seven days' journey away (31:23). He was adamant that even Isaac should never return to Haran (Genesis 24:5-8). Though evidently Abraham regarded it as a good place to find a wife (both Abraham and Isaac chose wives for their sons from the family of Bethuel), he did not regard it as a good place to visit. Sounds a lot like our current in-law family settings, doesn't it?

Earlier, Abraham had separated from his nephew Lot (13:8-11), with whom he had traveled, nomad-style, for years. Eventually, he even gave up Sarah, denying (lying) that she was his wife (20:1-18). This abandonment by denial was the more significant because God had already told Abraham that Sarah would bear him a son in the not-too-distant future (17:17).

In his symbolic abandonment of his family, Abraham revealed himself to be more like us than we would like to admit. When it comes right down to it, all of us have a tendency to be self-serving and self-protective. Many marital and family problems are maintained in family trees through self-serving and self-protective measures on the part of one or both parents. Such patterns often are parallel to Abraham's pattern of maintaining emotional separation from those inside the family while appearing to outsiders as loyal, compassionate, and sacrificing.

After Sarah's death, Abraham continued to distance himself from Isaac by producing an entirely different large family through Keturah, his new wife, and numerous concubines (25:1-6). To cap it off, Abraham was to die seemingly without ever passing on a patriarchal blessing to his son Isaac.

ENMESHED WITH HIS MOTHER SARAH

Because we do not live in a culture where women receive their identity almost solely through producing a male child (see the story of Rachel and Leah, 29:1–30:24), it is nearly impossible for us to fully understand what happened to Sarah when she finally bore her only son at the age of ninety. Not only did she experience the joy of those around her, she experienced the internal joy of at last achieving what she was always supposed to be able to do. She had finally arrived. She had borne a son.

So Isaac was doubly important to Sarah. He was important to her because her identity was excessively tied to producing a male child (16:1-6) and because he was her one and only chance at motherhood. Isaac was her "miracle baby." Today, any woman struggling with infertility who finally conceives and bears a son, the only one she can ever have, can relate to the emotions Sarah experienced. The natural protectiveness Sarah would have had toward Isaac, the pride she would feel, would have been indescribable. In a real sense, from her point of view, Isaac *belonged* to Sarah.

Sarah loved Isaac, maybe too much. She needed him, probably too much. The emotionally-charged atmosphere of this mother-son relationship is alluded to at Sarah's death (24:67): Abraham, the husband who had been married to her for more than one hundred years, grieved for the normal period of bereavement, but not Isaac. Sarah died when Isaac was thirty-seven (17:17; 23:1). At forty, *three years* after she was gone, when he married Rebekah (24:67; 25:20), he was still grieving. This enmeshment, or fusion (concepts more fully discussed in chapter 8), in the mother-son relationship of Isaac and Sarah helped set the stage for the later emotional separation of Isaac from Rebekah.

EMOTIONALLY DISTANT FROM HIS WIFE REBEKAH

Those who work with divorce and remarriage indicate that a second marriage is usually doomed if it follows too closely on the heels of the former one. The second marriage is commonly referred to as a "rebound relationship," an attempt to heal the pain of the loss of the previous relationship by becoming involved in a new one. The dynamics of a rebound relationship were at work in the marriage of Isaac and Rebekah.

The marriage was arranged by Abraham. Abraham, aware of how keenly Isaac felt the loss of his mother and probably trying to be helpful, decided to care for Isaac by finding him a wife. Perhaps there had not been room in Isaac's life for a wife while his mother was still alive. Relationships that are too close emotionally, i.e., that are *fused* or *enmeshed,* characteristically cut other individuals completely out of the picture. But now, in Isaac's case, Mom was gone, and marriage appeared to be a route to solace and comfort. Of course, we know that marriage as a substitute for the love of a deceased mother is only destined for pain and frustration (ask any woman who has married her mother-in-law's favorite only son), but Isaac—and Abraham—did not know that, and Abraham's servant was sent to Abraham's home country to find a wife for Isaac.

Often, individuals who are "stuck" in the grieving process will not change the environment the deceased person created. They keep the same living arrangements, drive the same car, and wear the same clothes as though the lost loved one is still present. It is easy to imagine that Isaac kept the tent exactly as his mother left it. After all, he had become accustomed to his mother's care and nurture for some thirty-seven years. Sarah was probably the most important woman in his life.

This loss of his mother, taken together with having an emotionally distant father, coupled with the trauma experienced at the altar on Mt. Moriah, left Isaac all alone. His separation was made more intense by his father's decision to remarry (Genesis 25:1). Now we have another blended family! Over the next thirty-eight years Abraham fathered at least six more sons (Genesis 25:2-6).

It is easy to imagine that at first, marriage to Rebekah was an intense bonding experience. Isaac was lonely and grieving; Rebekah was completely cut off from her family. Initially, they needed each other desperately. It was not long, however, before the unfinished business in the relationship of Isaac and his mother became apparent.

Rebekah soon realized that she needed to become "another Sarah" to Isaac. As she struggled with her relationship to Isaac and Isaac's relationship to his mother, her own identity began to disappear. In a culture where women's opinions did not really matter, she would have had to keep her frustrations bottled up inside. Coupled with her failure to become pregnant, it is obvious that Rebekah must have struggled with terrible feelings of inadequacy for the next twenty years (25:20-26). The one thing that she could do for Isaac as his wife—something Sarah, as his mother, could never do—was to provide him with children, and she was failing even in that.

The relief of finally becoming pregnant with Jacob and Esau must have been overwhelming for Rebekah. How she must have anticipated the joy of finally being fully appreciated for who she was, after providing the much sought-after sons. She must have thought, *Now that I have brought forth sons, my husband and I can focus on our relationship.* Imagine her pain and disappointment when Isaac chose instead to love one of the children, Esau—and the wrong one at that (25:28)! Rebekah found herself with no one else but Jacob. Instead of focusing on each other, she and Isaac each chose a son to love.

At his marriage, at the birth of his children, and finally at one of Rebekah's most difficult moments, Isaac continued to "abandon" his wife. When he was faced with possible death because of Rebekah's beauty, Isaac denied their marital relationship to King Abimelech (26:6-11). His sons, Jacob and Esau, had to have seen this abandonment through denial, for they were young men at the time. Through modeling, Isaac was adversely shaping his sons' attitudes toward women.

Where did Isaac get the idea of abandoning Rebekah? Was it just a common cultural practice? Did it come with his genes? My hypothesis is that Sarah, in her inappropriately close relationship to her son Isaac, at some point told him about the time Abraham had abandoned her to this very same Abimelech (Genesis 20). Even though he must surely have despised Abraham's tactics, Isaac was not above practicing them with his own spouse. A pattern of pain is likely to be passed down the line unless something concrete is done to interrupt it.

DESPISING THAT WHICH SHOULD BE VALUED

In both families, parents and children are learning to despise what is important. Isaac gave up his wife just after Esau actually gave up his birthright. Isaac's abandonment of his wife provided the groundwork for her mistrust of him. She could see that she did not always count with her husband. When the chips were down, he would place his security over hers. That concept, coupled with Isaac's attachment to Esau, pushed her later into taking matters into her own hands; if she could only get the inheritance for her son Jacob, her future would be secure. Surely her boy Jacob would take care of her all her life, even if her husband wouldn't.

This devaluing of what is important almost always underlies the development of family secrets, as well as contributing to dependency (addictions and compulsive behavior) and codependency (the need to have someone in the family responsible for another's irresponsibility). During the rest of this book, we'll examine these and related topics.

Enmeshed with His Son Esau, the One Whom God Rejected

Why would Isaac, himself the promised child—a type of Christ in the Old Testament—turn from the child God chose, Jacob, in favor of Esau? Was it only due to his taste for wild game (25:29)? Though that certainly played a part in Isaac's choice, there were also other factors at work.

First, Esau had a bent to be and do all that Isaac had never been able to be and do. Here was a chance for Isaac to vicariously become "a man's man." Here was the opportunity for this "mama's boy" to become a hunter through his son's excellent skills. Now he could feel what it was like to take risks. Now he could move out from under the smothering protection of being the "only" and favorite son. Now perhaps he could develop some self-identity through his son's achievement. After all, wasn't he Esau's father?

The favoritism Isaac showed toward Esau was initially probably simple fatherly pride in his son's achievements. That is normal for any dad. But it got out of hand when Isaac decided to bequeath the blessing differently from what God decreed (25:23). Isaac was never overtly angry, and was typically fearful of confrontation (see 26:18-22, where Isaac withdraws from several contested wells and digs new ones as opposed to standing up for what rightfully belongs to him). It was in keeping with Isaac's personality and the culture of the time for him to extend the blessing to the son he thought stood before him, his elder son, Esau, even though he well knew that such a blessing was contrary to explicit prophecy given before the sons were born (25:23).

Favoritism in a family is common. And, contrary to the opinion many people have, I think that as long as it does not lead to unjust treatment of the children, favoritism is not by itself wrong. Almost every family has a favorite child. That does not mean the parents love that child more than they love their other children. It only means that the favorite child *fits* better with the personality of the parents. They often see things alike or have shared interests that tie them together.

Jesus had favorites even among His disciples. The special three are well known for the times they alone shared with the Savior (Peter, James, and John in Gethsemane, Matthew 26:36-37; and at the Transfiguration, 17:1-8). Among that select group, John stood closer to Jesus than the rest (John 13:23-25; 21:20). Jesus didn't love John more than Peter; He just loved him differently. He and John fit together better. In the vernacular of our day, they were "on the same wave length."

But it was more than favoritism that Esau and Jacob faced at the giving of the blessing. On a spiritual level, the birthright given to the younger son reflected God's will that the family line should continue through Jacob and not Esau. On a personal level, the giving of the birthright involved intense competition for parental approval. Even after Jacob had stolen the birthright through deception, Esau still struggled to regain his parents' favor by marrying a woman of whom his parents approved (28:6-9; cf. 26:35; 27:46).

In the passing of the blessing, we see unfinished business, a family's secret that goes undiscussed and unaddressed until it flowers into the open. As a result, Jacob leaves the family, terrified (Genesis 27:42-45), and Esau leaves it angry and bitter, with plans to murder in his heart (27:41).

ISAAC SEPARATED FROM HIS SON JACOB

If we can step back a bit and look again at the relationship of Isaac and his sons when the boys were young, we can see again a negative pattern in the interaction of the family members. In keeping with the culture, Isaac preferred the eldest son as the recipient of the family blessing. He relegated Jacob, as the second born, to his mother to raise. As a result, the first picture we have of Jacob in the Scriptures is cooking food within the family compound (25:27-29). The arrangement sets up an exact replay of Isaac's own family experience (table 2.1).

Interestingly, we do not ever see Jacob express remorse over taking advantage of his father's old age and lying to him. After all, wasn't it his mother who had protected him all of his life? Hadn't she always been the one to whom he went when he was injured or in need? Knowing he was "the special one," Rebekah surely must have told her favorite son that God had chosen him. As mothers often do to reassure children, she most likely inadvertently played into the pattern by repeatedly telling Jacob the story of his birth and selection by God.

The rejection Jacob experienced when his father favored Esau would only intensify his questions and deepen his pain. *If Jehovah is the God of my father and Jehovah has chosen me, why has my father rejected me?* he might have asked himself, and his mother. *If God's plan is going to be fulfilled,* he must have thought, *my mother and I must cooperate in treachery.* Though she surely did not want con-

Table 2.1
Parallels in Isaac's and Jacob's Experience

PARALLELS	ISAAC	JACOB
Called of God	Genesis 17:21	Genesis 25:21-31
"Separated" from his father	At Mt. Moriah Genesis 22:2-7	Shortly after his birth Genesis 25:28
Enmeshed with his mother	Couldn't get over her death Genesis 24:67	He was her favorite son Genesis 27:6-10

sciously to do so, Rebekah's actions and advice in the matter of the birthright must have conveyed the view that God cannot be trusted to do what He says He will do (i.e., give Jacob the blessing). She ended up modeling mistrust of God—the exact opposite of the attitude she wanted Jacob to have as an adult.

Looking at this situation from a family systems view, as long as each child had a parent sympathetic with and partial to him, equilibrium in the family was maintained. It was only when Jacob was able to deceive Isaac and steal the birthright from Esau that the balance of power shifted in the family. Now Jacob had both parents on his side. Esau was cut off. Sibling rivalry soared to thoughts of premeditated murder. Throughout the period prior to the power shift, the family would have appeared to be normal. Things looked so good on the outside that no one would have suspected that the underlying dynamics that were to rip the family apart were already in place. And, for a while, it worked. As long as everyone stayed in his role, performed his task, carried out his life assignment, all was well. But the family structure was rigid, and as a result, fragile. When pressure came, as it inevitably does, the family shattered.

Not only did Rebekah not trust Esau, but Esau came to despise Rebekah when he realized that she was behind his brother's treachery. Jacob's and Esau's sibling rivalry brought to light rivalry that had existed between the parents for forty years. It was an undercover secret certainly, yet it was a powerful secret in a family that appeared—from the outside at least—to be at peace.

DYSFUNCTION TRANSMITTED TO JACOB'S DESCENDANTS

Though the families of Abraham and Isaac demonstrate inappropriate relationships and malignant secrets and dysfunctions, God continued to use them. He did not abandon them because of their dysfunction. We can take heart in that. God is faithful and will not abandon us in our dysfunctionality any more than He abandoned Isaac and his family tree. That is the mercy of God.

Nevertheless, the cycle of pain passed on to Jacob's family and later was repeated even more severely in the generations of the kings. We cannot examine those elements of dysfunction in detail now (you will find it useful to read the relevant passages in your Bible), but briefly here they are:

- The out-and-out performance-based mentality: Jacob and Laban (Genesis 30:25-43)

- The compulsion to earn the right to be loved: Rachel and Leah (Genesis 29:31–30:23)

- The unending manipulation of people within the family: Laban (Genesis 31:1-16, 26-35, 32)

- The ongoing abuse among siblings: Joseph (Genesis 37)

- The sexual molestation: Reuben (Genesis 35:22)

- Murder, treachery, and physical torture: Joseph (Genesis 37)

How the dysfunction present in Isaac's family was maintained and handed from generation to generation will be discussed fully in the next chapter, which examines just how dysfunction is passed down a family tree.

Questions for Reflection

Ask yourself the following questions, and make personal notes in the space provided.

1. What "religious experiences" did you have as a child or an adolescent that have impacted your relationship with God? Have you ever been able to talk about those experiences with anyone?

_____

_____

_____

2. Who was the favorite child in your family? What differences in treatment did the favorite receive?

_____

_____

_____

3. If you are a parent, who is your favorite child and why?

_____

_____

_____

4. What kind of inappropriate relationships exist in your immediate family history (grandparents, parents)? Who was inappropriately close? Who was withdrawn when it should have been the other way around? What impact have these relationships had on you, your relationship to your spouse, and your relationship with God?

_____

_____

_____

5. How do you feel as you read about and think about dysfunction in the family systems of the patriarchs? What have you learned? What concepts can you apply to your own family tree?

_____

_____

_____

Part 2

Contributing Factors in Family Dysfunction

3

Passing the Torch: The Multigenerational Transmission Process

By Dave Carder, M.A.

To Jim the pain of that night back when he was thirteen years old had been overwhelming. When Dad said he was leaving the family, that he had another girlfriend, and that he wouldn't be back, Jim couldn't believe it. He thought it was some cruel joke. His father's reassurance that he would still provide for them and would still see them on weekends were lost upon Jim's unbelieving numbness. When it finally sank in that Dad wasn't kidding, Jim fled upstairs to his bedroom sobbing.

Finally, he heard his dad's car start in the driveway. Going to the window, he saw the car back out and pull away. Tears streaming down his cheeks, Jim watched the tail lights until they were out of sight. The memory of that event still made Jim cry, and that was true even tonight, at forty-three, as he drove the U-Haul truck across the Kansas plains.

Back east were his wife and family, in emotional shambles. Following closely behind the truck was his girlfriend, Sally, driving her late-model car. They were headed west for a new life together. He was in his middle forties, she in her late twenties.

He had never intended to do this. In fact, on that night so long ago and many times thereafter, he vowed that for him marriage would be "forever." He would never abandon his kids. Growing up had been tough, but he had made it. He had always managed to keep his grades up, work part-time during school, and still play sports. After a great high school baseball season, he had won a college scholarship, then had gone on for his M.B.A. and marriage.

Jane had been great, and their early marriage had been, well, pretty good. Work had been tough, but Fortune 500 corporations demand long hours—besides, he wasn't scared of hard work. But things in their marriage went sour, and something snapped in him. Now he was going to try again with Sally. He knew Jim, Jr., was sobbing his heart out back home, just as he had done as a boy.

He hated even to think about that boyhood scene so long ago. Nobody had ever allowed him to talk about it. Mom had said that they just had to go on. The incident was over, she said, and they couldn't change it. Pastor had said that he should forgive his dad, and Jim thought he had. He did pray about it once, at least.

Now on this dark night it seemed so unfinished. Jim wondered if this was what his dad had felt like. Before long Jim had to pull to the shoulder of the highway because he was crying so hard. He felt like going back, in a way, but he didn't. He just couldn't. He didn't know why and, what's more, he wasn't sure he even wanted to know the answers to those questions.

When he had recovered somewhat, and after he had muttered some excuse for his behavior to a somewhat puzzled Sally, he and his girlfriend drove on into the lonely Kansas night.

THE "SONS OF THE FATHERS"

The pattern of a father (or a mother, for that matter) passing infidelity on to a child is heartbreaking. But until Jim figures it out, he very likely will pass on to his son what he hated most about his own childhood. The more an individual understands his or her past, the greater the possibility that he or she will be able to control what he or she passes on to the next generation. The term *understanding* here means more than just knowing the facts, though that is where you start, especially since dysfunctional families tend to hide hurtful facts.

LOOKING CLOSELY AT WHAT IS OFTEN "OVERLOOKED"

The following questions are ones you can use to find out more about your past. Most of these questions are painful to think about, but they deal with very influential people in a family tree, so it is important to consider them. Separating fact from fiction is sometimes like detective work, but it is a necessary first step in stopping a pattern of dysfunction. Otherwise, the secrets that are at the heart of a family's dysfunction will remain hidden in the family's version of events and thus be locked off from useful access. Only much later, after valuable time is lost, will anyone be able to sort it all out.

1. Who is/are the individual(s) in your family tree about whom other family members are the most quiet?

_____

_____

_____

2. Who is most frequently blamed for family problems, i.e., who is the "black sheep" or "the bad kid"?

_____

_____

_____

3. Who was unable to stay married for a very long time or, if presently married, has been unfaithful? Do you see a correlation of events in the present with what happened to that person in his or her childhood?

_____

_____

_____

4. Who is/was the addict in the family tree? What was his (her) pain? How does the family view him (her)?

_____

_____

_____

5. Who was cut off from the family tree? Who stayed away of his or her own volition? Who was ignored at family gatherings?

_____

_____

_____

6. Who (if anyone) in your family suffered from a serious or chronic illness? What purpose did the illness serve? How has the emotional pain it produced been "medicated"?

_____

_____

_____

7. Who in your family manifests the often stress-related illnesses such as allergies, chronic back pain, headaches, or gastrointestinal difficulties?

_____

_____

_____

8. Who in the family was depressed, suicidal, or even hospitalized for mental illness?

_____

_____

_____

9. Who was angry, mean, and/or controlling in your family?

_____

_____

_____

10. Which parent had the most power in your family? How did he/she use it? How did that parent maintain power and keep everybody in line?

_____

_____

_____

Working through these questions is not exactly what we think of as fun activity for a Saturday night, but we have to understand the dark side of our family tree as well as the sunny side. Familial aberrations exist to some degree in every family, and the Bible families we examined in chapters 1 and 2 were no exception. In this chapter we will examine how the "sins of the fathers" get passed down a family tree (Exodus 20:5; 34:7; Numbers 14:18).

First, though, we need to look at how unwritten rules enable family secrets to stay secret. When all family members "agree" to keep quiet about such secrets, those secrets become powerful, though unacknowledged, shapers of behavior.

FAMILY RULES GOVERNING FAMILY SECRETS

Claudia Black[1] has identified three almost universal family rules in dysfunctional families. They are:

- Don't Talk
- Don't Trust
- Don't Feel

We will examine these rules in detail below. But first let's look at how and when these rules are employed by families:

- Every family uses *some* of these rules *some* of the time. This point is related to the earlier observation that all families are somewhat dysfunctional.

- Some families use *some* of these rules *all* of the time. Families tend to see the rules they use as self-evident and always desirable, without question.

- Some families use *all* of these rules *some* of the time. That will usually occur in families with recurring stress patterns, for example, families which have experienced frequent job-related transfers, chronic illnesses, and so on.

- Some families use *all* of these rules *all* of the time. These families have in place the most lethal of family patterns. With no outlet for his feelings, a child in such a family never blossoms into full identity. He or she just strives to survive.

DON'T TALK

Family thinking under this rule goes something like this: "Don't talk to anyone outside our family about what you see going on in our family. This is normal family life. Everyone will think you are stupid if you see it otherwise. Within the family don't talk about it either, OK? Stay on safe subjects; pretend everything is OK. Who knows, maybe it will become OK if we pretend long enough. Don't ask questions! That is dangerous—you will get someone upset. Remember, we are a family. No one else really understands our family, so don't try to explain it to anyone. That would be foolish. Besides, you don't know who can be trusted outside the family."

The question of trustworthiness leads to the second rule.

DON'T TRUST

"Don't trust anybody outside the family. Who knows what they might do to or say about our family? You don't want to be responsible for that, do you? Besides, their families are just like ours. You need to care for us, not worry about them. Our family depends upon you—don't let us down. However, don't lean on me, as I am leaning on the bottle. So what if I got a little carried away last night? Everybody does that once in a while." (You can substitute any number of addictions for that last reference to drinking—for example, workaholism or hyperperfectionism.)

Trust is discouraged within the family through broken promises and failed commitments. The failure of parents to follow through with what is important to their children fuels this mistrust. The parents may be notable for their lack of attendance at their children's performances in sports, music, or drama. They may fail chronically to pick up their children on time (or at all) after events, thus keeping them waiting or dependent upon others to find transportation. They may impose an inordinately restrictive dress code on their children as a result of overly restrictive family standards in general or of parental distortions ("blue jeans are of the devil"). There are many ways a parent's dysfunction can grossly affect children. But whatever path is taken, the lack of trust built up through failed commitments develops hurt, shame, embarrassment, and anger in the child.

The child, unable to talk (the "Don't Talk" rule in operation), now experiences an eroding trust factor and emotional shut-down. She quietly asks herself, *If my parents—who are supposed to care for me—won't nurture me, who will?* She begins to shut down emotionally. It is too scary to risk herself emotionally in such an atmosphere.

DON'T FEEL

"If you won't allow yourself to think about the situation, it won't hurt so bad. After all, you really don't hurt that badly. Those are just silly, childish emotions. It's better to put them out of your head completely. That way you'll make it through life a lot better."

Denial begins to reshape the perceptions of the family. Some sense has to be made out of its craziness, so unfinished business goes underground to resurface in the next generation. The child begins to say to himself, *I am not going to get what others have* (for example, love and a normal level of family functionality), *but then again I guess I don't need it either.* Feelings freeze up. Spontaneity is lost. It doesn't hurt so badly anymore, but a key aspect of the child's nature—his emotional expression—has atrophied. It's a tragedy.

When a child shuts down his painful emotional side, he also loses the ability to express his joyous side. Emotions are a whole. With anger comes the ability to express delight; with sadness comes the ability to express lightheartedness. This is the breadth of emotion that allows an adult to experience intimacy with a spouse, with God, and with his children.

Some families actually use statements that squelch emotions. "If you don't quit crying, I'll give you something to cry about!" "You shouldn't feel that way." "Children should be seen and not heard." Other families discount children's hurts. "You'll get over it." "Be tough—it will happen many times, so get used to it." Other families don't see how insane it is for parents to expect their kids to be little adults. ACDFs often report the feeling of having had to grow up too fast. It is attitudes like these that help form aberrant patterns.

Though feelings are a package given to us by God, they are often influenced by culture. When internal spontaneity goes, the child as an adult will have to look externally to the culture to find out what is appropriate at a particular time in his development. For instance, our culture tells young males that anger is OK, but tears are not. Since young males often express their feelings through their hormones, sex and anger become their dominant emotions. With few feelings registering internally, that kind of man becomes insensitive to his own child's hurts. The process that damaged his life is already starting to reoccur in his child. Unless something is done to reverse the pattern, the next generation will be engulfed in it.

CHILDREN'S STYLES FOR COPING WITH FAMILY SECRETS

Dysfunction is passed down from generation to generation in a six-step process, outlined in table 3.1.

As the child develops in a family that structures its interactions around the rubric "Don't talk, don't trust, don't feel" (step 1), a personal pattern emerges. This pattern becomes a preference that later develops into a coping mechanism. It becomes deeply entrenched in behavior because it represents security, freedom from pain, and control over the environment (step 2).

As the child's coping mechanism becomes defined (step 3), a role emerges, the purpose of which is to reassure the child that he belongs (step 4). Regardless of how dysfunctional the role is, the family system becomes self-reinforcing—the more he practices it, the more he feels like he belongs to the family; the role becomes his critical link to the family group. That is why roles are so resistant to change, even if tremendous carnage has resulted. The adage "Don't rock the boat" (often used in dysfunctional families) means in this application, "Don't change your role! There is too much uncertainty and chance for pain if you do, so you must keep acting that way."

When a child grows up in such an environment, and enters adolescence with its dating and marriage involvements, he will attempt to build new relationships on the same dysfunctional pattern (step 5). Those relationships will work initially only if he is able to replicate the same family pattern he came from (remember, his style was forged within a specific family system). Now, as he faces marriage, with tool in hand (with its expected result of a sense of belonging), he will attempt to build a new family unit around his style (step 6).

But beware if the "match" is not perfect! Major problems occur when the new partner has not had the time to adjust, or having the time, refuses to fit into the role his spouse's family system "tool" requires. It's like trying to drive the proverbial square peg into a round hole. Success is practically impossible.

When the individual is not able to replicate his family style and is also unable to develop a new, mutually acceptable pattern with his spouse or child, intense conflict and the destruction of the relationship will occur. That is why ACDFs typically go through so many relationships prior to marriage and so many divorces afterward. Witness the woman who marries three alcoholic men in a row, all of whom mercilessly beat her. How could she have "the bad luck" to marry such men? we ask, but the "luck factor" was really very small. Rather,

Table 3.1
The Interactional Pattern That Passes Dysfunction from One Generation to the Next

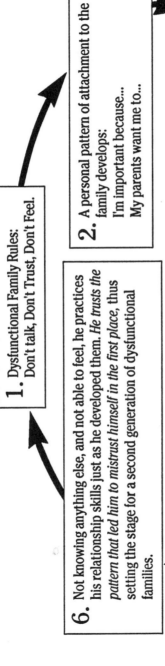

1. Dysfunctional Family Rules: Don't talk, Don't Trust, Don't Feel.

2. A personal pattern of attachment to the family develops:
I'm important because...
My parents want me to...

3. Unable to talk or to process this pattern, a child begins to shut off his emotional responses and develops an automatic coping mechanism.

4. The child refines the coping mechanism through the reinforcement his style receives from his parents. A role emerges.

5. This role determines relationship behavior both in the family of origin and after marriage.

6. Not knowing anything else, and not able to feel, he practices his relationship skills just as he developed them. *He trusts the pattern that led him to mistrust himself in the first place,* thus setting the stage for a second generation of dysfunctional families.

in her marriages, commitment to the relationship has been built on a coping mechanism: "I will stay with you as long as you allow me to live the way I learned to live at home." That is exactly why you hear so many times in troubled marriages, "You drive me crazy! You're *just like* your (expletive deleted) father/mother!"

The most important phrase in the process is found in step 6: *He trusts the pattern that led him to mistrust himself in the first place.* That is why the pattern becomes so important. There is nothing else to fall back on. The ACDF says to himself, *This is the only style I know. I am afraid to change because I can't trust. I can't feel, so I have no internal validation on which to rely as I go through the process. I can't talk about all that is going on, so I stay angry that the patterns are becoming different.* See the three "Don't" rules at work here?

COPING MECHANISMS

Change is extremely difficult for an ACDF. If he has only one rigidly held coping style, and if that style doesn't work under the new (changed) circumstances, the (usually unconscious) result is a terrifying sense of abandonment: *I don't fit in, therefore I don't belong, therefore I'm terribly and irreversibly alone.* He fails to see that it is not so much a problem of his not fitting in as a person as it is of his coping style not being appropriate to the new circumstances.

Two questions arise regarding coping styles:

1. Can they be identified?
2. Are they always dangerous?

Yes, they can be identified, but no, they are not always dangerous. In fact, each of us uses some of these coping mechanisms at various times in our lives. The danger lies in using a mechanism *exclusively* and *inappropriately.* Exclusively to the point that it becomes our style, our singular way of handling all relationships and all of life. Inappropriately in that we come to put increasingly greater demands on our coping response and expect it to provide increasingly greater benefits, even when we can see that the coping response isn't producing the results we want.

On a humorous level this type of behavior shows itself in the man who thinks that if he only talks louder the foreigner who doesn't know English very well will be able to understand him better. On the serious level this type of behavior shows itself in the unhappy wife.

She wants to change her husband and knows her nagging isn't working, but she still says to herself, *If I just try harder, I can make it work.* So she increases the behavior that was already driving a wedge between herself and her husband, often with disastrous results.

Now let's look at some of these coping mechanisms. The labels may sound a little heavy, but the concepts are easy to understand, especially since we all use each of them to some extent. I have decided to retain the technical labels for accuracy's sake, with everyday explanations attached. As you read the descriptions, try to think of the times you or others you know have used these processes. You might want also to look up the biblical passages illustrating these concepts. Remember, the concepts we are discussing become dysfunctional if they are the only options available in a given situation. Good emotional health in a family and in an individual's sphere of contact utilizes a variety of coping styles and responses.

REACTION FORMATION

This intimidating term simply means developing a reaction that is the opposite of what might be expected. A child growing up in an unhappy, painful atmosphere might develop a superficially positive attitude within the home. He provides all the happiness his family needs. His role becomes one of distracting other family members from their pain. He becomes their hope, the family hero, even though his health often shows signs of the stress that comes from trying to keep everyone else happy, when in reality no one is.

There are other kinds of reaction formations. One is to do everything in opposition to your family's norms:

- *never* spanking your children because you were spanked too much

- *never* drinking alcohol because your parents drank too much

- *compulsively* buying fancy new things because you felt embarrassed as a child over the poverty of your family of origin

- *refusing* ever to take a promotion that involves relocating because you moved too much as a child

Reaction formations usually include extremes that are detrimental to the one practicing them.

Look at a small part of the story of Amnon and Tamar (2 Samuel 13:1-22) discussed more fully in chapter 1. Before his assault on Tamar, Amnon was wildly in love with her ("in lust" would perhaps be more accurate), but what was his opinion after the attack? Through reaction formation, he suddenly came to hate her (v. 15)!

Not all reaction formations are so extreme, nor do they always have to do with covering up sin. They usually occur, though, in response to an emotionally painful experience. Often they involve vows an ACDF makes before God ("I will *never* again . . . ," or, "I will *never* do that to *my* kids") and are almost always a response to shame or guilt (see chapter 4 for a comprehensive discussion of shame). Certainly shame was a key element in the case of Amnon and Tamar.

The man discussed at the outset of this chapter is another good illustration. He vowed *never* to abandon his family, yet he wound up doing just that. The apostle Paul's words (in Romans 7:15*b*-16, 19-20) apply here: "For I am not practicing what I would like to do, but I am doing the very thing I hate" (v. 15).

DISPLACEMENT

Displacement often occurs in settings where it is not safe to express feelings to the one who needs to hear them. The classic and somewhat facetious example is the person who kicks the dog instead of the boss.

But the less humorous, indeed the dangerous, example of displacement occurs when family members displace their anger on one another. When a child cannot talk out his feelings without fear of punishment, shame, or denial, he may come to believe that the only mode of expression available to him is to act out his feelings. The result is that he displaces unsafe feelings onto safe or neutral objects. That is why a child's anger or pain will often show itself in drawings, play therapy, or even in bullying younger children. Unfortunately, this acting out of stifled emotions becomes more dangerous as the child matures, for older children can do much more harm than can younger ones, as witnessed by the shocking increase in gang killings among teens.

Families in which displacement is widely used often produce the "problem child," or "identified patient," as counselors call him. The rest of the family sees this "identified patient" as the only one who really needs help. A parent calls in with a "problem teen," whereas after we delve into the family system, we find that all members of the family need some degree of help. The parents of a girl we'll call Valerie came to us with the complaint that she was "boy crazy" and headed for unwedded pregnancy, but when we examined the case it turned out that her parents were the ones obsessed with illicit sex (see chapter 11).

The object of the displacement, the "identified patient" or "problem child," becomes the family scapegoat. Just as in the Old Testament practice of sending a goat out into the wilderness (Leviticus 16:8-10) to bear away the sins of the nation, so the "identified patient" essentially "carries" the sins of the family. Disparaging comments are typically made: "If it weren't for Billy, we'd have a good family." Sarcastic remarks abound. Sadly, and ironically, the child's sense of belonging is enhanced as he misbehaves, becomes psychosomatically ill, displaces his feelings, or carries out whatever role he and his family have unconsciously (but nevertheless cooperatively) worked out.

Julie's family, noted in the introduction to this book, illustrates this coping style. In her family system she was the only one who was seen as deserving punishment. She was the identified patient or scapegoat. And yet in spite of this mistreatment she felt that at least she had a role (versus no role at all) in her family by acting as the scapegoat of displacement.

The biblical character Samson practiced displacement. Probably the most obvious instance occured when, in anger at his new wife, he killed thirty men in Ashkelon to pay a debt to the men of Timnah, who had given the correct answer to his riddle (Judges 14:1-20). Now many times it is actually healthier to displace angry or hurt feelings than to express them directly, but in a relationship it is critical to be able to talk these kinds of feelings through. This is where the practice of praying out loud to the Lord can be relieving to the believer who feels unable at the moment (due to boiling feelings of anger, for example) to talk directly with the individual involved.

PROJECTION

Projection is the act of blaming others for your own faults. Projection means seeing in others what is impossible for you to see in yourself (much like seeing the speck in your neighbor's eye and missing the log in yours [see Matthew 7:1-5]). If you think about what the word "projectile" means (the idea of motion from one point to another, as in a missile), you'll be able to see how in this coping mechanism blame is *projected* onto another.

Usually projection takes place where there are grievances of a similar nature. Remember Adam and Eve in the Garden? Both had eaten the same fruit, but when they were caught, Adam blamed Eve and God for what he himself had done (Genesis 3:1-13).

Another example of projection is the "dry drunk" syndrome. An ACDF often doesn't drink at all (reaction formation) but does exhibit the behavior pattern of an alcoholic. The ACDF might be just as belligerent, angry, controlling, and intimidating as was his (or her) drinking parent, but he doesn't drink; hence the term "dry drunk." He may be as selfish, demanding, stubborn, and sullen as was his alcoholic parent, but he doesn't beat his kids or his wife. So he thinks he is doing OK. But when you think about it, the only thing missing is the booze. Because he attaches (projects) onto his drinking parent all the personality traits he hates, and because he doesn't drink, he is oblivious to those same traits in himself.

As a child, he (or she) typically told himself that if his dad would just quit drinking, things *would be* OK. As an adult, he doesn't drink, so he thinks that things *must be* OK. He often sees himself and his family atmosphere as being radically different from his family of origin. It is not uncommon for him to tell his chidren, "You don't know how good you have it," or "If you think this is bad, you ought to have seen (my drinking parent)."

Another pattern of blame is to hold someone else accountable for "all" that has happened to you. Parents of ACDFs are often the focus of this rage. We all know adults who practice this style. They manage to find someone to blame for everything that is difficult in their lives. They themselves are always cast as the victims (of course, since they're the casting directors!). An obvious benefit of this coping style is that the one who uses it doesn't have to take responsibility for his action or inaction; whatever he does is always somebody else's fault.

The New Testament records a conversation between Jesus and a man practicing a form of projection, the lame man lying by the pool at Bethesda (John 5:1-15). The lame man was afraid of change. After all, he had been in the same environment for thirty-eight years. To change now was scary. Most of us would have imagined that the lame man would have shouted a desperate "Yes!" to Jesus' question, "Do you wish to get well?" Instead, the lame man offered the excuse that he had "no man to put [him] into the pool when the water is stirred up" (v. 7). He had accommodated himself to his painful condition and was projecting blame for his continuing to stay unhealed onto another—that missing person who wouldn't help him get to the waters in time. His blaming, or projection, guaranteed that he received exactly what he really wanted: the appearance of an effort to be healed without ever having really to change his life-style or to use all his resources in an attempt to improve his situation.

INTROJECTION

Introjection means the adoption of another's pattern as your own. It has to do with assimilation of another's pattern or role, regardless of how healthy it is, or how you feel about it.

Consider Kathy. With her lower jaw quivering and eyes puffy from crying all night, Kathy just couldn't figure it out. Why would Dan leave her? *He had had it so good. I took good care of him and the kids, didn't I? We were a perfect family. The house was always straight. Dinner was fixed and on time every night. The bills were always paid when they were due. Why, I even shopped for his clothes to save him time and keep him looking sharp. Why would he want someone else? I wasn't bad in bed either. All our friends think I look terrific, especially after having three children. Everything was so right—what went wrong?*

Starting in her family of origin during her childhood, Kathy had always done everything perfectly. As the oldest child and with both parents working, it wasn't long before she was heavily involved in chores around the house. Her day started by getting herself up and fixing her dad's lunch while her mom was still at the hospital working the night shift. After that, she got dressed, straightened her room, fixed breakfast for the family (she was glad when they got a microwave), fed their cocker spaniel (he always made her feel happy), and then waited on the couch, watching TV until the school bus came.

After school, it was time to help Mom with dinner and around the house before Dad came home and they all ate together. Mom left for work after supper, so Kathy always did the dishes. She filled in partially for Mom in parenting her younger brothers and sisters, too. In short, Kathy was a hyperresponsible child and received much praise as caretaker, even at such a young age.

When she married it was no problem for her to bring all this overwrought caretaking into her new family, for she had been doing it all her life, as she often observed to herself. Dan's parents (especially his mother) thought she was the perfect wife. Didn't Dan?

Now it all seemed so empty and useless. Gradually, though, through insight gained in counseling and other sources, she came to see that she had always taken care of everybody else. Now don't get me wrong. Some normal amount of caring for others is desired by God. But in Kathy's case this good thing was carried to an extreme, so that it became dysfunctional.

Kathy found that in her caring she always managed to *control* exactly what went on in her family—both in her family of origin and in her family as an adult. She never realized how smothering this out-of-control mothering was to her husband—and to herself. She had not intended for it to be that way, but not knowing anything else, and because of introjection, she had simply adopted the pattern as her own. She wound up mothering/smothering everyone near and dear to her. And she paid the price for it, in a dysfunctional marriage relationship.

REPRESSION

When something is repeated long enough and often enough, adults and children alike will believe it. Repression relies on that premise. Repression means the denial of your own perceptions. It is also called "selective forgetting." For example, dysfunctional families often insist they are well and healthy. They often attempt to look great on the outside. But to make their perceptions and feelings match, repression has to go to work. The child begins to believe the lie of "health" and denies his own perceptions and feelings about his family's true health and functionality. He makes his experience conform to the "party line," the picture his family wants to present. Only later, often in mid-adult life, do nagging doubts surface.

Two forms of repression occur in the most painfully dysfunctional families, those that include abuse. Some ACDFs can recall the physical abuse, beatings, or cruel punishment they received without any emotion whatever (unusual in itself), but they discount and minimize its impact upon them. Others don't discount the abuse—they just remove from conscious memory (repress) all the painful experiences of their childhood.

As a result, these adults often have large time gaps in their childhood memories. Alas, not only are the painful memories gone, but so are memories of many other events, too. As far as memories go, childhood is often a black hole to these adults, who as children felt compelled to use the strategy of repression. It's the result of the "go on, forget it, get out, and don't look back" approach to handling problems so often urged on us by our culture and by our need to survive.

Some younger children initially attempt to stay close to the abusing parent out of desperation for any small nurturance they might accidentally receive. Eventually, though, anger sets in, and the abused ACDF often becomes the abuser, thus transmitting the cycle of pain to succeeding generations. Recovery usually is painful and difficult for the adult who as a child repressed his painful experiences. Under the right conditions, those memories can return with a vengeance. Like a flash flood, they can overrun the adult child in an overwhelming and unexpected way.

A beautiful picture of healing that finally occurs after years of repression appears in the story of Joseph and his brothers (Genesis 37:1-36; 39:1–50:26), culminating in the account of their meeting after their father's death (Genesis 50:15-21).

Repressed memories began to return to Joseph and his brothers in the initial confrontation when the brothers first arrive in to Egypt to buy grain (Genesis 42:1-24; 43:16-31; 45:1-15). The power of the repressed secret was broken as Joseph gently led his brothers symbolically through his own experience. He required one of the brothers to be left in prison as a guarantee that the youngest would arrive in Egypt. Immediately the scene of Joseph in the well flashed before the brothers' eyes, and they recalled his pain and their own guilt. All the long-buried secrets they had hidden in a conscious, collaborative effort suddenly resurfaced—and Joseph was listening (42:21-24).

For full recovery to take place Joseph needed to hear their acknowledgment of their sin, and they needed to feel his pain. Before he could forgive his brothers he had to be convinced that they felt *his* pain and terror at its outset, not just the pain and terror they felt now that they had been caught. Once he could see and hear that they did feel his pain, he could forgive them. Then he could reveal himself. All of this took time, and the process itself is expanded over chapter 12.

Repression has classically been compared to a boiling kettle with the top tightly clamped down, the energy inside just waiting to explode. It is interesting to note the amount of weeping that goes on in the various passages dealing with the restoration of Joseph to his brothers (45:2-3, 14-15), showing the degree of emotion pent up in their repressed memories.

FAMILY STRUCTURE THAT PROTECTS
AND PASSES ALONG FAMILY SECRETS

The combination of coping style, family secrets, and shame is by itself inadequate to guarantee the transmission of distortions across generations. For that to occur there must be a family structure in place to maintain and actually transmit the distortions.

Family *structure* is different from family *style*. Family style is concerned with how the family comes across to others. It has to do with who appears to be in charge of the family and who *appears* to be responsible for certain items (maybe in accordance with a particular Christian denomination's tradition).

Family structure has to do with the way the family organizes itself around certain individuals. Family structure has to do with who really has power in this family, who really calls the shots. The healthier the family, the less difference there is between style and structure. In a healthy family things are as they appear to be. The greater the differences between style and structure, however, the greater and more powerful the family secrets and dysfunction.

Indeed, family secrets can often take on a life of their own. They become a force within the family simply because so many individuals put so much energy into ignoring, denying, or distorting what has actually happened within the family. As the family tree grows up it incorporates this distortion.

Family structure was initiated in the Garden of Eden when the first family composed of Adam, Eve, and God was established. They were close and enjoyed unrestricted intimacy. The Fall changed not only that relationship but also the regulations that govern family systems. An understanding of those changes is essential to grasping how and why families develop healthy or unhealthy systems. Let us look at how relationships in the family changed after the Fall.

Notice the triangular diagrams (tables 3.2, 3.3, 3.4). They are examples of triad models, diagrams helpful in interpreting relationships in a family. The models operate according to the following assumptions:

1. Often it is helpful to view family relationships in threesomes (triads).

2. Relational intimacy can only be built along one axis at a time. That is why time alone with each family member and time alone with God is important.

Table 3.2
Triad Relationship of Adam, Eve, and God

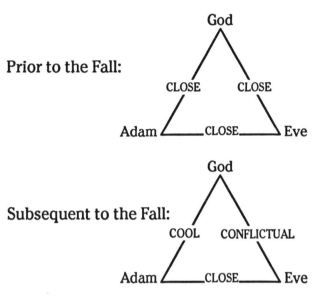

3. The relationship between any set of three individuals (a triad) can be evaluated along varying degrees of closeness: *close, cool,* or *conflictual.* All three terms are relative and flex with each family system. *Close* is simply the closest of the relationships, whereas *cool* is slightly more distant or withdrawn than the close relationship, and *conflictual* is more tense, with more open disagreement than in the close relationship.

4. Each triad can only have one *close* relationship, one *cool* relationship and one *conflictual* relationship at any given time. When a different relationship in a set becomes *close,* the entire pattern changes.

5. The more dysfunctional the family is, the more marked the contrasts between the three relationships.

6. Circumstances can temporarily change the usual pattern of relationships within the triad (for example, the loss of a job, moving to a new city, a major illness, financial reversal, the

aging of parents, children moving in/out of the home, and so on).

7. All three relationships are subject to change when one individual in the triad is replaced by another (divorce, death, older parents, children moving in and out of the home, and so on).

Table 3.2 shows one way the family system in Eden before and after the Fall could be diagrammed. Note that the relationships between Adam/God and Eve/God are different. Eve led the rebellion by eating the fruit, so her relationship with God immediately after the disobedience was the rockier one. Adam joined in eating, too, and he must bear responsibility with Eve to be sure, but at least he and God were still on speaking terms, as evident in God's asking, "Adam, where art thou?" (3:9, KJV*). Adam and Eve then collaborated in hiding and in clothing their nakedness.

The post-Fall triangle only describes the experience just before Adam and Eve left the Garden. Relationships are constantly changing, are constantly subject to ebb and flow. Any triad evaluation is only good for the moment. It is simply a snapshot of the relationship. That is true of the triads given above. Eve's relationship with God warmed after she left the Garden, as is shown in Genesis 4:1, 25, when she gives credit and thanks to God. A triad evaluation made then might look quite different from the one given in table 3.2.

The relationship between any two persons at the bottom of the triangle will vary depending on the identity of the party at the top (by the way, placement at the top doesn't necessarily imply elevated status). Think about how your family shifts when the two different mothers-in-law come to visit (table 3.3)!

Now please note that in figure 3.3 I did not label the axes for level of intimacy. That is because I want you to plug in your own (or a hypothetical) situation. If you and your spouse have a solid relationship, you would label the husband-wife axis *close.* But say you are newly married, or you and your spouse are having problems in the relationship with an in-law. Then you might place the *close* label on another axis. (Pick your poison: do you want to define the mother/daughter axis as *close,* or mother-in-law/son-in-law axis? The possibilities are excrutiatingly endless.) You would have to decide if the

---

*King James Version.

Table 3.3

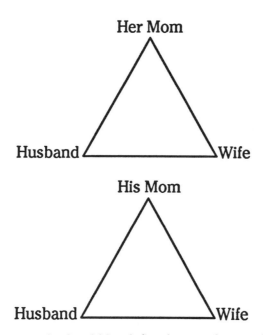

Her Mom

Husband   Wife

His Mom

Husband   Wife

spouse/spouse axis should be defined as *cool* or *conflictual.* Add the scenario "favorite-son-marries-wife-whom-Mom-detests," and you really have a mess on your hands!

Triad relationships have a built-in tension, as you can see. As a counteractive to this confusion, boundaries need to be constructed between the various members of the triad (for a fuller examination of boundaries, see chapter 8). God Himself recognized the trauma of trying to bring parental relationships into the triad relationship of man and wife and gave an explicit command to newly marrieds: for family health, the couple must separate from their respective families of origin and "cleave" to one another (2:24; see also chapter 10 of this book).

The triad system of examining relationships is dynamic and flexible. That is because relationships themselves are dynamic and subject to change. When one relationship in a triad changes, the entire system changes to accommodate it.

The capacity in a family setting for flexibility of triads is an indication of health. If relationships cannot flex and change, dysfunction may be setting in. For example, if in figure 3.3 the spouse/spouse axis is *cool* or *conflictual* due to problems in the relationship, the couple might seek marriage counseling to correct the axis. That would be a good step for the couple to take, as they sought to bring the triad again into a biblically correct mode. But if, say, the wife/mother axis was *permanently close,* that is, if she had not yet left her family of origin to "cleave" to her new husband, as the Bible exhorts, the system would not be able to flex sufficiently to allow for the spouse/spouse axis to become *close.* If the wife could not release her (inappropriately) *close* relationship to her mother, the best relationship she and her husband could achieve would be *cool* or *conflictual* —hardly God's ideal!

Now a question is probably surfacing: if relationships operate in triads, how would you diagram an entire family system at once? Table 3.4 provides an answer. Look at all of those triangles! And each axis of each triad has one of three characteristics. No wonder successful family living is so complicated!

As you study table 3.4, try labeling each axis from your point of view as it pertains to your present family or your family of origin. Then have your spouse make his/her assessment independently of yours, and compare notes. Or ask your adolescent children to label as many triangles as they can. It will make for interesting conversa-

Table 3.4
Triad Relationships in a Family

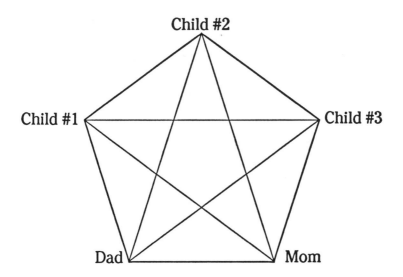

tion! The exercise can lead to significant discoveries and, ultimately, toward the healing of dysfunctional relationships.

PASSING THE TORCH UNCONSCIOUSLY

In summarizing the process that passes dysfunction from one generation to another, we see several elements. We see destructive family rules (don't talk, don't trust, don't feel), coping mechanisms (reaction formation, displacement, projection, introjection, and repression), and structures (triads). We also see human society deciding to disregard God's guidelines for healthy family living (for example, a man's not "leaving" father and mother to "cleave" to his spouse). Destructive elements in our personal and family life, combined with rejection of God's guidelines for living, result in the "sins of the fathers" being passed down the family tree with alarming predictability.

Let me close this chapter by calling attention to an entertaining observation that also carries with it a sobering truth. In the many years of marriage and premarital counseling I have done, I have found that it can take a new couple many years (Would you believe up to twenty in some cases?) to sort out which patterns they want to keep from their respective families of origin. The influence of their families extends to every sphere in the marital relationship.

Which is why I say that when you hop into bed on your wedding night, you will find six people in there: *her* mom and dad, *your* mom and dad, and the two of you!

Questions for Reflection

Ask yourself the following questions, and make personal notes in the space provided.

1. Which one of the three "don't" rules did your family employ most? What recurring circumstance caused all of the rules to be employed at once in your family?

_____

_____

_____

2. As you look back on your childhood, what coping mechanism did you utilize most? Which mechanism was most prevalent in the other individuals in your family of origin? Have they been able to adjust in later life? Have you?

---

3. As you review the cyclical pattern in table 3.1, how do you feel about the statement "The child begins to trust the system that caused him to mistrust himself in the first place"? What impact has this phenomenon had on your current adult patterns?

---

4. If this chapter seems to fit your family of origin, what specific relationship styles do you see your siblings carrying into their dating-/marital relationships? How about yourself?

---

5. How did the particular religious views of your church and family of origin impact the family system in your (original) marriage? What particulars of that religious system kept your family from changing? What has been hard for you to change in your current family as a result of your religious training?

---

6. The section on triads says that it is possible to develop intimacy with only one person at a time. How do you feel about that? What regular shifts do you see in your key relationships? What one individual seems to have the most influence in your relationships?

Why? Is it appropriate for that individual to have that much influence? If not, what options do you have?

_____

_____

_____

    7. On a scale of 1 to 10 (with 10 being high), how close was your family's style (the way it looked from the outside) to its structure (the way it actually functioned)? Did the individual who was supposed to be responsible for certain behavior actually carry it out? If he didn't, who "covered" for him? How would your other siblings answer this question?

_____

_____

_____

Note

1. Claudia Black, *It Will Never Happen to Me* (Denver: M.A.C. Printing, 1982), pp. 31-49.

4

Guilt-ridden Baggage: The Role of Religious Shame

By Earl Henslin, PsyD.

Grab a pencil and check yes or no to the following questions; you'll total the results below. Be honest—this is only a private assessment of your feelings and has proved helpful to many people who have taken it.

Shame Quiz

1. Do you have difficulty feeling relief when you confess your sin to God or to another person? In other words, do you have lingering feelings of guilt that you've never been quite able to shed?

   _____ Yes   _____ No

2. When other people are having fun, do you feel uncomfortable?

   _____ Yes   _____ No

3. When you feel hurt or angry, do you automatically experience guilt for feeling that way?

   _____ Yes   _____ No

4. Is it hard for you to tell another person how you are feeling because you think he might think you are a bad Christian?

_____ Yes   _____ No

5. Do you feel embarrassed when you experience success?

_____ Yes   _____ No

6. Is it hard for you to totally relax/have fun?

_____ Yes   _____ No

7. Do you want to withdraw from friends and family when you feel hurt or when you have done something wrong?

_____ Yes   _____ No

8. Do you view God as a stern and unfeeling Judge you will never be able to please?

_____ Yes   _____ No

9. Do you feel uncomfortable with and/or have difficulty enjoying your sexuality?

_____ Yes   _____ No

10. Do you always feel like you will never be a "good enough Christian"?

_____ Yes   _____ No

11. Are you too quick to criticize and/or judge others?

_____ Yes   _____ No

12. Do you become defensive quickly whenever someone asks you a question and/or tries to offer constructive feedback?

_____ Yes   _____ No

13. Are you now depressed and/or angry after reading this list?

_____ Yes   _____ No

Total up your "yes" answers. Here's an analysis of how you may stand with regard to religious shame:

0-2 "yes" answers: You've been extremely fortunate in not encountering religious shame. You should read this chapter to better understand your spouse, your friends, and your colleagues, who probably have been shamed significantly—or take the week off and go to Hawaii. You deserve it—and you won't feel guilty about it—so go for it!

3-5 "yes" answers: You probably have significant levels of religious shame in your thinking and emotions. You should read this chapter carefully.

6-13 "yes" answers: You'd better find a support group right away!

A SERIOUS MATTER

Even though you may have detected a bit of good-natured humor above, shame is a serious problem for ACDFs, and religious shame even more so, since the power of the Bible or God is purported to back up the shamer. In other words, nonreligious parents may simply invoke their rank as parents (or invoke generalized societal traditions) as their authority in making a child feel false guilt over something. But when religious parents use (misuse) the Bible or other Christian teachings as their authority, the effect is far more powerful, long-lasting, and resistant to correction. For not only is Mom or Dad shaming the child, but God Himself is seen as being in on it, too!

Religious shame is pervasive in our culture. If you have been a Christian for five years or more, you very probably have experienced religious shaming, particularly if you grew up in a fundamentalistic, evangelical background and are more than twenty-five years of age. Unfortunately, it seems that the longer a person is a Christian, the greater the load of religious shame he carries.

Religious shaming is not something churches or Christians do intentionally or maliciously. Rather, it reflects a theology that somewhere along the line left out concern for feelings and one's inner, emotional life. Emotions are seen as evil enemies needing to be fought off, subdued, and controlled; legalism and condemnation are seen as virtues.

Those who have been subject to this philosophy have had to live with contradictory religious messages:

"I'm as worthless as rags" ——	"I'm of immense value as a person because Christ died for me"
"I'm deserving of hell" ——	"I'm made in God's image"

It is easy to see why there is widespread confusion among Christians on this subject and why religious shame is so powerful. Without a Messiah we definitely *are* as worthless as rags in comparison to a holy, sovereign God (Isaiah 64:6). However, too many Christians have been so obsessed with the fact that they have a sin nature that they never allow themselves to feel any of the good that does exist. They have been afraid that if Christians let up on the teaching that apart from Christ we deserve hell, the church will turn into a raging herd of humanists!

I think it would be great if we could all say at the beginning of a Sunday school class, as in an A.A. meeting, "Hi, my name is Earl, and I am a sinner." Then everyone would respond in unison with an affirming, "Hi, Earl." That way we'd have that particular theological fact covered and could get on to the main tasks in such a setting: sharing what God is doing in our lives, sharing our pain and our struggles, and exploring ways to better glorify God in our lives.

But we are not there yet. We tend to focus on our worthlessness before God to the extent that we never acknowledge Christ's work in our life and the depth and beauty of what that means. We never acknowledge the light and goodness there is in the world. The Bible says, "If we walk in the light as He Himself is in the light, we have fellowship with one another, and the blood of Jesus His Son cleanses us from all sin. If we say that we have no sin, we are deceiving ourselves, and the truth is not in us" (1 John 1:7-8). If I am to be in the light and have fellowship with other people, I need to bring my sinfulness into the light and not deny it. Likewise, I should not deny the good part of the gospel, for example, the truth that I am of immense worth because of Christ. So let's move out of denial and have fellowship in the light together.

As a therapist I find that religious shame keeps many Christians from getting help for their problems and keeps them isolated from others, bearing all alone terrible hurts and secrets. When they do come in for therapy, they must struggle through issues of religious shame before they can begin to deal with the immediate problems that made them seek help.

RELIGIOUS SHAME VERSUS TRUE GUILT

True guilt is that voice we hear inside—and it could be either the Holy Spirit prompting us or our conscience—letting us know that we have done something wrong. When we hear that prompting we need to take steps to deal with the offense we have committed. The process is stated clearly in 1 John 1:9. All we need to do is to acknowledge, or confess, our sin to God and repent of it, and we are cleansed, based on the work of Christ on the cross. Forgiveness is accomplished.

However, many do not feel forgiven even after they have confessed their sin to Christ. The culprit is usually shame, or false guilt. Shame is the line of thinking that often mistakenly equates normal life conditions with true guilt. For example, a four-year-old's room is generally messy. A religious, shame-based parent would scold the child and say, "God thinks that Jamie is a very bad, wicked, and lazy girl, since her room is so messy because she didn't pick up her toys!" (Such a statement is usually accompanied by a fierce-looking frown on the parent's face.) You can imagine the view of God this practice gives a young, impressionable child!

ACDFs who have been brought up in a shaming home environment find it almost impossible to experience true relief and closeness to God after confession of sin. Try as they may, they cannot conjure up the relief they so desperately need.

TWO TYPES OF RELIGIOUS SHAME

There are two types of religious shame: *external* and *internal.* External religious shame is experienced in relation to a person, group, or organization. Internal religious shame is a process that goes on within us, and has to do with messages and feelings dictating our reaction to certain events or activities.

EXTERNAL RELIGIOUS SHAME

External religious shame occurs in many forms: a comment or look of superiority, a set of shoulds or should nots, or a set of rules for daily living. For example, religious shame can influence the type of church we choose. We are likely to choose a church that reflects the level of religious shame within us. If we feel more comfortable with an external, rule-governed spirituality that dictates how we are to live, then we will choose that type of church. Legalistic churches, which are highly controlling of its members, feel safer and more comfortable to the person dominated by religious shame. Where to go and what to do—life is easier if those choices are already made for him. In a religious organization characterized by shame-based thinking, people don't have to take so much personal responsibility for deciding their personal conduct under God. They just follow the code and assume they've "got it."

When I was sixteen years old, I had a friend several years older than I. He came from a painful family background and had a hostile relationship with his father. In spite of the turmoil in his home, he managed to make it to church regularly and was involved in the youth group.

This was during the Vietnam War, and our whole country was in a period of upheaval. The stable '50s were giving way to the unstable '60s: the Beatles were popular, as were radically different hair styles, dress, and entertainment—you name it. My friend wore his hair long, and when he came to church he didn't always wear the traditional "Sunday best." He looked different from everyone else.

That brought reactions and "Christian" confrontation—accusations of his being on drugs and being a hippie, neither of which was true at the time. These accusations communicated judgment and condemnation. They cast him in the role of a "bad" Christian. Needless to say, he stopped coming to church. Later, he become addicted to drugs and did not get sober until he was well into his thirties.

When I look back at the rude, uncaring, and unchristian treatment given to this teenager, it is obvious that the church members had little idea what my friend really needed. What he needed then was caring relationships with folks who would stick with him through the difficult times he was experiencing in his family and the fear he felt that he might be sent off to the Vietnam War. Yet that is not what he got. Shamed by his church family, he began practicing what they accused him of by becoming a drug addict and a hippie. Now don't get me wrong—each person is responsible for his choices and actions—but in this case his church must share some of the responsibility for the way they treated him at a critical juncture in his life.

It goes back to what I said at the outset of this chapter. We are sometimes so obsessed with the bad that we can't see the good. The church couldn't see the good in my friend's life: that he was a teen-ager with serious family problems yet still made it to church regularly on his own and was involved in the youth group. They were "all good" and he "all bad" (chapter 9 will discuss this goodness/bad-ness theme in more detail). Funny, isn't it? When you sit down with a person and get to know him, his outer appearance becomes less im-portant. What really matters is his inner person.

One couple I know who had recently become Christians began to attend an evangelical church near their home. They became in-volved in one of the adult fellowships and made friends with some of the couples in the fellowship, on occasion going out to the movies with them.

The class decided to go on a retreat, and this couple signed up. At the retreat in various conversations they innocently mentioned the movies they had attended. To their utter amazement, the couples with whom they had attended the movies acted as though they had not gone with them. This reaction was uncomfortable and puzzling to the new Christians.

To make matters worse, as the ski weekend wore on, some peo-ple criticized the wife because her ski clothes were colorful (note that I say *colorful*; they were not too tight or sexually suggestive).

Soon the pastor cornered them and began to sermonize about the evils of movies and provocative dress. The couple was mortified when they realized that it was not OK to be open about attending a movie, and they recognized the hypocrisy of their new-found friends, who acted as though they had not gone. By the end of the weekend they felt as though there must be something wrong with their Chris-tianity and that they must not be as spiritual as the other couples. Yet at the same time they were hurt at the treatment they received—and all over brightly colored ski clothes and attending a movie. It was the last time they attended that church. (See Galatians 2:11-21 for a first-century parallel.)

External religious shame fosters and encourages secrets. Once the Christian discovers the hidden list of rules used to define people as "all bad" or "all good," the secrets start. There is no talking about the things you do, for shame floods in from shame-based Christians. It becomes increasingly difficult to share anything about yourself. Talk is limited to a spiritualese that communicates nothing about who you are and what you are going through as a person. People become experts at hiding and covering up their pain in, for example, superficial prayer requests labeled "unspoken."

INTERNAL RELIGIOUS SHAME

Internal religious shame is the inner voice that communicates how bad a person you are. It is an inner set of beliefs, values, and experiences based on distorted messages or experiences in life. These beliefs usually originate in churches or with other Christians and are shame-based in their orientation. Seemingly insignificant events, thoughts, or feelings can tip off a "shame attack" that spirals into depression or anger.

I grew up in an environment where playing cards was seen as evil and sinful. There was one exception, however: the card deck associated with the board game "Rook." Our family enjoyed playing it. (I often wondered if Rook cards were invented by the same person who spread the story of the evils connected to regular playing cards as a means of increasing sales!) I even attended a Christian college for one year where if you were caught using regular playing cards you would get demerits and risk expulsion from school.

Imagine my confusion a couple of years later when I attended a college fellowship at a nearby state university where for fun the students played cards (no gambling, just such games as bridge). The students in this fellowship were alive, joyful Christians who shared their faith eagerly, and yet they played cards. Some of them even went dancing! Yet their lives did not disintegrate into debauchery, as I had been told would happen to people who practiced such evils. Were my parents wrong, or were my friends wrong?

Now please understand me. I am all for holding the line on behavior that God explicitly says in His Word is sinful or unhealthy. My Christian friends at the university had to make choices. They avoided some movies as unhealthy and some places as off limits when it came to dancing. But there was nothing lustful about the way they danced; in fact, it seemed to me that more unmarried girls got pregnant at the Christian college I had attended than at that secular university!

But back to my cards-are-evil-except-for-Rook complex. Until I resolved the shame problem in my own thinking, playing cards brought over me a wave of shame, as though I were doing something evil. I felt guilty and depressed and withdrew from those around me. I experienced a sense of shame, yet it was a shame that had its foundation in distortion and not in truth. When I carried this load of shame inside, it was hard for me to experience grace or forgiveness —I felt like such a bad person. It would take me days or even a week to pull up out of the shame nosedive.

CHARACTERISTICS OF RELIGIOUS SHAME

Shame-based people and religious organizations have a characteristic way of looking at life that is different from a healthy spiritual view. Look at the columns below, and see if you can identify with some the statements in the column "Religious Shame View."

Religious Shame View	Healthy Spirituality View
"Emotions are sinful."	Emotions are neither good nor bad. It is what you do with them that is important; for example, following Paul's advice in Ephesians 4:26-27: "Be angry and yet do not sin; do not let the sun go down on your anger, and do not give the devil an opportunity."
"Having problems is sinful."	Having problems is a part of my human condition. I can take my struggles to God and my fellow Christians for support and encouragement.
"Compulsive disease[1] is sin.[2]"	Compulsions such as alcoholism, drug addiction, eating disorders, or sexual addiction are complex

Religious Shame View	Healthy Spirituality View
	disease processes that impact a person spiritually, emotionally, and physically. I need to attend to all levels in order for recovery to occur.

Let's look at each of these three messages in more detail.

"EMOTIONS ARE SINFUL"

Many Christians feel sinful when they experience anger or hurt. They were taught that the emotion itself is sin, rather than looking at a person's response to the emotion and what brought it about. If you grew up in a dysfunctional family where it was not OK to feel certain ways, you were hit with a double whammy if your parents claimed the authority of God to communicate such family rules as "don't feel." It is sad but true that many times Christians have to go through more to begin to recover than non-Christians. They have to separate the messages they received from their parents into two categories: those that were biblically true and those that were biblically wrapped but untrue.

Many Christians were severely traumatized as they grew up. Even though their parents were Christians, alcoholism, sexual addiction, sexual abuse, and physical or emotional abuse were present in their homes.

One woman whom I'll call Judy struggled with depression and suicidal thoughts from the time she was a teenager. In our first counseling session she told me that although she grew up in a "Christian home," her father was an alcoholic. That one piece of information was extremely difficult for her to share. She saw it as sinful and inwardly shaming to acknowledge her father's condition to someone outside the family. Surely it would dishonor her father and mother for her to talk about what had caused her such pain in her growing up years. As a further extension of the rule, she found it immensely difficult to attend a support group for ACDFs—the very thing that would later contribute greatly to her recovery.

Judy needed to separate biblically wrapped messages from biblically true messages. She needed to distinguish obeying the fifth commandment ("Honor your father and your mother" [Exodus 20:12]) from talking about family pain to an outsider (remember the "don't talk" rule from chapter 3). In breaking the code of silence, Judy was indeed knocking down a barrier, but it was not a barrier erected by God. It was a barrier erected by her father's alcoholism.

It is tragic that Judy had to carry her pain alone for many years. Inwardly the shame was so intense that isolation from others and, later, suicide seemed a better choice than breaking the barrier erected by her father's alcoholism and religious shame. After several months of recovery work, memories returned to Judy of having been sexually abused by her father. With those memories came crushing anguish and inner pain that made her feel as though her very soul were being torn apart.

After days and weeks of crying and weeping, anger began to surface. She began to feel rage toward her father for the way he had victimized her as a little girl. After the anger was directed toward the man who had hurt her, she began to accept what had taken place and was later able to forgive him.

I have condensed Judy's story. The healing process took several years. She had to change many perceptions about herself, her sexuality, and her relationship with God. She also had to surmount numerous roadblocks in order to work through the process of healing the deep hurt, and religious shame was one of the most significant of those roadblocks.

Judy's hurt and anger was intense. She had learned in her youth that anger was sin; now she had to learn that the anger and hurt she was feeling was a normal response to having been abused. She had to experience for the first time the feelings she had to repress as a little girl.

The strength of her feelings was hard for her Christian friends to accept. When someone in Christian circles is hurting, it brings out the codependent "rescuers" in the crowd. They want to rush in and "fix" the pain. That was the case here. Judy's friends told her she needed to let go of her anger and forgive her father. In one sense her friends were right: forgiveness is the ultimate goal. But when a person is first becoming aware of intense anger, he needs time to go through the process of dealing with those feelings.

Whenever Judy tried to let go of the pain prematurely, as her friends suggested, she became depressed and suicidal. That only made her feel more defective as a Christian. She thought that if only she had more faith, she would not have such intense feelings of hurt and anger and could easily forgive her father. Her friends' attempt to help only shamed her and prolonged the agony.

Her friends were right in one sense, though. Forgiveness *is* the key—but only in due time and only after the individual has passed through the appropriate steps. Eventually Judy was able to accept that it was all right for her to face the anger and hurt she had carried around inside for so long. For the first time she could see in Scripture that Jesus was a man of great emotion. She could identify with the rage Jesus felt when He saw the Temple being used wrongly. His response was one of righteous anger, and He threw the money changers out. He expressed His outrage clearly and directly to the ones who were desecrating God's Temple. As she connected that scriptural reality with her own experience, the religious shame lifted. Now she was truly in recovery from the abuse she had experienced.

"HAVING PROBLEMS IS SINFUL"

Somewhere along the line we have lost a sense of humanness in the Christian community. An image of perfection has become the goal of spirituality rather than an attitude of acceptance of ourselves and others and an understanding that we are all imperfect. We have lost the sense that all of us need a Savior—and need each other, too.

Who has not struggled with depression? Who has not had times when he wondered if being married to her particular spouse was really the right thing? Who has not wanted to ship his teenagers off to some unknown place until they were ready to support themselves? Who has not wanted to run away and hide when life became overwhelming? Who has not struggled with her own "secrets," certain that if people really knew her they would not want to be around her?

It is normal to have struggles, to have hurts to get over. There is no such thing as a perfect marriage or a perfect family. Our parents were imperfect, and we are as well. We live in a world much different from the one in which our parents grew up. We have a much greater opportunity than they did to deal honestly with feelings, intimacy, closeness, and self-esteem. The tragedy is that we still continue to struggle alone, rather than letting Christ become real to us through the actions of a caring, supportive Christian community.

Sometimes the view that "having problems is sin" gets institutionalized in our churches. I know of a church where the official teaching is based on an antipsychology attitude. The pastor preaches against the evils of psychology and argues that only pastors are qualified to counsel others. He strongly implies that it is disobedience to

God for a Christian to see a psychologist or psychiatrist for help. The cure he proposes, of course, is strictly a matter of faith and trust in God.

One of the men from that congregation arrived home from work and as was his custom most days after work went directly to his shop before going into the house for dinner. Time went by, and his wife glanced out the kitchen window, wondering why he had not yet come in. Fifteen minutes later, he was still in the shop, so she went to find out why. She found him—dead. He had killed himself.

No one—not even his closest friends—knew that he had been struggling with depression. He had not felt comfortable sharing his emotional struggles with his pastor or any of his friends, or even with his wife, the first one to whom he could have gone, so he struggled in isolation. I have had patients who feel that even being on antidepressant medication implies sinfulness and defective spirituality. Most times people have no idea what is causing them to struggle so deeply. They need someone who can help them sort things out. If that help is not available, and if it's not "OK" to access it, what ends up being most important is looking good and dressing nicely, giving the impression that all is well, even though everything on the inside is falling apart.

Now I'm not saying that the pastor was responsible for this man's suicide; the man himself was ultimately responsible to let others know he needed help. Nevertheless, the attitude in the body of believers with whom the man fellowshipped was not one of acceptance of or warmth toward those who were struggling. The message those believers conveyed, overtly and covertly, was that struggling with emotions was a sign that somehow you were deficient in your Christianity. That is truly a shame.

Please don't misunderstand me on this. God is the cornerstone of any healing process. No lasting change or healing occurs without the Lord. Yet as Rich Buhler, a popular radio pastor in California, often says, "If you were a lousy cook before you became a Christian, more than likely you will be a lousy cook after you become a Christian." If you did not have the skills to express your feelings, to be close, to be intimate, or to resolve conflicts before you became a Christian, more than likely you will have trouble in those areas after you become a Christian, too. The difference, though, is that as a Christian you will have the power of the Holy Spirit in your life. He can empower you and motivate you to learn and make the changes needed in relationships.

Having problems means having the opportunity to experience God working within your life in a manner that you are not accustomed to. As my friend and coauthor Dave Carder often says, "If you *always* do what you have *always* done, you will *always* get what you have *always* got." Making a change might mean taking the risk of going to a support group in your church (or in the church of a friend) where honest sharing takes place. It might mean taking the risk of talking with a recovery-literate pastor or similarly qualified Christian therapist. It does not mean staying alone and isolated with your hurt.

"COMPULSIVE DISEASE IS SINFUL"

This particular attitude has probably killed more people in the Christian community than any other. By restricting our view of compulsive disease to the purely spiritual realm, or by not paying enough attention to the addictive physiological aspects of compulsive disease, we shame Christians who struggle with these addictions and prolong their agony.

Most of us either know or by now have read about individuals like these:

- The person who struggles with alcoholism and who feels defective as a Christian. He walks the aisle, gives his life to Christ, and within twenty-four hours is using alcohol again.

- The Christian who struggles with bulimia (an eating disorder involving binging and purging on food), recommitting herself to Christ over and over again, only to begin compulsively eating again once she is alone.

- The Christian woman who strugles with anorexia (an eating disorder where the person starves him/herself to death), eating normally when she is around her Christian friends but going back to starvation when she is alone.

- The Christian man who vows before God to never buy another pornographic magazine or video but the next day finds himself in an adult bookstore.

- The woman who is unable to face her prescription drug addiction, getting two prescriptions filled from two different doctors for the same medication.

- The man who has to have a cigarette every time he steps out of the house. He is more nervous and disagreeable with his family on weekends because he is accustomed to smoking whenever he wants to at work.

- The man who compulsively works sixty to seventy hours a week and manages to fit in several meetings at church besides. He is addicted to the rush of adrenalin he gets from compulsively working and from having a high profile at church. His family does not know him anymore.

Such people struggle within a cycle of "using," attempting reform, and then returning to "using." Unless intervention takes place, the cycle will continue indefinitely. The alcoholic/addict returns to his "drug of choice" (whether it be food, alcohol, TV, sex, gambling, work, or shopping is irrelevant) because withdrawal sets him or her up for that. His entire day is wrapped around the moment he can "use" again. His attachment in life is not to God or to people but to his drug of choice.

To walk up to an obese individual and tell him that if he just "gives his life to the Lord" he will be thin is the same as ignoring the devastating physiological struggle the addict endures when he withdraws from alcohol or drugs. The eating-disordered person may be able to keep from binging for twelve or twenty-four hours, but after that his body begins to go through withdrawal, just as in the case of the alcoholic/addict. The physical process of withdrawal leads to continued mental obsession with the particular food he prefers, since his prime desire at that point is to satisfy his withdrawal feelings. The first bite he takes of the food of choice—sugar, bread, whatever—brings relief. That in turn leads to a binge that may leave the eating-disordered person out of control over food for days, weeks, months, or even years.

That is why 12-step groups are so crucial. We need to be around other people struggling with the same disorder in order to learn how to be sober one day at a time. We need to be around others who are struggling honestly and who know all the games, rationalizations, and tricks we perpetrate on ourselves and others in order to stay in the disease cycle.

For a long time Christians frowned upon participation in 12-step programs such as Alcoholics Anonymous (A.A.), charging that foul language was sometimes used in the meetings, that people sometimes smoked when they were there, and that the phrase "Higher Power as we understand Him" was used as a reference to God. That negative attitude has kept many Christians in bondage to compulsive disease and has kept multitudes of families in pain. Although I think it is better to get in touch with an overtly Christian program like Overcomers Anonymous, much wisdom can be learned from conventional 12-step programs, especially if those are the only programs available.

STEPS TO TAKE IN CLIMBING OUT OF THE PIT OF RELIGIOUS SHAME

Recovery is a process, not an event. In honest recovery there are no quick fixes or cures. Recovery requires openness and honesty before God and a group of people whom you can trust. Recovery does not occur in isolation. It occurs in relationship with God and other people. The steps listed below incorporate these principles of relationships.

1. *Write down a list of shame-based attitudes, beliefs, and experiences and contrast them with Scripture.* Writing is one of the important tools of recovery. When you write something down it becomes more real and manageable for you to deal with. Your list may look something like the following:

Religious Shame View	Healthy Spirituality View
I'm worthless and no good, and deserve nothing.	I am a son of God and in Christ (Galatians 3:26, 28).
I'm not as good a Christian as (Jane). She's thin and I'm not.	I have a compulsive disease. I can allow God to minister to me through (Overeaters Anonymous), which is helping me to get through today and be abstinent from (too much chocolate) (1 Corinthians 12:25-26).
My friends say I can be delivered from my alcoholism. I pray and give it to God but still want to drink.	God can help me stay sober one day at a time through A.A. and a group of other recovering Christians (Matthew 6:34). Paul had a thorn in the flesh for which he did not receive

Religious Shame View	Healthy Spirituality View
	healing but through which he learned to let God be glorified (2 Corinthians 12:7).
I am divorced and can no longer be used by God.	God accepts me as I am no matter what happens in my life. I can continue to grow in Him and be open to His leading. (Consider the life of David: although he had much struggle and pain in his life, he was used mightily by God.)

2. *Find a support group, preferably one based on the 12-step model, where you can share your feelings of religious shame.* I hope that in your reading of this book one message has come through: you need other people in your life to recover. There are many types of support groups. Attend the support group appropriate for you and, in time, take the risk and begin to share what hurts. If you can't find a support group, start one.

3. *Learn to respond and not react to external religious shame.* It is not uncommon for a person to feel angry or hurt as he begins to deal with religious shame. It is important that you direct the anger you feel where it belongs. Don't use that anger as an excuse to pull away from God or the church. In most instances religious shame comes from people and churches who have not had the opportunity to learn any other way of acting. As you become aware of religious shame, you may need to graciously confront people who have shamed you. Now there is a risk in doing this: the relationship you have with that person or church may change. But that does not mean that you need to give up the process. You may need to find a church that is more recovery-oriented and accepting of people who hurt. Sometimes people stay in the same church and attend a support group in another community or church. As you grow in your recovery, you may find other people in your congregation who are in recovery. All it takes is two or three people to start a support group.

4. *Read the scriptural account of Jesus and the woman at the well.* It's in John 4:5-26. This is one of the most important and powerful scriptures with regard to shame. In simply talking to a woman, Jesus was breaking the rules. At that time Jews steered clear of Samaritans, so the fact that she was from Samaria meant that He was breaking still more rules. Jesus tells the woman to call her husband. He shows His supernatural nature in knowing of her extensive history of failed marriages. As they talk, she asks Jesus for the water that will never leave her thirsty again. He goes on to tell her more, and by the end of the passage she apparently accepts the Living Water.

Now for the interesting part with regard to shame: do you see Jesus judging her? Does He condemn her? Not at all! She simply acknowledges that she does not have a husband. She is truthful with Him, and He accepts that and goes on because He is more concerned about her inner spiritual condition. He does not focus exclusively on what her dysfunctional behavior has been. He goes right to what her true need is: to find the Living Water.

What a contrast to the way we view life! What is your first reaction when you find out someone is in his second marriage? What would be your reaction to a member of your congregation who had had five husbands and was now living with another man? What would be your reaction if you found out that a member of your church was an alcoholic or a sex addict? It is fascinating that in Jesus' conversation with the woman at the well all it took was for her to honestly acknowledge the truth about her life, and then Christ moved on to deal with the most crucial need.

Reread the story of the woman at the well, substituting your own name whenever you see the words *Samaritan woman.* When the passage talks about her issues (marriage-related), substitute your own issues. Let it sink in that Jesus understands your situation and wants to bring you out of shame and into healing. This exercise can help move this from an intellectual understanding to something you can feel within.

Imagine being at the well with Jesus. You look into His eyes and can feel the love and compassion He has for you.

The little boy (or girl) within you feels understood and supported for the first time. You say to Him, "Sir, give me this water so I won't get thirsty again and have to keep coming back to the well."

Jesus says to you, "Ted, bring the sweets from your home here so that we may eat together and talk about the Living Water." You hang your head and look at the ground and stammer, "I've eaten them all . . . I have nothing left to share with you."

Jesus says to you, "Ted, you have answered well, for in fact your eating has been out of control for years. You have kept it a secret from others and have tried to hide it from Me. You have kept it from those who can love and support you through your overeating and into recovery."

You say, "I can see You are the Son of God, the risen Savior—I understand and accept Your Living Water to help fill me, one day at a time."

Questions for Reflection

Ask yourself the following questions, and make personal notes in the space provided.

1. Look over the Shame Quiz at the beginning of this chapter. Which questions can you identify with? What significance does that have for your recovery?

_____

_____

_____

2. Write down the experiences you have had of religious shame, and then contrast those experiences with Scripture.

_____

_____

_____

3. Which of your shaming experiences might you be able to share soon with a trusted friend or a support group?

_____

_____

_____

Notes

1. Let me explain my use of the term *disease* here and in my other chapters. Many Christians get uneasy at the use of the word to apply to such compulsions as alcoholism or drug abuse. They think, incorrectly, that using the term implies the idea of dismissing personal responsibility for addictive behavior. Alcoholics could then say, in effect, that their behavior wasn't their responsibility any more than their exhibiting flu symptoms would be. But that's not what I mean. By using the term *compulsive disease,* I am saying that the complex of behaviors, symptoms, and transmission patterns characteristic of the syndrome is very much parallel to the patterns characteristic of such conventional diseases as smallpox or even cancer. Compulsive disease is a complex set of biological, emotional, and spiritual variables that can destroy a person's life and the lives of those around him if left untreated. Those who work in the recovery movement have found the disease paradigm a helpful construct in dealing with this life-threatening pattern of behavior.

2. For years the so-called Christian view of such problems as eating disorders, sexual addiction, alcoholism, and so on, was that if you prayed long and hard enough and confessed enough sin, you would be delivered from these addictive diseases. It is true that some Christians have experienced instantaneous deliverance. The problem is that we have held up these miracles as the norm. Anything short of them we consider inferior. What if we applied the same sort of thinking to cancer? Many Christians have been miraculously and instantaneously healed of cancer. Do we assume that all healings should occur that way? No, we are just as pleased to see millions of Christians healed by God's working through competent medical treatment. Yes, sin may play a role in the alcoholic's taking that first drink, and, yes, the alcoholic/addict will sin during the course of his alcoholism and will sin again after sobriety. But labeling alcoholism as sin and simply prescribing repentance has proved to be ineffective and to delay recovery.

5

Helping the Helpers: Dysfunctional Families in "The Ministry"

By Alice Brawand, M.A.

The car screeched to a halt in the church parking lot. An angry, red-as-a-beet father bolted out of the car, slammed the door behind him, and hurried toward the church. As he dashed along, he straightened his tie, mumbling vague obscenities under his breath as he hurried to his appointed place.

When he actually entered the church, Pastor Rusty quickly adjusted his mask. Now all "business as usual," he faced his parishioners with his usual broad smile, cheerfully greeting people right and left. To the amazement of those in the know, his seething anger had dropped out of sight, safely hidden beneath an affable exterior.

Stunned and quiet, Rusty's wife and children lingered in the car for a moment, too numb to move. Then their anger erupted: "He's always blaming us for upsetting him and making him late. For making *him* look bad. . . . It's not fair!"

Slowly the hurting family climbed out of the car as four-year-old Steven blurted out: "Mommy, why is Daddy mean to *us* and nice to church people?"

The wounded wife and mother responded: "Honey, I honestly don't know. Ask your daddy."

With heavy, slow steps Bill made his way through the thronging crowds of a hot city street in Nigeria. Sticky with perspiration and sighing heavily, he pondered: *Nothing's going right. Cindy and I had hepatitis last year, and we've been exhausted ever since. The romance has gone out of our marriage. Seems like we're always angry at each other. There's never time or strength or money to do anything special together.*

Then the children: the baby doesn't sleep at night, and the others are having adjustment problems in the MK school in South Africa. Never-ending dysentery plagues us all. And the kids are missing their friends back in the U.S. Guess we all are, actually.

Yeah, and then there's that workaholic boss of mine. I never can seem to please him no matter how hard I work.

And, oh, this language! It's impossible. I'll never learn it. And the people we minister to here . . . well, they smell!

I'm a failure. What'll the folks back home think?

Bill was still grumbling under his breath when suddenly, seemingly out of nowhere, an attractive woman appeared in front of him. Her seductive glance and body movements caught him by surprise. In a weak, vulnerable moment, with no forethought or particular plan in mind, he began to follow her, his curiosity teasing him. *This little pursuit won't get out of hand,* he assured himself. *Besides, even if it did, in this crowd no one would ever see or know.*

Caught up in the excitement of the moment, he continued to follow the woman. He wondered where in town she might live. He was curious, that's all.

But soon she turned and began to speak to him, motioning him into her small apartment building. She entered a small, hot, candlelit room, turned, and moved closer to him, her shapely body brushing against his. His heart pounded as stinging beads of perspiration ran into his eyes.

Suddenly, in his mind's eye, he saw his wife, Cindy, his children, his calling in life. Instantly he turned and fled. With shortness of breath and racing heart, he disappeared among the hordes of people roaming the city street.

I came too close to falling into that pit. Bolting into a cafe for some desperately-needed coffee, he recalled verses he had memorized long ago:

> With persuasive words she led him astray;
>> she seduced him with her smooth talk.
> All at once he followed her
>> like an ox going to the slaughter,
> like a deer stepping into a noose
>> till an arrow pierces his liver,
> like a bird darting into a snare,
>> little knowing it will cost him his life.
>> (Proverbs 7:21-23, NIV)

Staring into the blackness of his coffee, Bill realized that he needed to get help in handling the stresses of his life, even though he was a missionary. He had narrowly missed self-destruction. It was time to heed the red flag before it was too late.

SCATTERED WRECKAGE, DISTURBING TRENDS

Such sad stories are all too familiar. I know, because I counsel troubled families of vocational Christian workers day in and day out. Rusty's story and the story of the discouraged missionary are fictitious in the strictest sense, but they are based on real-life experience with counselees. My clients are typically returning missionaries, but I also minister to U.S. pastors and their families, as well as to parachurch workers. Since we tend to idolize our Christian leaders, it is hard to realize that many of them are adult children of dysfunctional families, but it's true.

Shipwreck (and impending shipwreck) in the ministry is usually kept quiet in evangelical circles, but the truth is it is far from uncommon. Almost everyone knows of a pastor or other Christian leader who has suffered a divorce or other family crisis. Very often non-Christians remember such scandals for life—who hasn't tried to witness to the unsaved person who says he can't buy into Christianity because the pastor of the church down the block ran off with the organist?

The list of disgraces to Christ's church could go on:

- The youth pastor who leaves the ministry because he has sexually molested young boys in his church

- The missionary family that must suddenly return from the field because their unmarried daughter is pregnant

- The church that is shaken to learn that their pastor is leaving because of an illicit relationship he had with the wife of an elder

- The two single missionary women who must abruptly leave the mission field after falling into the trap of a homosexual relationship with each other

It is sobering to realize that today far too many shepherds, themselves led astray by the deceptive enticements of the world, are inadvertently leading their flocks away from the true Pastor, the Lord Jesus. Jeremiah wept for these shepherds many centuries ago, as we should be weeping for our own Christian workers today.

> My people have been lost sheep;
>   their shepherds have led them astray
>   and caused them to roam on the mountains.
> They wandered over mountain and hill
>   and forgot their own resting place.
> Whoever found them devoured them;
>   their enemies said, "We are not guilty,
> for they sinned against the Lord, their true pasture,
>   the Lord, the hope of their fathers."
>   (Jeremiah 50:6-7, NIV)

THE FACTS SPEAK FOR THEMSELVES

The statistics are shocking. Outside the church in the United States, 50 to 65 percent of husbands and 45 to 55 percent of wives say they had experienced extramarital affairs by the time they were fifty.[1] In our sex-saturated society, strong temptations from the world loom everywhere.

Yet it seems the line between the world and the church is blurring; mission and church leaders agree that the world is invading the church. In a survey of three hundred pastors by *Christianity Today*, researchers discovered that an alarming *23 percent* admitted they had been sexually inappropriate at some time. Of those, more than half acknowledged that they had succumbed to extramarital sexual intercourse. Eighteen percent of those surveyed admitted they had participated in other forms of illicit contact, such as passionate kissing or fondling/mutual masturbation. Of this total, only 4 percent said they had been found out.[2]

NO GUARANTEE

The mere act of serving in Christian ministry does not diminish one's temptation to be involved in sexual sins. The psalmist David, known as a "man after [God's own] heart" (Acts 13:22), was at the pinnacle of success in the kingdom. He had it all: fame, success, fortune. Anything, and anyone, he wanted was available to him. Then the enemy struck. You know the story: David's eyes fell upon Bathsheba, the couple committed adultery, and David then committed murder. Pain and shame ensued. Their baby died.

God's man Nathan pointed the finger at David. "Thou art the man," he cried (2 Samuel 12:7, KJV). In agony and grief over his baby's death, David repented of his sin against God. Fellowship with God was restored, but David never regained his former glory. True, he was forgiven, but in many ways his life turned sour, and his sin brought serious consequences into his life and into the lives of his descendants. Perversion ran rampant in his family: the scandal of Amnon and Tamar (examined in chapter 1), Amnon's murder by his brother, and Absalom's rebellion and subsequent death. In the incident with Bathsheba, the tide in David's life turned. His kingdom was never the same.

Are Christian workers today any different from those in David's time? Peter Steinke, director of clergy care for a large Protestant denomination in Texas, worked therapeutically with 350 ministers over a period of seven years.[3] Sixty-five of those ministers had been involved in extramarital affairs before or at the time of therapy. Fully 75 percent admitted to having difficulties in their own marriages. Their affairs usually involved partners in close proximity to work: church organists, secretaries, staff members or their spouses, counselees, or church members. Steinke found that as a group, the ministers had underestimated their own emotional needs and had overestimated their ability to disentangle themselves from their illicit relationships. Such statistics are in no way unique to Steinke's denomination; the cancer is, unfortunately, spreading throughout the church.

WHAT IS AT THE ROOT OF THESE PROBLEMS?

Each case is unique, but in my research I have found these common denominators:

1. *Hidden or repressed anger, often involving unresolved conflicts from the past.* These individuals habitually explode in anger as a way of letting off steam.

2. *Endless living in the fast lane.* The pattern of ceaseless activity, constantly being on the go, and cultivating experiences of great exhilaration and great exhaustion can cause Christian leaders to thrive on risk-taking and even to consider this on-the-edge life-style as normative. Then, when temptations come, their spiritual resources have already been drained and they are more likely to fall into sin.

3. *The superstar syndrome.* These individuals thrive on the praise of others and become heroes to their admirers. "Ministry for God" (and the resultant praise) often becomes an escape from family responsibilities and an artificial way of having personal needs met.

4. *Habitually hiding one's own deep needs.* These Christian leaders end up neglecting their own need for intimacy by not allowing themselves to appear human to others. They continue to give to others even when their own emotional "tanks" are empty.

5. *Operating without a personal support system.* No matter where Christian leaders live, in the homeland or abroad, they often experience intense stress and loneliness. Not daring to share on a deep level with anyone, they open themselves up to fierce attacks from the Adversary.

6. *Establishing only superficial relationships with others.* In not being real with others and in throwing up barriers to intimacy, these leaders increasingly cut themselves off from support and begin a lonely, downward spiral.

7. *Allowing expectations of oneself and others to drive one to the point of exhaustion and burnout.* These leaders can no longer cope with life's heavy demands. Their lives and ministries no longer have meaning, and they experience hopelessness.

Pastor Rusty's anger was causing extreme difficulty in his most important roles, those of husband and father. His unreasonable outbursts distanced him from his wife and children. Research has shown that when a Christian leader does not deal constructively with his anger, he will distance himself from his wife and family.[4] As a result, he may seek emotional support outside his marriage. Then it isn't long until temptation can overtake him.

God created each of us with deep needs for intimacy. The primary source of filling these needs ought to be our relationship with the Lord Himself and then with our spouse. In Pastor Rusty's case, his anger separated him from his wife and children, and therefore his own needs for intimacy were blocked. He struggled with denial of his need for intimacy, of the general conflict in his family life, of his resentment against people in the church who demanded too much of him, and of his hostility against the world in general. He expended an inordinate amount of emotional energy guarding the volatile secret of his explosive anger. He and all the people around him suffered the consequences.

If Rusty does not get help to reverse this dysfunctional pattern, he will pass it on to his children, even though he desperately does not want to do so. He may eventually find himself asking the question: "What shall it profit a man to gain the whole world and lose his own family?"

Bill, isolated on the foreign mission field, was experiencing intense stress and aloneness when sharp attacks from the Adversary struck. His discouragement had alienated him from his best support system, the Lord Himself, and then his wife and family. That was when temptation presented its insidious enchantment.

Investigators have found that emotional deficits and low self-worth from childhood are major contributing factors when Christian leaders have affairs.[5] An emotionally distant and unavailable father who seldom affirms his son contributes to a lack of masculine strength and identity in the son. We do not know for sure about Rusty's and Bill's childhood. We can only guess, but it is highly disturbing to see what they are doing in the lives of their own families. Their grievous behavior pattern likely will repeat itself in succeeding generations.

LET HIM WITHOUT SIN CAST THE FIRST STONE

What of *our* attitudes? Before we condemn Pastor Rusty, we need to ask ourselves how many times we have hostile, cruel disagreements with our spouses and/or our children. Sullen, angry words can pierce the heart of every family. We, too, need to deal with unresolved anger before it ruins our families.

We know that our Christian leaders have needs; let us maintain an attitude of understanding and compassion for them. We all stand in great need and are all guilty. Perhaps our problem is unexpressed, hidden anger that comes out in a hostile, bitter spirit. Perhaps the problem is pornography, homosexuality, or another type of sexual preoccupation. Or maybe it is not a sexual sin. Perhaps it involves pride or selfishness. As Christians, we and our families are not exempt. We, too, may be prime targets for the enemy's darts.

What Are Some of the Characteristics
of Those in Vocational Christian Ministry?

Many people who enter the ministry do so for dysfunctional reasons. It's a shock to hear that, but it's true. All of us think it is admirable to be kind, gentle, patient, forgiving, and helpful to others. But is it possible to overdo those qualities? In the case of ACDFs who enter the ministry, it *is* possible—they are often living proof!

People who enter the ministry are often "people helpers" at heart, which is admirable. But when they carry people-helping to such an extreme that they cannot feel good about themselves unless they are continually doing good for others, even to the point of joylessness and exhaustion, they have fallen into a dysfunctional pattern. Eventually, a slow resentment will build in them as they find themselves "manipulated" by unreasonable demands. Unless their own deeper needs are satisfied and unless they learn some of the healthy patterns described in this book, burnout and dropout will almost surely result.

They should beware of the following traps:

- Feeling undue responsibility for others, a compulsion always to "fix" what ails these people. This is a significant characteristic, for ministers are typically seen by nearly all of society as "fixers." But only God can truly "fix" people, as they cooperate with Him.

- Saying yes when they mean no; being "people-pleasers."

- Doing for others what they (others) are capable of doing for themselves.

- Seeking to be "all things to all people." Many people in vocational Christian service misapply 1 Corinthians 9:22 in a noble effort to "minister" to everyone they can. But they sometimes forget that the context of the verse has to do with evangelism, not with attempting to "fix" every person who has a need. Paul was speaking about adapting his evangelistic approach to Jews and Gentiles, not of compulsively meeting every human being's needs. Doing that is impossible for men; only God can do so.

- Feeling good about themselves only when they are giving to others.

- Being primarily motivated by interpersonal and social rewards. Rather, we need to be motivated by God's approval (2 Timothy 2:15).

- Feeling exclusively attracted to needy people.

- Feeling bored, empty, and even worthless if there isn't a problem to solve or someone needing help.

- Continually abandoning a schedule or important project for the sake of someone else's needs; "dropping everything" because someone needs "fixing."

- Overcommitting themselves and then feeling harassed and under pressure.

- Consistently rejecting praise and yet becoming depressed when none is given.

- Often feeling guilty when spending money on personal needs.

- Fearing rejection (or feeling guilty) if not constantly ministering to others.

- Too easily taking things personally.

- Being overly afraid of making mistakes.

- Being driven by perfectionistic, self-imposed standards.

A codependent person is one who depends on satisfying the needs of others in order to feel his or her own value. Taken to the extreme, the codependent Christian worker is drinking from a dry well and will never be satisfied. In the long run his efforts will not be as effective as he imagines, for he is promoting his own dysfunction. The codependent's needs can only be met by the true Source of Living Water. In Him he will find a personal sense of value simply because he is God's child, not because he is "needed."

WHAT ARE SOME SOLUTIONS?

FIRST, A WORD TO LAY CHRISTIANS

Unwittingly, Christian laymen may be feeding into the problem. When those in Christian ministry are placed on a pedestal (as discussed in chapter 10), unrealistic expectations are imposed on them. True, those in ministry are to be examples, but that does not mean that they must be paragons of perfection. They and their families should be free to be themselves and to enjoy life within biblical parameters without harsh judgment from their followers.

Christian leaders provide encouragement and support for the laity, but they have needs, too. They need the following things from those around them:

- Faithful prayer support

- Respectful treatment

- Encouragement and communication between themselves and their people

- Lightening of the load when possible

- Appreciation expressed verbally and in writing

- Consideration of their reputation even when they aren't present

- Respect for their privacy

- Freedom from unnecessary demands on their time and energy

- Protection from the "appearance of evil" with the opposite sex

We are too often unaware that our spiritual leaders struggle and sometimes fall. God's plan is build, and rebuild, them. The road may be arduous, but the Lord promises:

> I know the plans I have for you. . . . plans to prosper you and not to harm you, plans to give you hope and a future. (Jeremiah 29:11, NIV)

And also:

> "I will satisfy the priests with abundance,
> and my people will be filled with my bounty,"
> declares the Lord.
>
> (Jeremiah 31:14, NIV)

FOR THE STRUGGLING CHRISTIAN WORKER

The Christian worker is not without resources in the battle. The following needs to be kept in mind:

1. *You are not alone.* All the heroes in God's hall of fame struggled. Some fell. We don't have to fall. God Himself says:

   > The wrong desires that come into your life aren't anything new and different. Many others have faced exactly the same problems before you. (1 Corinthians 10:13a, TLB*)

2. *There is hope.* The saying goes: "The darkest hour is the hour before the dawn." You may have struggled for a long time and failed again and again, but remember, a fresh start, a new hope, is always available. God hasn't given up on you, so don't give up on yourself!

   > But as for me, I watch in hope for the Lord,
   > I wait for God my Savior;
   > my God will hear me. . . .
   > Though I have fallen, I will rise.
   > Though I sit in darkness,
   > the Lord will be my light.
   >
   > (Micah 7:7-8, NIV)

3. *You cannot change on your own.* You may be able to make a change for a few days or a few weeks, but you need outside help for long-lasting change. Primarily, of course, it's the Holy Spirit's power you need, but God never intended for you to struggle alone on the human level. It's OK to need someone else. Although ultimate responsibility rests on you, a relationship of accountability and support with a godly brother or sister (of the same sex) can help assure you the victory.

* The Living Bible.

Share each other's troubles and problems, and so obey our Lord's command. (Galatians 6:2, TLB)

4. *Seek a new depth in your relationship with God.* Commit to living a holy life free from those attractions that on the surface may seem to be harmless but are actually debilitating. Involvement in sin will corrode your inner being and render you ineffective in your life and ministry.

Therefore, I urge you, brothers, in view of God's mercy, to offer your bodies as living sacrifices, holy and pleasing to God—this is your spiritual act of worship. (Romans 12:1, NIV)

5. *Seek a new depth of emotional intimacy in your marriage.* Cultivate the habit of openly exchanging feelings-level parts of yourself. Let yourself be vulnerable with your spouse. Work toward allowing yourself to say such things as

"Sometimes I'm lonely."
"Sometimes I get discouraged."
"Sometimes I feel shut out of your life."
"I don't always do it right. Can you help me?"

As you mutually encourage and nurture each other, neither of you will be as likely to look outside your marriage for satisfaction of your inner needs. As you grow in intimacy with each other, you will grow closer to the Lord.

6. *Make a checklist of sinful practices or seemingly neutral practices that do not contribute to a godly life.* Be sure to include thoughts, fantasies, feelings, and actions that stimulate or gratify you sexually. Also, include TV programs or magazines that may not seem overtly pornographic but still appeal to the flesh. These programs and magazines may not appear to be all that bad, but you can become enslaved to them if you are not careful.

7. *Don't give up.* Satan will try to convince you that it's a hopeless cause. Daily encourage yourself, and receive encouragement from the Lord and others.

No temptation is irresistible. You can trust God to keep the temptation from becoming so strong that you can't stand up against it, for He has promised this and will do what He says. He will show you how to escape temptation's power so that you can bear up patiently against it. (1 Corinthians 10:13*b*, TLB)

8. *Write down your commitment, and keep it in a visible place where you'll see it often.* Commit on a moment-by-moment basis. That is the way effective change comes about.

> Your word is a lamp to my feet
> and a light for my path.
> (Psalm 119:105, NIV)

9. *Continually be renewed in your mind by meditating on Scripture.* Memorize it. Flood your mind with God's Word, for it is your greatest weapon against the onslaughts of the evil one. It will enable you to put to death the first thoughts of temptation.

> Do not conform any longer to the pattern of this world, but be transformed by the renewing of your mind. (Romans 12:2*a*, NIV)

10. *Take time for recreation, enjoyment, fun, and, most important, exercise.* A balanced life that includes diversion will bring untold spiritual, emotional, and physical benefits. After a time of ministry, the apostles reported to Jesus their many impressive accomplishments. In fact, they were so busy they didn't even have time to eat. Jesus saw their predicament, and in loving concern He advised:

> Come with me by yourselves to a quiet place and get some rest. (Mark 6:31*b*, NIV)

11. *Develop a relationship of mutual accountability.* Many find a relationship with a mature Christian of the same sex to be significant in overcoming undesirable habits and weaknesses. In the sharing of temptations or illicit fantasies, the stronghold of such desires can be broken. Being tempted is not sinful; the sinfulness lies in how that temptation is han-

dled. Hebrews 3:12-13 speaks of our needing one another in order that we not be "hardened by sin's deceitfulness." Give yourself permission to be accountable to a trusted individual.

A Challenge to Both Clergy and Laity

What family secrets and unfinished business are hidden in each of us? What powerful hold needs to be faced? Is there a pattern you do not want to replicate in the future? If these issues are not dealt with, the cycle of sin will probably continue. In searching our own hearts, let us remember that families reproduce in kind, and let that motivate us.

Christ longs to "make all things new" for us, and He has given us the freedom of choice. He never forces His will on us. In the light of God's holiness, let us choose to resolve our unfinished business by confronting, resolving, and releasing our secrets. Then we will no longer be bound by them and will not pass them on to our children.

Be It Resolved . . .

Below you will find five key principles followed by "I" statements. These principles will help you immensely if you make them your own. Whether you're dealing with a sexual problem, anger, an unruly tongue, jealousy, pride, or a thousand other sins, resolve, by God's grace, to

- *be alert to the presence of the evil one and aware of his brilliant strategies for demoralizing, discouraging, and defeating you in any way possible*

I will never forget that I am in a spiritual battle.

> Be self-controlled and alert. Your enemy the devil prowls around like a roaring lion looking for someone to devour. Resist him, standing firm in the faith. (1 Peter 5:8-9*a*, NIV)

- *remain fervent in prayer, never hesitating to call down power from God Almighty*

I will first take my problems to God. I will fight my best battles on my knees.

The effectual fervent prayer of a righteous man availeth much. (James 5:16*b*, KJV)

- *refuse to retaliate or take revenge in the energy of the flesh*

I will decide to be accountable to God and some other spiritually mature individual of the same sex, remembering that alone I am inadequate to fight my own battles.

Confess your faults one to another, and pray one for another, that ye may be healed. (James 5:16*a*, KJV)

- *refuse to slacken, surrender, or quit*

I will follow the path of obedience no matter how intense the pressure, and I will remember this whenever temptation confronts me.

Therefore, my dear brothers, stand firm. Let nothing move you. Always give yourselves fully to the work of the Lord, because you know that your labor in the Lord is not in vain. (1 Corinthians 15:58, NIV)

- *glorify your Lord and God and trust His Word regardless of your circumstances*

I will aim to please God more than people. I will enjoy life within biblical guidelines with a free conscience. I will not be bound by "the traditions of men." I will always remember that in Christ there is victory.

May there be shouts of joy when we hear the news of your victory, flags flying with praise to God for all that He has done for you. (Psalm 20:5*a*, TLB)

To Him who is able to keep you from falling and to present you before His glorious presence without fault and with great joy—to the only God our Savior be glory, majesty, power and authority, through Jesus Christ our Lord, before all ages, now and forevermore! Amen. (Jude 24-25, NIV)

Questions for Reflection

Ask yourself the following questions, and make personal notes in the space provided.

1. Why is it that those in ministry may be even more vulnerable to certain sins than lay people? What special temptations do they face?

_____

_____

_____

2. Why does it matter how one's family interacts in private?

_____

_____

_____

3. Why is it that a Christian leader's severe anger may lead to immorality?

_____

_____

_____

4. How does superficiality often bring defeat in one's ministry?

_____

_____

_____

5. How do lay people sometimes contribute to the stress and occasional downfall of those in ministry?

_____

_____

_____

6. Why is it that the past can have such a hold on the present and the future? Aren't "all things made new in Christ?" Why won't "forgetting the past" heal the pain with its consequences?

_____

_____

_____

7. How might woundedness and shame in one's background affect his or her present life and ministry?

_____

_____

_____

8. Discuss the sphere of influence that fallen spiritual leaders have. How have you been affected by their fall? What can the laity learn from such experiences?

_____

_____

_____

9. Do you have unresolved personal problems that could lead you into a downward spiral?

_____

_____

_____

10. Aren't lay people seen as spiritual leaders in their places of work and in their homes? How might some of the concepts discussed in this chapter apply to laypersons as well?

_____

_____

_____

Notes

1. Grant Martin, "Relationship, Romance and Sexual Addiction in Extramarital Affairs," *Journal of Psychology and Christianity* 8, no. 4 (1989): 5.
2. R. Exley, *Perils of Power: Immorality in the Ministry* (Tulsa: Harrison, 1988), pp. 10-11.
3. Peter L. Steinke, "Clergy Affairs," *Journal of Psychology and Christianity* 8, no. 4 (1989): 56.
4. Raymond T. Brock and Horace C. Lukens, "Affair Prevention in the Ministry," *Journal of Psychology and Christianity* 8, no. 4 (1989): 44.
5. Steinke, "Clergy Affairs," p. 57.

6

Blest Be the Tie That Binds: Local Church "Family" Patterns

By Dave Carder, M.A.

One does not have to attend very many churches to realize that each has its own distinctive personality. By personality I mean the pattern the church uses to express itself to those outside, the way it conducts its business within, and the hierarchy of values it establishes for those who belong.

We can tell fairly quickly whether or not we will fit in with a particular group of believers. And that is important, for the better the fit and the more numerous the points of contact, the greater the level of comfort and commitment we will feel. So the church has a vested interest in our commitment, just as we have a vested interest in our comfort. But what exactly are the "points of comfort" or "fit" that get the ball rolling in the first place?

THE SEARCH FOR A CHURCH FAMILY "FIT"

Just as people look for spouses who will allow them to practice the relational styles they learned in their dysfunctional childhoods (see chapter 3), so, too, do they look for churches built on relationship styles with which they are familiar. The way the members of a person's family related to each other and to the power base of the family will determine the type of church family that will attract him. It is all he knows of relationships. People who grew up in homes headed by extremely powerful fathers who were accountable to no one are likely to gravitate eventually to churches where the senior pastor operates the same way. I say eventually, because often new converts are initially caught up in the environment where they first trusted Christ as Savior.

UNFINISHED BUSINESS

Many times unfinished business from a family of origin will be acted out within the church family. An individual who left home angry at his father may well find a church home much like his family home and act out lingering resentment toward his father by aggravating the pastor: continually disagreeing with him, being belligerent, spreading damaging rumors. He will not confront his own father, but he is more than happy to confront the often bewildered surrogate, his pastor.

The comfort level the new believer seeks from his new church family can become the source of his greatest disappointment. Having chosen a church family relationship style much like the one he knew at home, he fails to realize that each style has its own craziness. It will not be long before a sense of déjà vu permeates his thinking. What he had hoped to leave behind, he now experiences on an even larger scale in the church. Business meetings become replicas of old family feuds, deacons' meetings replace the family council, and the sermons parallel his parents' lectures.

This dread of getting caught in the same family system one experienced as a child drives some people from church to church, forever looking for the right kind of church family experience. These people are running around issues, not working through them. Individuals who work through their unfinished business and settle down do not have to keep up the endless compulsion to join new fellowships. This is evident when we consider the marriage relationship. It is easy enough for us to see a problem in the individual who cannot find the right spouse and runs from relationship to relationship until he is fifty, never marrying because he has not found the "right one." Decades of church hopping are little different, though we tend to be less critical of it.

UNMET NEEDS

Individuals from dysfunctional families often report feeling a void and an uncertainty over family relationships. Having never had supportive functional relationships of the kind we all yearn for (see chapter 7), these new believers often see in the church a chance to "re-family." Finally, the opportunity to get what they have never experienced looms in front of them. It is almost more than they can take in. They have a new Father and His representative, the pastor; a new family, the local church; and a new "me" with a new nature. One can almost hear the hallelujahs.

Though such a view is true in some respects, it may set up the ACDF for disappointment. A new-found relationship with Christ and His church can provide a wonderful experience, but it can never make up for the deficits one brings to salvation. Don't forget: the church itself is composed of imperfect people, all with their own hurts and unresolved issues.

Many times new believers do initially experience what they so desperately need, and recovery begins. The church is healthy, accepts their hurting, and provides a place of recovery. Others experience a less positive scenario. In fact, their disappointment in their church may be so severe that it leads to bewilderment and even greater despair. Often the only recourse they see is simply to look good on the outside and figure out their troubles as best they can on the inside. *Feelings are not important,* they say to themselves. *Just think straight, look sharp, and keep your failures a secret. Things probably aren't any better for anyone else.* Or so the thinking goes.

THE UNCERTAINTY

Since relationship skills are basically caught, not taught (though they can be enhanced by teaching), the new Christian sometimes feels lost. Knowing he should not repeat the patterns he experienced as a child, and hearing about a new set of guidelines without ever having practiced them himself or seen them in practice, the new believer often feels inadequate, confused, and uncertain about what "normal" Christian relationships are all about.

One of the more common illustrations of this uncertainty has to do with the concept that Christian men are to be the "spiritual leaders" of their homes. None of the ACDF men ever experienced that sort of godly leadership in their own homes as they were growing up. They feel successful if they can just numb the effect of some of the painful things inflicted upon them as children. They're surviving, not thriving. Now they have a wife who, taking her cues from the pastor and women's Bible study leader, feels strongly that the hindrance to the development of Christlikeness in their home is his failure to be a spiritual leader. After all, she can't be responsible for that area. God has assigned that task to her husband.

But her husband is extremely uncertain about venturing into these uncharted waters. He has no idea if he is doing it right or even if he is on course. And he is not alone. If the truth be known, most evangelical men feel as though their spouses have much higher expectations of them as spiritual leaders than they can meet. They see their best efforts as paltry. So why try when you know you are going to fail? Add to this the fact that the husband can see all kinds of dysfunctional relationships in the church families around him, and it is no wonder he settles for a musty old role rather than a new fresh experience with God and others.

CHURCH FAMILY ROLES

People in a church tend to gravitate toward the same family roles they had in their families of origin. To this familiar role are added unfamiliar roles of Christian service: teacher, children's worker, bus driver, usher, parking lot attendant. Add to that the encouragement the new believer receives to join an adult fellowship or Sunday school class, and you have all the external trappings of being important and belonging to a family.

It's a pretty good feeling when viewed from the exterior. Internally, however, little has changed. True, the roles given the new believer reassure him that he is important as an individual and that he belongs to the group. But as explained in chapter 3, he has already picked a church characterized by a relationship style already familiar to him, and where he's likely to find a sense of security based on predictability. So it won't be surprising to find that pretty soon he's settled into a relationship role not too different from the one he had in his family of origin or the one he has in his own family.

The following four role categories are taken from Claudia Black.[1] As you work your way through the descriptions of these categories, remember that the reassurance the roles provide the individual about his attachment to the group is what is important.

OVERLY-RESPONSIBLE MEMBERS

Each church has its overly responsible children who support it, lead it, and contribute to it, all following the "party line" with fatherly pastoral support. Statements such as "If only everybody could be like (person's name), wouldn't it be great?" abound. These individuals take it upon themselves to keep everybody happy, to do all the serving, and to anticipate ahead of time whatever needs to be fixed. In small churches this role often is filled by the pastor's wife.

The only problem is that the role is never appreciated or noticed except through a departure or loss. It is just assumed that the overly responsible ones in the Body will carry out their role. And, until these types leave or die (or have a heart attack), they will continue to do everything needed. Let's face it, healthy or not, this system works. But dues will be paid in the long run in terms of dysfunction and burnout.

ACTING-OUT MEMBERS

These are the ones who continue to stay in the church family but who cannot live up to its codes of behavior and appearance. They are the members of whom it is said, "If it weren't for (person's name), we would be doing pretty well." This individual's "besetting sin" is the focus of the church family's prayer life and the talk among its members.

As in a dysfunctional family, acting-out members (or entire families) "act out" the church's pain. Their role is so necessary and ingrained that the more the church attempts to change their behavior, the worse they have to become. If they were well, and therefore "like everybody else," they would no longer be the object of everyone's concern, prayer life, and interest. They would lose their sense of specialness and belonging. And besides, the church body would lose the caretaking mission they have adopted.

A strange twist can take place when healing does begin to occur. Because the acting-out role has such permanence in the life of the individual (or family) who adopts it, sometimes just as he begins to experience improvement, a crisis "happens" to come along to reassure him that things really have not changed after all (remember, ACDFs are shy of change) and that his relationship to the church is still intact. As is the case with ACDF issues, often the status quo is preferable to any change at all, even if that change leads to health.

MASCOTS

These are the loyal "pets" of the local church family. Everyone enjoys their presence, admires their personality, and keeps them locked into a role. Mascots are the ones who accept the responsibility for acting as though the family is functioning as it is supposed to. They don't do the necessary hard labor. That is not their task. Their responsibility is to make everybody feel good about belonging to the Lord's family. As in the dysfunctional family, these folks are often the center of everybody's attention and affection, while the hyper-responsible ones are killing themselves without recognition from anyone.

THE ADJUSTING MEMBERS

These are the folks who move in and out of the church family, depending on how well it is going. If another church family has a better program going, they move; if another preacher is saying what they want to hear, they go to listen. When things are good at the "home" church, they come. If things are not so good, they go elsewhere or just stay at home, much like the "adjusting child" who stays in her room, or practically lives at her friend's house, when things are rocky. Adjusting members are in and out of the church and not very committed, yet they are not so distant that they lose their membership, either.

Just as in the dysfunctional family, when any recovering member begins to respond in a new way, difficulties usually ensue. Many times the recovering member feels that he needs to find a new church that will allow for the new identity and different relationship style he feels. When that happens, the "church family of origin" often feels abandoned or betrayed and senses a need to develop its own version of why the individual left. This version is often designed to protect the family image and to convey the idea that the *faithful stayed* while the *unfaithful strayed.*

FAMILY RULES AND CHURCH WORSHIP STYLES

As in dysfunctional families, so dysfunctional churches practice the rules described in chapter 3: don't talk, don't trust, don't feel. Notice in table 6.1 how these three rules play themselves out in the church's life.

LITURGICAL

Individuals who grew up in a family lacking trust (dependability and security) often seek out a church atmosphere that contributes to that emotional deficit. In the liturgical worship style, the process is predictable. Everyone knows ahead of time what will happen during the service, and the service repeats itself week after week. For those growing up in chaos, confusion, and unpredictability, the liturgy is a haven, a safe place to relax.

Table 6.1
Dysfunctional Family Rules and Church Preference

Dysfunctional Family Rule	Worship Role	Style
Don't Trust	Liturgical	Calm, tranquil, predictable
Don't Talk	Evangelistic	Noisy, formula-intensive, hyperlogical
Don't Feel	Charismatic	Rhythmical, exciting, bordering on the unpredictable

EVANGELISTIC

Just the opposite is true for children who were to be seen and not heard. Children from families emphasizing the "don't talk" rule often gravitate to the evangelistic style of worship. Here they find encouragement to talk and are given the exact message to say. Many times this message is a formula, making it easy for them to express their feelings about spiritual subjects. Most times these churches are noisy with casual conversation. After all, the members now have the license to talk with their new family. The church becomes a gathering place, a key ingredient in the social structure binding these individuals together. Many times the new church family becomes so significant that it actually assumes greater importance to the individual than does his family of origin.

CHARISMATIC

Individuals whose family life acknowledged little of their feelings as children may find themselves attending charismatic fellowships. Emotional expression has been denied them for so long that they find the experience of freedom offered by the charismatic church breathtaking. It is all part of doing it differently, of finally having permission to express oneself in ways one always knew one wanted to. Deep within them rhythm and music always existed, but neither was tolerated in their family of origin. Or if rhythm and music was tolerated, it was stifled in them because they had to take care of too many others at too early an age. Now the new family recognizes this behavior as normal and natural and actually makes it mandatory for attachment.

No wonder the church often holds more significance for these individuals then does their family of origin. They have found what all their lives they have been searching for in a family.

Individuals with an ACDF background often confuse good and bad with stylistic preference. If a charismatic brother without qualification calls a liturgical style of worship "of the devil," that's confusing good and bad with preference. That's why we have more than one brand of automobile and more than one type of soft drink. We each have different tastes, and the sooner we acknowledge that, the less likely we will be to pronounce as wrong somebody else's church preference.

EVANGELICAL CHURCH PERSONALITIES

As you read this chapter, you may think that I enjoy throwing rocks at the local church or that I see all churches as dysfunctional. Nothing could be further from the truth. I have spent all of my adult life (more than twenty years) in full-time local church ministry. I (along with the other authors of this book) share this material for the building up of a needy Body of Christ. It is stiff medicine, but necessary stuff. It is part of our effort to buttress the church we love.

The material in this chapter has been developed over the course of twenty years in a society that seems to fragment itself more each passing day. Fortunately, the more a church reaches out in such a society, the more it will be able to attract fragmented and dysfunctional families. Yet at the same time, the more such families populate the church, the greater the danger of fragmentation in the church. Churches in some ways are too much like families. Many times pastors and other church leaders have their own unfinished business to process, just as the parishioners do, all with negative results for the congregation as a whole.

Tom remembers the night his anger finally exploded at his father. For years he had lain awake at night listening to his parents' arguments turn to fights that finally ended with his mom lying help-less on the floor, battered and bleeding. Sometimes she lay there all night. Other times she was able to make it to the bedroom before the children woke up in the morning.

On this particular night, something snapped inside. He ran downstairs screaming at his dad to leave her alone and get out of the house. Surprisingly, Dad did. But he never came back.

Tom stepped into the role his dad had vacated, and the family did pretty well. Bible school, marriage, and full-time Christian minis-try followed for Tom. It all seemed to happen in such an easy progression.

Suddenly the van lurched, and Tom was jerked back to reality by painful handcuffs around his wrists. He was in a police paddy wagon on his way to the station to be booked for soliciting prostitu-tion. It was scary, sure, but also in a strange way relieving. His secret life had been going on for years, and he had not been sure how much longer his nerves could take it. He had learned his lessons well at his father's knee: women are sex objects. Neither Bible school training nor years in the pulpit had magically cured him of this dys-functional pattern, instilled in him when he was only a child.

Remember what was said in chapter 3 ("Passing the Torch") about relationship styles? The same holds true for pastors looking for churches. They will seek out a church that allows them to practice the only relationship style they know, the one they learned in their family of origin.

This process suggests that different churches will attract differ-ent kinds of parishioners and pastors. Whereas a person enters the family of origin without any choice, he does have a choice when he joins a local church. That choice has to be a mutually satisfying one, or long-term bonding cannot take place. Put another way, the choice must be mutually satisfying in that he agrees to the rules by which the new family practices family togetherness.

This selection process helps a person identify his relationship style, and it guarantees that the power base determining the church family rules will remain unthreatened. *The dynamics of relationship styles is so foundational it is often at the root of church splits, for church splits almost always occur over family rules and not family beliefs, as is commonly believed.* Doctrine rarely splits a church anymore.

CHURCH FAMILY SPLITS

As in any family, many dynamics have the potential to fracture the structure. Two are of special significance, however: the age and the adaptability of the family. As a family ages and passes through different life cycles, family relationship styles also have to adjust. When the family cannot flex, and parents continue to control young adults (adolescents) as though they were small children, anger and resentment set in. (See Ephesians 6:4 [NIV], "Do not exasperate your children.")

Many parents correctly recognize that they are in reality almost finished parenting by the time a child reaches late elementary age. By that I don't mean we should give up parenting—rather, that by then they will have communicated the lion's share of attitudes and values their children will pick up. Wise parents will realize as well that even when their children leave home in late adolescence the job won't be over completely. None of us can "finish off" our children in some eighteen-odd years; God Himself says it takes Him an entire lifetime (Philippians 1:6).

When a family of origin won't adjust, its individual members often find a family that will. This they may do by starting families of their own through early marriages. Or they may run away as adolescents. Some children will cope while they are still living at the home by finding a surrogate family in the neighborhood. Did your mother or father ever complain that you or one of your siblings were "always over at _____'s house"? That same pattern is found in churches: splitting, running away (called backsliding), and church hopping!

Some individuals respond to rigidity in their church family in just the opposite way. Though they are unhappy with their church family, they fear abandonment and rejection so much that they just resign themselves to the situation. They mutter to themselves, "It's the best church around," or "It's the only church around," or "At least their doctrine is good." When these individuals make up the majority of a church family, an even more rigid personality begins to evolve.

CHURCH FAMILY PATTERNS

Table 6.2 categorizes several church family patterns. Skeptics looking at the table may say the conditions described in it are overstated or that their church doesn't fit into any of the categories. That may be true, or it may be denial on their part; in any case, I have seen these patterns proved over many years. A better way to evaluate one's experience might be to view the chart as a description of tendencies. The church family does not have to behave a particular way all of the time. In fact, the primary pattern is made more acceptable by an occasional exception. For example, in a church that typifies the first category in table 6.2 (The Church Terrified), the tyrannical father-style pastor may occasionally act in an unrestrictive, hang loose manner just to take a break from the stifling style that normally pervades the setting. But after he and/or the membership have had a short break, it's back to business as usual.

The amazing thing is that hundreds (often thousands) of church members in a local assembly even tolerate bizarre behavior, often for an unbelievably long time. Overabundant loyalty and other factors common in dysfunctional families cause individual church members to accept the unacceptable in church behavior, all of this under the guise of "being biblical" or "practicing New Testament Christianity."

Churches and families often mirror one another. Secrets, abuse, and immorality tolerated in the one can be practiced in the other. *Anything that can run in families can run in churches.* The pastor who lives in immorality will attract families who tolerate immorality. Similarly, abusive families will tolerate abusive church leadership.

Just like a family, church leadership often develops an official interpretation of the family patterns they practice. Secrets are ignored, and the church goes on, often with only a slight pause to detour around them. Just as a compass one degree off course on a long journey can lead to a destination miles from the desired original objective, so, too, can the collective detours around the secrets of the church and its member families take it places it would have never chosen to go in the beginning.

To paraphrase the apostle James: Brethren, these things should not be! (James 3:10). My prayer is that the concepts shared in this chapter and the others in this book might help us to reverse these worrisome trends and make the local church family less dysfunctional and therefore more glorifying to the Lord Jesus Christ, whose name we bear.

Table 6.2
Church Family Patterns

Description	Feeling	Primary Behavior
The Church Terrified	Regimented	Tyrannical father, everyone in line
The Church Compulsive	Overwhelmed	Program-oriented, exhausted
The Church Seen, but Not Heard	Constricted	Quiet, compliant, conforming
The Church Disconnected	Detached	Cold, professional, austere
The Church in Denial	Intolerant	Slick, no hurting members, happy looking

Questions for Reflection

Ask yourself the following questions, and make personal notes in the space provided.

1. What kind of church family have you chosen now? In the past? What do you foresee for the future?

_____

_____

_____

2. Was your initial church family parallel to your family of origin, or the opposite of it? How long did you stay? Why? What did it take for you to leave? Was your departure parallel in any way to your other departures—from family of origin, initial marriage, job, school, and so on? What common patterns might be emerging?

_____

_____

_____

3. How do you feel about the effort of this chapter to make our church family selection process more natural? For example, does this chapter generate in you misgivings as to whether God led you to your present church? What feelings does this chapter create in you? Does it make you feel more/less free, more/less responsible, more-/less eager to stay? Does this chapter relieve you because the material makes sense?

_____

_____

_____

4. What runs in your church family? Are there patterns in your church's history? Do you see balance in the lives of individuals who participate in your fellowship? What percentage of the members of your church stay there to stay away from something else?

_____

_____

_____

5. Where do you fit in? What role do you play in your church family? Do you like that role? How does it compare with the role you had in your family of origin?

---

6. What do you think about the comments about husbands' uncertainty over wives' expectations for being the spiritual leader in their homes? Have you and your spouse talked about this issue? If not, try it.

---

7. How do you feel about the illustration of Pastor Tom on his way to jail? If he was your pastor, what would happen in your church when the news got out? What would you urge your church to do? Why?

Note

1. Claudia Black, *It Will Never Happen to Me* (Denver.: M.A.C. Printing, 1982), pp. 13-27.

Part 3

**Family Health:
How to Do It Right
When You Learned It Wrong**

7

Learning to Bond

By John Townsend, Ph.D.

The story is told of a little girl in a Christian family who, when frightened at night by noises in the dark, called out to her mother, "Mommy, Mommy, come here! I'm scared. There are big monsters in here!" The mother, not wanting to miss an opportunity to give a spiritual object lesson, replied, "Don't worry, honey, Jesus is there with you." After a moment of reflection, the little girl called back frantically, "But Mommy, I need someone with skin on!"

In this little vignette an important family principle unfolds that will be the guiding thought for this chapter: *the first and most fundamental human need the family should meet is the need for forming deep and loving attachments,* the need to develop the feeling of being close to someone "with skin on."

Many people assume that because they came from a family whose members spent time together, attachment automatically occurred. In reality, nothing could be further from the truth. Many people report the sensation of being "alone in a crowd," or of "not belonging" or "fitting in," as part of their everyday experience. This sort of experience reflects a basic lack in their ability to feel welcome and connected to others, or, put another way, reflects a lack in their sense of belonging. But what is "belonging," and how can we deter-

John Townsend (chapters 7 and 8) and Henry Cloud (chapters 9 and 10) work closely together as therapists and writers with the Minirth-Meier Clinic West. The topics examined in these four chapters have also been addressed in Henry Cloud, *When Your World Makes No Sense* (Nashville: Oliver Nelson, 1990).

mine if "belonging" is an area of struggle in our lives? The following section gives us a working definition of the term.

WHAT IS "BONDING"?

A bond between two people is an emotional and intellectual investment they have in one another. It is a relationship in which all of the parts of the soul—feelings, thoughts, values, beliefs, joys, and sorrows—are shared with and valued by another. To be known at this level is to be truly understood in all of one's complexity, the complexity David speaks of in Psalm 139:14 when he states, "I am fearfully and wonderfully made." The best way to define bonding at its core is to say that when I am bonded, I "matter" to someone.

When we are bonded to another person, we feel that we make a difference to him, that our presence is desired when we are around and missed when we are absent. This sense of "mattering" is in direct contrast to feeling overlooked, forgotten, or even simply tolerated by others.

EXAMPLES OF FAMILY BONDING

A family should be a place where its members can count on the safe nurturance of others to fuel their emotional needs. It should be a "filling station" where needs for love are met so that its members have the strength to go out and interact with the world, to accomplish the heavenly Father's command to "subdue" and "rule" the world (Genesis 1:28). These needs for love and interaction are met through

- warm times of telling stories and saying prayers at bedtime

- times of conversation over the dinner table about the day's events

- moments of sharing painful hurts at work or at school and of having tears wiped away

- times for assurance that no matter how hard things are in the outside world, at home everything is OK

- times when parents show their children their own vulnerability and thus let their children know that their parents are human, too

THE PRIMACY OF BONDS IN THE FAMILY

Why are human attachments so important? Because none of us is complete in ourselves. God has fashioned His universe so that relationship is the fuel for all growth. Without connections, we always experience a deficit.

BIBLICAL EVIDENCE

The very nature of God indicates how important bonding is. Consider the Trinity: God the Father, Son, and Spirit (Matthew 28:19; 2 Corinthians 13:14). The mystery of the divine interrelationship of the three Persons of the Trinity models for us the truth that God by nature is in relationship. And the beauty of this truth for us is that though God may *desire* connection with us, He does not *need* us. He is, at all times, bonded to the other parts of the Trinity. We are not responsible for God's relational needs; He has taken care of them Himself.

Being made in His image, man is also in need of bonding. We are incomplete in isolation. Though Adam's creation was a "good" thing, it was "not good" that he be alone (Genesis 2:18). God focuses on relationships, of which marriage is an example. Solomon warns, "Woe to the one who falls when there is not another to lift him up" (Ecclesiastes 4:10). Difficult times are made even harder when we go through them without attachments.

The entire New Testament teaching on the church emphasizes the fundamental need we have for connection with each other: "And the eye cannot say to the hand, 'I have no need of you'; or again the head to the feet, 'I have no need of you'"(1 Corinthians 12:21).

The little girl described at the beginning of this chapter was made by God with an inner need to be soothed from panic brought on by darkness and isolation. We all need to be bonded with loving, attachment-forming people.

Many Christians going through losses or trials have been unintentionally injured by well-meaning friends who have told them, "Just trust God, and leave it with Him." This sort of advice denies the hurting person one of God's primary avenues of comfort and support: the incarnational healing of His Body on earth. God does not intend for us to struggle alone with our sorrow. He has specifically made a place in our hearts for Him and for His people. When one of those places is isolated or ignored, we suffer.

PHYSICAL EVIDENCE

God's physical universe illustrates the primacy of the need for attachment. Consider the workings of plants, for example. A plant grows when the correct ingredients (food, water, air, sunlight, and soil) are provided. If one of these primary ingredients is denied, the plant wilts and begins to die. In addition, different parts of the plant need each other. Jesus refers to this principle of attachment in John 15:4 when He says, "As the branch cannot bear fruit of itself, unless it abides in the vine, so neither can you, unless you abide in Me." Quite often, a family with bonding deficits sends its members out into the world "unnurtured" and thus unprepared for the demands of life. These people often feel rootless and lost as a result.

"I'm a thirty-two-year-old zero," said Sandra quietly in her first session at the counselor's office. "All my friends are marrying and settling down, enjoying their careers and lives, and I can't even hold a job longer than six months. . . . I don't know how to be close, or what I need in a relationship. I guess I just don't feel a part of the human race." Sandra's understated desperation reflects a deep lack of belonging—a lack of bonding—in her life.

PERSONAL EVIDENCE

Consider for a moment your own life history. Think back over the hardest year of your life. Chances are that, whatever your circumstances, a major factor in that year was some sort of relational loss, either of a loved person or through a season of extreme isolation from others. Even in the physical presence of others, many Christians carry the burden of a problem, secret, or loss that has never been shared with another "person with skin on."

"But you don't understand," sobbed Joan to her counselor as she attempted to grapple with a painful divorce, a troubled daughter, and job stresses. "It's just not right to bother others with these problems. They've got problems of their own. Besides, I should be able to handle this by myself, shouldn't I?" Listen to the isolation in Joan's life: the aloneness of being a single parent coupled with the sense of being cut off from others who could help her in her struggle. No wonder she feels an almost unbearable burden.

If bonding is such a deep need in our hearts, what part does the family play in it? It is the crucible in which our "bondedness" is either developed or injured. God has made the family an incubator in which our sense of basic trust and dependency is formed in thousands of experiences over time. If we find that our emotional needs are welcome in the family, we will experience a sense of bondedness throughout our lives. But if our emotional needs are ignored or are met inconsistently, we will experience instead a feeling of aloneness and emptiness.

COMPONENTS OF FAMILY BONDING

SAFETY

Just as plants need protection from storms, disease, and privation, so we need a place of emotional shelter. The family's job is to provide its members, especially its young children, a sense of unconditional cherishing. There should be an atmosphere of feeling "connected" no matter what conflicts exist. This is partially what Paul means in Ephesians 3:17 when he speaks of our being "rooted and grounded in love."

Have you ever noticed what an infant does when he or she is startled by a loud noise? Say an adult sneezes suddenly near a baby. After an initial startled response, some infants will only require a few seconds of holding and comforting before they relax again. Other babies will require several minutes of calming by a parent before they regain their equilibrium. What makes the two groups respond differently?

Often, it is the number of consistent, predictably loving experiences the parents have given to the child. The baby who feels safe recovers quickly because he has a foundation of safe memories on which to draw. The baby who feels unsafe is shaky and ungrounded for a long time because he is deficient in that store of safe memories. The experience of the first child is parallel to that of the man in Luke 6:48 who built his house upon a rock. The "flood rose, the torrent burst," but the house could not be shaken, "because it had been well built." The child whose life rests upon a solid foundation of love will enjoy a sense of safety as he journeys through life.

Safety in the family also means that

- the parents give their children the assurance that they are loved by Mom and Dad no matter what they do or say

- family members reinforce vulnerability among themselves by taking the initiative to ask about each others' feelings

- the parents are consistent in their behavior and promises; the children know that their family is a predictably safe environment, not a chaotic or confusing one

- the family makes anger and sadness acceptable as part of the vocabulary of its conversation

- the parents understand the roots of conflicts before taking action to punish them

- family members are emotionally warm and gentle when hurt feelings are expressed

Unfortunately, many Christians find deficits existed in the emotional safety of their original families. These deficits likely showed up in two forms, as *emotional withdrawal,* in which the children learned that expressing their needs and feelings resulted in a parent detaching from them, and as *emotional attack,* in which the children learned that expressing their needs and feelings caused a parent to become emotionally or physically hostile. Both of these reactions will seriously undermine a child's ability to feel secure in who he is.

MODELING

The second component of the bonded family is the ability of the parents to "teach by doing" through being vulnerable with their joys, sorrows, and conflicts. When children hear Mom and Dad sharing hurts, losses, and failures, they learn that feelings and needs are normal parts of life. Parents should certainly be discreet in what they share with their children, for children often try to take responsibility for the emotional needs of their parents, but they should still persevere in teaching their children by example how to confess problems and solve them in a family. God is an example of a parent who shared His losses, as when Jesus wept over lost Jerusalem (Luke 19:41-44).

A lack of modeling in the family tends to cause the members of that family to regard their feelings as bad or weak. Children, especially, will assume that if their parents don't talk about their struggles or emotions, they must not have any problems. One woman expressed it this way: "When my father died, there was no warning beforehand, and no grieving afterwards on my mother's part. It was as if a TV channel had been switched: one day he was here, one day he was not. And since I never saw her sadness and anguish, I figured the feelings I experienced were bad and inappropriate. The shame I felt over my emotions was overwhelming."

Note the "double tragedy" here: not only did this woman feel unsafe with her grief, but the lack of modeling by her mother provided no "picture" through which she could learn what the season of mourning described in Ecclesiastes 3:4 actually looks like. The result was a feeling of badness and shame.

EMOTIONAL OPENNESS

This third component is at the heart of bonding. Whereas safety provides a place for bonding, and modeling offers object-lessons, the ability to communicate our needs and struggles in an environment of receptivity and trust is the essence of family attachment. Table 7.1 diagrams deepening levels of emotional openness among people. As you study the table, try to pinpoint your family's predominant level of intimacy.

Let's observe a few things about these differing levels of closeness. First, one level is not worse than another; instead, different levels meet different needs. We need relationships on all five levels. Jesus loved the world, but He had twelve deep relationships, the disciples. And of that dozen, three—Peter, James, and John—were singled out. Of those three, John was recognized as being "the disciple whom Jesus loved" (John 21:20). So we need and enjoy casual acquaintances as a means of relaxing, but at the same time experience a sense of internal isolation and emptiness if our family never addresses issues deeper than current events.

Second, as the levels of bonding increase, the number of relationships at each level decreases. In other words, we can have many acquaintances, but only a few truly deep bonds. Why is this? Simply because it takes an incredible amount of time, many shared experi-

Table 7.1
Levels of Intimacy

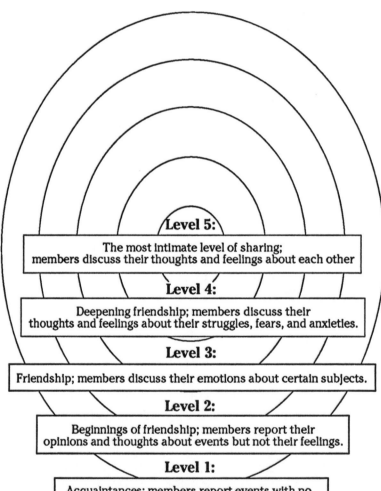

Level 5:
The most intimate level of sharing;
members discuss their thoughts and feelings about each other

Level 4:
Deepening friendship; members discuss their
thoughts and feelings about their struggles, fears, and anxieties.

Level 3:
Friendship; members discuss their emotions about certain subjects.

Level 2:
Beginnings of friendship; members report their
opinions and thoughts about events but not their feelings.

Level 1:
Acquaintances; members report events with no
opinions or emotions connected. Sports, weather,
and news are permissible topics of conversation.

ences, a good deal of work, and solid commitment if we are to take a relationship to the fifth level of intimacy. We should consider ourselves blessed if we can count a handful of these closest relationships by the end of our lives. As shown above, our Lord's pattern of human relationships was similar.

The second point brings us to the third: because the family is the incubator where bonding is learned, the quality of the years spent in our family of origin determines, to a large extent, our predominant level of intimacy in subsequent, adult relationships. That is not to say that this level is set in stone forever. It is only to say that it is helpful to see that our relational problems are not without origins. Detached families do tend to produce detached children.

The bottom line is that our struggles have roots. True, we are all sinners, being born of Adam. There is indeed a generational component to our sinfulness. But the types and kinds of problems we have tend as well to be a reaction to our most important relationships: those within our family of origin.

SYMPTOMS OF BONDING DEFICITS

Bonding deficits reveal themselves in characteristic ways. Look through the following checklist of signs that a family is having difficulty in achieving closeness. As you read the list, ask yourself: Do any of these symptoms characterize my present family, my family of origin, or both?

- Whenever all of the members of the family are at home, they spend all of their time in different rooms.

- When the members of the family need comfort, they turn to food, drugs, work, hobbies, or other nonrelational substitutes.

- Conversations in the home center around what a person is doing as opposed to how he is doing.

- Relationships outside the home take precedence over relationships inside the home.

Individual family members may also experience symptoms that point to a problem in bonding:

- Feelings of isolation

- Loss of meaning

- Substance abuse

- Shallow relationships

- Depression

- Obsessions with activity or work

- Suicidal thoughts or actions

WHAT DO THE SYMPTOMS MEAN?

If you have experienced some of these symptoms in your family of origin or your present family, consider the symptoms a red flag signaling that something has gone wrong. Jesus said, "Every good tree bears good fruit; but the bad tree bears bad fruit" (Matthew 7:17). In other words, use the symptoms list to help yourself understand the bonding problem.

The symptoms tell us that when love and closeness are absent, the family has no firm roots upon which to build everything else. When Dad loses his job he will not think of his home as a safe place to refuel before launching out to find another job. When Johnny feels shut out by the peer group at his new school, he will isolate himself in his room and listen to music instead of coming to dinner with everyone else and sharing his hurt. When Debbie's boyfriend breaks up with her, she will hide her loneliness and sadness in a binge of overeating but not share with the rest of her family the hurt that caused that overeating.

DEVALUATION AS A RESPONSE TO FEAR OF INTIMACY

Let's suppose you have been able to identify several symptoms of bonding deficits in your family. Often, in order to survive the sense of loneliness and emptiness brought on by bonding deficits, Christians develop barriers to intimacy that soothe the pain but prevent the problem from being resolved. These barriers can be described in one word: devaluation, or undervaluing our need for close, loving relationships.

We don't come out of the womb devaluing love. On the contrary, we are born empty, frightened, needy beings. We want love. But after repeatedly being punished for having needs, seeing others withdraw from our needs, and having our trust betrayed, most of us inwardly decide that numbness is the best policy: *To protect myself, I must live without needing others. And to live without needing others, I must not feel my own needs.* Devaluating our needs has the personal usefulness of protecting us from the pain of needing caring and grace from others and not being able to have it. There is no more excruciating emotional pain in the world than this.

The problem is that this protective device (called a coping style in chapter 3) becomes a prison. Devaluation of the people who didn't bond properly with us generalizes to a habit of withdrawing from anyone who has something to offer. As a result, we increase our isolation. Paul addresses this self-induced isolation in 2 Corinthians 6:11-13 when he speaks of a lack of love returned:

> Our mouth has spoken freely to you, O Corinthians, our heart is opened wide. You are not restrained by us, but you are restrained in your own affections. Now in a like exchange—I speak as to children— open wide to us also.

I find Paul's reference to children particularly significant, since we tend to learn this prison-making behavior early in life.

We can see this defense mechanism in action in Phil, whose wife had left him. "I think you guys have it all wrong," Phil protested to his concerned friends. "I'm really fine," he continued. "She wasn't that great a wife anyway, and I really didn't love her. It's no great loss." Not until several months later, when Phil developed a severe drinking problem, did the lie (devaluation) became apparent.

Certainly even some of our closest relationships can be unsatisfying at times. In addition, feelings of love are mercurial. It is normal for one sinner to have a hard time constantly feeling close to another sinner! But did you notice Phil's devaluation of how important his wife was to him? He used it to protect himself from the anguish of his loss.

DEVALUATION AS A WAY OF EXPLAINING OUR WITHDRAWAL

While devaluation of our need for others is often a response to a fear of attachment, other kinds of devaluation come about as a means of explaining and justifying our withdrawal. These devaluations revolve around the three primary relationships we have: with God, with others, and with ourselves. Consider the following devaluative statements:

Devaluations about God:

"God isn't trustworthy since He allowed me to be badly hurt."
"God doesn't care about me personally."
"God is more concerned about what I do than who I am inside."

Devaluations about others:

"People can't be trusted."
"There is no one who truly cares about my needs."
"If I am vulnerable, I will be hurt."

Devaluations about ourselves:

"I have no need for others; I am fine alone."
"Closeness is an illusion."
"I am too bad to be loved."
"It is wrong and selfish for me to ask for comfort."

Observe that most of these beliefs have a kernel of truth to them. The statement "I am too bad to be loved" is certainly true in the sense that all of us are sinful. All of us carry guilt in our soul that testifies to our sinfulness. But there is also much to love in each of us. The lie is that our eligibility for love depends on our performance, and often a completely perfect performance at that. Phil conveniently used his wife's human imperfection (the kernel of truth) to devalue her importance to him (the lie).

The problem is that these beliefs generally develop from experiences at an early age and then graduate from truths within the dysfunctional family to truths about the universe. What was once a way to protect us from further hurt becomes an isolative wall around our hearts, sealing us off from the grace of God and His Body, the church.

Understanding My Bonding Deficits

We have seen God's ideal for family bonding and what can go wrong. Now let's turn to our own personal situation and learn about what may have gone wrong. Let's examine how our past affects our present. As you read this section of the chapter, use the blank lines below each subsection to make personal notes for yourself.

1. A Personal Inventory

   In prayer, ask God to help you have insight into your own struggles with intimacy: "Search me, O God, and know my heart; Try me and know my anxious thoughts" (Psalm 139:23). Look through this chapter, and note which parts of the discussion relate to your life.

   _____

   _____

   _____

2. List of Symptoms

   Begin with the behaviors, attitudes, and feelings that trouble you most. Do these aspects of your life point to isolation? Are they substitutes for attachment to others?

   _____

   _____

   _____

3. Underlying Problems

   In this section of the inventory, deal directly with your experience of isolation. Do you find that you struggle with devaluations of love? What sort of thoughts do you find recurring that tend to push away your need for closeness?

   _____

   _____

   _____

4. Causes of Bonding Deficits

Evaluate your family of origin's ability to bond (i.e., its capacity to provide safety, modeling, and levels of openness). Was the family emotionally cold? Was there instead a pseudointimacy that masked isolation? Was emotional vulnerability met by indifference, hostility, anxiety, or withdrawal?

_____

_____

_____

5. Linking Past to Present

Take a look at how you may be repeating the isolating patterns you learned in your original family. Do you expect inconsistency in those you are close to? Are you afraid to trust because you expect to be let down, betrayed, attacked, or made to feel guilty?

_____

_____

_____

SKILLS FOR REPAIRING BONDING DEFICITS

If you survived the bad news of learning about your injuries in the last section, good for you! The following section will deal with the good news: God wants to help you heal. Your ability to connect emotionally with others is like a torn or injured muscle. It is atrophied and undeveloped, but it can be repaired and strengthened. Here are some ways you can restore this God-given "muscle."

1. Find a safe, uncritical relationship (or two) in which you can begin to learn to bond. This relationship may be with your spouse, a friend, a pastor, or a counselor. Just remember that bonding wilts in the face of detachment or criticism, but flowers in the presence of acceptance and warmth.

2. Become aware of your resistance to intimacy. Do you withdraw when you find yourself becoming needy? Do you find yourself devaluing relationships when you are hurt?

3. Take risks with emotional issues. Are there experiences, memories, thoughts, or feelings you have never shared with anyone? Allow someone to care about this isolated and unloved part of yourself. James 5:16 says, "Confess your sins to one another . . . so that you may be healed." In the context of this chapter the verse might be paraphrased, "Confess your lacks to one another . . . so that you may be healed."

4. Begin to allow yourself to make relationships in which it is OK to share emotions at a deep level.

5. Allow yourself to feel the need for closeness. Allow yourself to need uncritical relationships and to be comforted by them. Jesus said, "Blessed are those who mourn, for they shall be comforted" (Matthew 5:4).

6. Pray on a personal rather than a grocery list level.

7. Meditate on who God is rather than simply on what He does.

8. Begin to forgive your family for injuring your "bonding muscle." Forgiveness is a process and takes a great deal of healing to accomplish. Beginning this step brings you further out of the bondage of repeating the dysfunctional patterns you learned there. Remember, our parents were probably also injured by their parents!

9. Allow for mistakes. Practicing bonding means sometimes getting hurt when we attempt to be close, and sometimes even withdrawing when we need to get close. But we learn by mistakes. Hebrews 5:14 states that "solid food is for the mature, who because of *practice* have their senses trained to discern good and evil" (italics added). With practice, we learn who is safe and who isn't. With practice, we learn the skill of taking emotional risks. And with practice, we begin to receive and give what God has intended for us from the beginning: ourselves.

ARE YOU A "BONDING CASUALTY"?

As this chapter on family bonding closes, you may have identified yourself as a bonding casualty. You may feel that your life is typified by emotional isolation. And if you have experienced deficits in the bonding patterns of your original family, you may also feel some sense of confusion about bonding or tend to trivialize the need for finding close relationships. That is normal and is due to a tendency to be frightened of intimacy ("being") and more at ease with activities ("doing").

Chet was struggling with family bonding problems. He had begun to experience deep feelings of sadness about some major losses in his life. After wrestling with his agonizing emotions, he decided to phone his counselor. Taking the initiative by calling his therapist after hours was highly significant in that it was the first time in his life that he had ever *asked for* a personal connection to share his pain. Chet poured out his sadness and feelings of loss, then asked for advice on what to do with his emotional pain. He expected his counselor to suggest some kind of action like "get more organized, put it behind you, do something positive . . ."

The therapist replied, "Chet, you're doing what you need to do."

It gradually dawned on Chet that during the lengthy conversation his pain had been understood and shared. In making such an intimate connection with his counselor, he felt immense emotional relief.

In seeking the healing God wants to provide for bonding deficits, we need to learn the lesson of simply allowing others to care about us without performing; we need to be Marys instead of Marthas (Luke 10:38-42).

Is this an easy task? No! In fact, it will probably be one of the most difficult tasks you will ever encounter, especially if you suffer from bonding difficulties.

As you begin the process of learning bonding, ask God to direct you to safe, attaching, forgiving people. We can't repair this injury in a vacuum. God made people a part of the process. As you search for those few people with whom you can begin to learn to trust, look in your church, your social circles, your work, and your family. Ask yourself, *Would he or she be gentle with or critical of my emotions? Would I be understood, or would I be judged?* Then, after careful and prayerful evaluation, take a risk—a small one, but a risk nonetheless—and let yourself be vulnerable with that person.

Questions for Reflection

Ask yourself the following questions, and make personal notes in the space provided.

1. In which of the three components of bonding (safety, modeling, and openness) have I experienced problems? How has this affected my life?

_____

_____

_____

2. What activities, good or bad, do I find myself substituting for intimacy?

_____

_____

_____

3. When are my bonding injuries most painfully apparent to me (social situations, alone at night, and so on)? Use these times as a barometer of your spiritual and emotional well-being. As you identify the situations in which you become most aware of bonding deficits, ask God to reveal ways of relating that will help you make it through the tough times (for example, calling a friend, taking a risk to share feelings, or honestly discussing your needs with God in prayer).

_____

_____

_____

4. Who is the person in my life right now with whom it would be the safest to begin a vulnerable relationship?

_____

_____

_____

5. Which of the bonding skills can I begin to learn this week? What would be a first step in building this skill?

_____

_____

_____

8

Learning to Set Boundaries

By John Townsend, Ph.D.

A young mother confided tearfully to a friend that she has been having problems with her eighteen-month-old son. "We've been so close ever since he was born, but now it seems so hard. He disobeys and disagrees with me. I miss my 'easy baby.' I guess we're entering the 'terrible twos.'"

The woman's friend responded, "Well, I can understand your frustration, but I see this stage differently. I call it the 'terrific twos.' I love to see my child's personality emerge and begin to blossom."

What a radical difference in the child-rearing perspectives of the two women! The first wishes her baby was once again compliant and cuddly and resents the stubborn willfulness of her child. The second sees the child's emerging energy as a joy. Their conversation illustrates a problem many Christians (and non-Christians) have about what a "good baby" and a "bad baby" are. Passive, obedient, cooperative babies get the white hats; those who are more self-directed and oppositional (the "strong-willed child" James Dobson talks about) get the black hats.

And yet it is this active willfulness that sets the stage for the second developmental need designed by God to be nurtured in the family: the need for separateness. Boundaries help us make responsible choices, but we need strength of will to set them. So, within

---

For further treatment of the material in this chapter, refer to Henry Cloud, *When Your World Makes No Sense* (Nashville: Oliver Nelson, 1990).

biblical limits (as we shall explore here and elsewhere), some degree of what people commonly call "willfulness" is God-given and essential.

What makes the will so important? Simply this: our will has both a positive and a negative function: *it helps us to choose the good and refuse the bad.* Without it, we easily cave in to sin and have difficulty standing for righteousness. When it is totally undeveloped, and especially when overly compliant behavior is praised (particularly during childhood), the ability to set healthy boundaries is impaired. Dysfunctional or codependent relationships almost always result.

OUR NEED FOR SEPARATENESS

To understand separateness, let's return to bonding, the developmental need mentioned in chapter 7. Many people feel they are "people persons," that they are able to bond and connect with others. Yet these same people often feel overwhelmed, anxious, and frustrated about the obligations and responsibilities their bonded relationships seem to demand. The reason for this is that bonding alone is not enough. We also need self ownership—self-determination of what we are to do with our lives and resources. In a phrase, we need stewardship over how we use our lives (Matthew 25:14-30).

A good example of bonding without separateness is found in a Christian man in his mid-thirties I'll call Bill. He began seeing a counselor for symptoms of depression. As he explored his life and circumstances, he began to notice a pattern in his important relationships. "I'm realizing now that all my life I've been so afraid to disappoint people that I've never said no to anyone," he said. "In order not to let down my family, my wife, my boss, and my friends, I've worked later, longer, and harder than anyone I know. I even feel that God depends on me for everything, too. And I'm so busy taking care of everyone else's requests for my time that I've been ignoring my own needs. No wonder I've felt burned out for years."

As time went on, Bill began to recognize the source of his problem with separateness. He had come from a family where differences of opinion were seen as rebellion and where compliance was rewarded. This injury to his will manifested itself in Bill's adult life as chronic depression.

How do mistreatments of the will lead to depression? In this way: when we don't feel free to be honest and truthful with others about our opinions and values, we set in motion the process of allowing ourselves to be controlled by the feelings and desires of others. That in turn leads to a deep sense of powerlessness and resentment, based on a feeling of helplessness. If this sense of powerlessness and resentment is not checked, one's hope of being in normal control of one's life begins to die. Depression is the result of the death of hope. Proverbs 13:12 says, "Hope deferred makes the heart sick." When we feel constantly owned and controlled by others, our heart suffers.

BLOCKS TO BONDING

The interaction of the abilities developed in chapters 7 and 8, the capacity to bond with others and yet establish boundaries, is shown in the table 8.1.

The value across the top, "Bonding," represents the presence or absence of deep attachments in a person's life. The value at the left of the chart, "Boundaries," represents the presence or absence of clear separateness and autonomy. The results that occur when these elements are combined are listed inside the four blocks. Let's examine each of the blocks in turn. Give some thought to which pattern, if any, applies to your life.

Table 8.1
Interrelationship of the Capacity to Bond and the Capacity to Set Boundaries

		BONDING	
		HIGH	LOW
BOUNDARIES	HIGH	Block 1 Intimacy	Block 3 Isolation
	LOW	Block 2 Fusion	Block 4 Chaos

BLOCK 1

Block 1, "Intimacy," indicates that *closeness plus clear separateness produces a healthy intimacy.* In such a relationship differences of opinion and even arguments do not disturb the sense of being "rooted and grounded in love" (Ephesians 3:17).

After several weeks of intensive counseling for severe depression at a Christian psychiatric hospital program, Mary began to grasp the deep relational conflicts underlying her condition. "I've always feared that differences between me and *anybody* would cause me to be abandoned forever, whether it was my husband, my children, or even the paper boy. Working so hard to avoid conflict burned me out. Now, as a result of the learning I've done as a result of therapy, I can 'speak the truth in love' and still feel connected to people I disagree with."

What was the epochal "truth telling" event that made all the difference for Mary? Simply that when a staff member invited her to a field trip to the beach, she declined because she wanted to do some reading. When the staff member, to whom Mary felt close, did not become angry or hurt and reject her over her choice, Mary actually wept in surprised relief! Having a relationship where differences of opinion or desire didn't result in rejection was something she'd never experienced in her family of origin.

BLOCK 2

Block 2, "Fusion," indicates what happens when bonding without boundaries occurs. One or both people in a relationship are unable to be free and separate. In fused relationships, differences of opinion and normal degrees of conflict are either denied or punished. We saw an example of a fused parent-child relationship in chapter 2 in the relationship of Isaac and his mother, Sarah. Fused relationships among adults can be seen in the suffocating heat of romantic infatuation, when romantic partners do not know where one person starts and the other ends. The couple is "lost" in love for one another. Their relationship is fused, which is in large part why such relationships are usually rocky, unfruitful, and short-lived.

BLOCK 3

Block 3, "Isolation," shows what happens when boundaries exist but not bonding. An isolated individual may be very much in charge of his or her life and have a well-developed ability to say no, but at the same time not have any deep emotional relationships. People in this pattern tend to "die on the vine," withering from a lack of normal interaction and love. We saw in chapter 1 how David's son Absalom felt isolated from his father. Absalom thought it was necessary to do drastic things to get his father's attention, such as setting a wheat field on fire. The workaholic or loner is a modern-day example of this type.

BLOCK 4

Block 4, "Chaos," describes the relational capacity of a person who is injured in both attachment (bonding) and separateness (boundaries). He feels lost in relation to others and to himself. He is neither connected nor self-directed, but is in a spiritual and relational limbo.

This is the most injured category, for in it both connectedness (the basis for feeling loved) and self-responsibility (the basis for self-control) are at low-functioning levels. Today we see many adolescents with these two deficits. They are unable to form deep attachments and have extreme problems in delaying gratification and being responsible for themselves. It is no wonder that drugs have become so prevalent in our culture, with their promise of helping the user to feel loved (connectedness) and to experience instant gratification (a result of having weak boundaries, which form the basis for self-control).

BOUNDARIES: THE SEPARATENESS TOOL

Given that we need both attachment and freedom, how does this second ability, the ability to be separate, develop in the family?

The family was designed by God to develop our wills for two purposes: (1) to protect us against evil, and (2) to give us the freedom to choose how we will live our lives under God. The mechanism for building our wills is called a *boundary*. Let us understand what we mean by this term. A boundary is that which distinguishes one person from another person. It is that which sets him apart. Just as we can tell property lines of ownership by legal boundaries, in the same way spiritual and emotional boundaries exist to show us what is "mine" and what is "not mine."

Our skin is a boundary. It keeps us separate from others. It keeps bad things out (infections, dust, and germs) and good things in (our organs, muscles, and so on).

The word *no* is a boundary. When we say no, we are keeping something out, perhaps an unwanted obligation or a demand on our time or money that would be debilitating. When we use the word *no* skillfully and without fear or guilt, we help to define and protect ourselves. Using *no* is like developing a muscle. The skill improves with practice. The "no muscle" takes a great deal of time to mature, and it is susceptible to injury, particularly as we are growing up in our families of origin.

A word of caution. I am not saying that Christians should not be helpful. The New Testament is replete with admonitions to "die to self" and "love one another," and I heartily agree with those admonitions. Rather, I am talking about dysfunctional (and unscriptural) behavioral patterns that hinder us from practically *ever* saying no. It's a balance I'm urging.

PROPERTY LINES, KNAPSACKS, AND BOULDERS

If we look at boundaries as spiritual "property lines," we can see that boundaries determine what we *are* responsible for and what we are *not* responsible for. God has made us responsible for those things, and only those things, that are within our boundaries. We encounter conflicts with ourselves and with others when we make one (or both) of the following mistakes:

- not taking care of the things that are within our boundaries

   or

- taking care of the things that are outside our boundaries

Galatians 6 is a good chapter to study in connection with this point. There Paul asserts that "each one shall bear his own load" (v. 5). The Greek word for "load" means *knapsack,* or what we carry daily on our journey through life. It is the same "burden" that Jesus spoke of when He said, "My yoke is easy, and my burden is light" (Matthew 11:30, KJV). This "load" comprises that responsibility we should shoulder for ourselves.

Our individual knapsacks include such items as our thoughts, attitudes, opinions, beliefs, needs, choices, feelings, values, time, possessions, money, gifts, talents, behavior, and bodies. We are to set limits around these parts of our lives and should protect and maintain them *ourselves.* It is our responsibility to care for them.

The converse is also true. Just as we are positively to take care of the elements of our lives that are properly within our own boundaries, so we are to refrain from taking care of the things that are inside other persons' boundaries. If we fail to observe this restraint two negative results are likely to take place:

- We will sabotage the spiritual growth of another person (Ephesians 4:15)

  and

- We will neglect our own God-given responsibilities and become poor stewards of ourselves (Matthew 25:14-30).

The important thing about our knapsacks is that they are "divinely sewn" on our backs by God. In other words, we should not "carry" (take responsibility for) someone else's knapsack. God Himself doesn't do that. For example, He allows people to refuse His gift of salvation. Think of Jesus' words in Luke 13:34:

> O Jerusalem, Jerusalem, the city that kills the prophets and stones those sent to her! How often I wanted to gather your children together, just as a hen gathers her brood under her wings, and you would not have it!

Just as Jesus allows others to make destructive decisions for themselves, so we have to accept the reality that we aren't strong enough, nor do we have the right, to take responsibility for others. We are to love them but not to parent them (unless we are legally responsible for them, as in parent-child relationships). When one adult "parents" another (even when the two adults are related), co-dependent, dysfunctional relationships almost always follow.

In contrast to our knapsacks, Paul describes a different "load" in verse 2 of the same chapter. This Greek term is the word for *boulders:* heavy, crushing burdens that cannot be borne alone. These are the tragedies, crises, and losses that befall us and that are not our fault. As best we can, we are to help one another with these boulders. Doing so is practically the definition of brotherly love and pleases God greatly.

Thus we see that God wants us to make a clear distinction: to handle boulders differently from knapsacks. Whereas we can only love, but not take responsibility for, someone whose knapsack is giving him problems, it is entirely proper for the Body of Christ to surround the stricken, crushed member with caring and support until he or she can get back on his feet.

The story of the Good Samaritan illustrates this perfectly (Luke 10:30-37). The Samaritan, finding the injured man, didn't put him up in a hotel for the rest of his life. Instead, he provided enough funds for the man to be healed and assumed that after an appropriate time, he'd be on his way. The Samaritan loved the wounded man but did not take permanent responsibility for him. To do so would have been to deny the injured man his own identity and autonomy.

To summarize: Paul is saying in Galatians that we are fully responsible *for* ourselves (bearing our knapsacks) but only partially responsible *to* others (helping them with their boulders when we are able). Put another way, God's plan for growing up involves taking full responsibility for our lives and helping others in crisis, but we are not responsible for the normal loads of others (i.e., their knapsacks).

We will hurt ourselves and others if we shoulder the wrong load. If we try to pick up their boulders instead of our knapsacks, we will end up denying others their adulthood and prevent them from learning that their actions have consequences. We will make them dependent on us and ourselves codependent with them.

THE FAMILY AND BOUNDARIES

The second great function of the family, after bonding, is to help its members take responsibility for their "loads" by setting boundaries and developing the ability to make wise and responsible choices.

How does the family provide this need? These are some of the ways:

- by allowing family members to state their opinions
- by making it safe to disagree without fear of criticism, rejection, or isolation
- by encouraging members to think for themselves
- by helping members discover and train themselves to use their unique gifts and abilities
- by allowing anger to be expressed appropriately (Ephesians 4:28)
- by setting limits with consequences, not guilt or fear
- by respecting each other's "no" choices

- by allowing age-appropriate choices:
    condition of a bedroom (sloppy or well-kept)
    choice of relationships (within biblical guidelines)
    development of Christian values
    how to spend money
    when to be with friends instead of family

The family has a tricky job: it needs to keep members intimately attached yet simultaneously separate.

WHAT GOES WRONG?

Many Christian families do not produce members who can set limits with others. What happens in these families that impairs the growth of the "no muscle," thus hindering the development of healthy boundaries?

Basically, parents who are confused about boundaries tend to produce children who are confused about boundaries. There are several source points of this confusion, some of which are given below:

- Parents who feel abandoned when their children begin to make autonomous choices. These parents respond to autonomy in their children by conveying guilt or shame messages about their lack of love and loyalty to the family or to the parents.

- Parents who feel threatened by the increasing loss of control they have over their children. These parents use anger or criticism, not guilt or shame messages, to convey their unhappiness over the childrens' new-found separateness.

- Families that equate disagreement with sin.

- Families that are afraid of the anger of their children.

- Families that are hostile toward the anger of their children.

- Families that praise compliance in the name of togetherness over healthy independence.

- Families in which emotional, physical, and sexual abuse occur. These kinds of abuse cause severe damage to the children's sense of ownership of their bodies and themselves.

- Families in which the children feel responsible for the happiness of the parents.

- Families that rescue children from experiencing the consequences of their behavior.

- Families that are inconsistent in limit-setting with the children.

- Families that continue to take responsibility for the children in adulthood.

Let me illustrate the first of the points listed above. Cynthia was a loving Christian wife and mother of two who could not understand why a growing, gradual sense of isolation increased in her as her children grew older. Finally, in therapy for depression, she began to realize that she was feeling abandoned by her children as they became more and more autonomous. "But why in the world would my kids' growth make me feel lonely?" she asked.

Digging deeper, she began to see that her mother had made her the center of her life. If Cynthia was around to support her, Mom was happy. But if Cynthia wanted to spend time away from home with friends, Mom became sad and depressed.

When Cynthia married and moved out of state, her mother began isolating herself, developing physical problems, and making sure that all letters and phone conversations to Cynthia were directed toward how empty life was without her. Those messages were like a knife in Cynthia's heart, full of guilt and shame messages about what a neglectful daughter she was.

Cynthia's mother felt abandoned because she made Cynthia responsible to take care of her loneliness instead of developing her own adult friendships. As a result, Cynthia was conflicted about her own autonomy. Her boundaries were fuzzy. This pattern was repeated in Cynthia's own family when she married and had children. She felt the same feelings toward her own children that her mother had felt toward her. That is why she came into counseling as her children matured. There was a difference, however: Cynthia wanted the family pattern stopped in her generation and worked hard to allow her kids age-appropriate freedom without feeling responsible for her loneliness. She wanted to halt the cycle of transmission (discussed in chapter 3) so that godly patterns might be sent down the line instead of ungodly ones.

As we can see, where the family makes the child (1) responsible for what is not his, and/or (2) not responsible for what is his, boundary injuries ensue. Note that we say boundary "injuries" and not simply "confusions." Errors in this area do a grievous injury to a developing human being. Just as some people suffer from untreated childhood physical injuries well into adult years (for example, unset broken bones or untreated tooth decay), many Christians take boundary injuries into their mature years, where the deficits wreak immeasurable havoc in their lives. Nowhere is the principle Jesus articulated in Matthew 7:17, that good trees produce good fruit (corresponding to appropriately responsible children) and bad trees produce bad fruit (corresponding to children who take too much or too little responsibility for their lives), more evident than in the case of boundary problems.

WHAT IS THE RESULT?

When a family has not provided clear "ownership" guidelines to its children, the children learn to say yes to what is not theirs (yes to the bad) and no to what is theirs (no to the good). Although some families produce children with one or the other patterns, many more families produce children who live out both extremes.

"There's just no hope for me," Phyllis said bitterly in her therapist's office. An attractive woman in her late forties, she was grieving the demise of her third marriage. "I always end up with the same type of man: charming, flashy, and totally irresponsible. Am I a magnet for these losers?"

Phyllis's latest failure had come about when she found that her husband of three years was having an affair (in addition to being chronically unable to hold down a job for more than a few months). She had been the stable breadwinner in all three marriages. Was she a magnet?

In a way, yes. Both of Phyllis's parents had been alcoholics, loving in their intentions but consistently inconsistent in following up on their promises. Phyllis had painful memories of being left at school without a ride, of meals she had to make herself, and of promises of gifts that never materialized and special events that never occurred.

Yet Phyllis had never learned that this pattern was not her fault, but her parents'. In one session she remarked, "I figured they didn't follow through because I wasn't being good enough, so I became better than good. . . . I became the most responsible little girl in the world."

Then the responsible little girl entered adulthood. Typically, when these types of conflicts are not noticed and worked through, there is a repetition of the pattern in the next generation, and that is what happened in Phyllis's case. She married men like her parents, who "talked their talk" but didn't "walk their walk."

Why? She put it together one day: "I've been trying to *fix* these men with my love, the way I *couldn't* fix Mom and Dad." She had developed a hallmark symptom of codependent relationships, the need to "fix" other adults.

Phyllis is an example of someone who had been trained by her environment to allow irresponsible people into her life, thinking their irresponsibility was hers to repair. Put in our boundary discussion terms, she had learned to say yes to the bad.

It's sad. Think of all the mature, reliable, consistent men who had possibly been interested in Phyllis but in whom she was not interested. There was nothing to fix in their lives! Phyllis was not only saying yes to the bad, she was also saying no to the good.

RESULTS OF BOUNDARY PROBLEMS

Table 8.2 illustrates the types of boundary problems individuals contend with, both in relation to themselves and to others. Let's look at the diagram. Perhaps you'll see yourself, elements of yourself, or your loved ones here.

BLOCK 1

Block 1 represents the person who can't say no to others because of guilt, fear, or an excessive desire to please. This person gives up stewardship of his life to the control of others' wishes, needs, and demands. Though he is active in helping others, the inability he has in setting limits for himself often causes him intense confusion, anxiety, and frustration because of a lack of direction. Bill, cited earlier as a workaholic who didn't want to disappoint anyone, fit into this category. In contrast, God warns us against "seeking

Table 8.2
Boundary Problems

	CAN'T SAY	CAN'T HEAR
"No"	**Block 1** Feels guilty and/or controlled by others	**Block 3** Wants others to take responsibility for him
"Yes"	**Block 2** Self-absorbed; doesn't respond to others' needs	**Block 4** Can't receive caring from others

the favor of men" too much (Galatians 1:10) but rather urges us to seek to please Him as the number one priority in our lives.

BLOCK 2

Block 2 refers to the individual who does not respond to others' boulders, the "excessive loads" of Galatians 6:2. He does not say yes to valid needs of others. His behavior is in direct contrast to the pattern exhorted in Proverbs 3:27: "Do not withhold good from those to whom it is due, when it is in your power [note the condition here] to do it."

The neglect of caring characteristic of persons in this category is usually due to one of two causes:

- a critical spirit toward others' needs (Pharisaism)

- a self-absorption in one's own desires and needs to the point of excluding others (narcissism)

It is important here not to confuse this self-absorption with a God-given sense of taking care of one's own needs first so that one is then able to love others.

Whereas Blocks 1 and 4 have to do with the codependent person, Blocks 2 and 3 have to do with the dependent person, the one who takes little responsibility for his own life but instead seeks to make others bear the load. Dependent people tend to gravitate toward codependents, because a codependent's lack of proper boundaries is likely to cause him to neglect himself and "rescue" the dependent individual. That is what had happened to Bill. He had a dependent mother, wife, and boss, and he could not care for all of them and himself, too. The result was depression and burnout. Phyllis illustrated the other half of the equation. She consistently found dependent types to marry so that she, in her codependence, could rescue them.

BLOCK 3

Whereas Block 1 refers to the person who can't *say* no, Block 3 refers to the person who can't *hear* no. People with this boundary problem tend to project responsibility for their lives onto others and either through manipulation or demand get others to carry the load God intended for them alone. These people generally have not had consistent limits set for them by their families and so tend to exploit others to get their needs met, thus violating the boundaries of others. They have extreme difficulty in taking ownership for their actions, indeed for their whole lives.

Roger grew up in a well-to-do family where all normal responsibilities had been taken care of by his parents or the hired help. He had never held a summer job, nor had he been held accountable to make good grades in school. After a few months of marriage, his wife was amazed to find that he had run up thousands of dollars of credit card purchases and was writing bad checks. When she angrily confronted him over it, he said resentfully, "Don't worry, someone will take care of it."

That someone had always been his parents, who, because of their own boundary conflicts, had acted as Roger's financial safety net. They took responsibility for things inside Roger's boundary. He had always assumed that someone would absorb the consequences of his actions, but that someone was never himself. Now Roger's inability to delay gratification was causing him to violate his wife's financial boundaries. He couldn't hear "no" from her regarding his excesses.

God sees a situation like this quite differently from the way Roger did. He has ordained a law of the universe we informally call the "law of sowing and reaping." Responsibility brings success; irresponsibility brings failure. As Paul wrote in 2 Thessalonians 3:10*b*, "If anyone will not work, neither let him eat." An empty stomach would quickly help teach Roger to respect his wife's boundaries more!

BLOCK 4

Block 4 refers to the person who denies God-given needs because of guilt, a desire to please others (Colossians 3:22-23), or a fear of emotional abandonment. This is a matter of setting boundaries where none should be. The person believes it's not OK to have needs, whereas in actuality no such barrier or boundary exists. People who have difficulty in being direct with others about their needs for comfort, support, encouragement, and caring fall into this category.

People in Block 4 usually fall into two groups:

- those who are afraid of, or feel guilty about, asking for what they need (in contrast to Jesus' encouragement in Luke 1:8 to "ask," "seek," and "knock")

  and/or

- those who are unaware that they have emotional, spiritual, or relational needs (in contrast to Jesus' blessing in Matthew 5:6 on those who "hunger and thirst for righteousness, for they shall be satisfied")

The people who fall simultaneously into Blocks 1 and 4 are codependent. They take responsibility for others' needs but neglect their own. And yes, it seems that Bill, our people-pleasing workaholic, fits both blocks himself. Bill was much more attuned and sensitive to what others wanted from him than what he would need if he were to grow.

The boundary confusion these people suffer is technically known as a "reversal," since there *are* boundaries where there should not be, but *no* boundaries where there should be. The condition can lead to workaholism, depression, eating disorders, substance abuse, and panic attacks.

OBSTACLES TO TAKING OWNERSHIP

The heart of the problem of ownership is *responsibility*, determining what is and is not mine. It is failing to take appropriate ownership within appropriate boundaries. Part of what hinders us from doing so is a reliance on myths about God, others, and ourselves:

Boundary confusion about God:

- God should always say yes to me ("Genie in a lamp")
- God is responsible to keep me from suffering loss, whether or not I take responsibility for my life
- God expects me to love Him and others without being responsible for my own legitimate, God-given needs

Boundary confusion about others:

- If I say no to others, I'm being selfish
- I am indispensable to the needs of others
- My happiness is the responsibility of someone else in my life

Boundary confusion about ourselves:

- If I am needy, I am bad
- If I love, I should be loved in return
- My life is not my responsibility

Fundamental to these myths is a confusion about the relationship of love and limits. Many families operate on the unspoken assumption that love and limits are antagonistic. One wife told her husband tearfully, "You never provide enough money for us to have traveling vacations. If you really loved me and the family, you'd do something about it." Yet at this point in their married life, the husband was trying to work their way out of severe debt problems, and it was tough going.

Why did the wife fail to see that? Because she interpreted her husband's appropriate limits (i.e., "no fancy vacations until we're out of debt") as an absence of love, whereas in reality it was healthy responsibility. Strange though it may seem, often people with firm (healthy) boundaries are characterized by people around them with unhealthy boundaries as being selfish, uncaring, or unloving. Instances of this are not uncommon. Their frequency indicates how far we as a society have strayed from God's healthy design.

People who have good boundaries tend to be the most loving people in the world. Why? Because they don't give from obligation or fear, but as "cheerful giver[s] " (2 Corinthians 9:7). Loving people are to have firm boundaries, and firm people are to love. That is growth into the image of God.

ATTITUDES TO ADOPT AND
ACTIONS TO TAKE TO REPAIR BOUNDARIES

By now you may feel a bit overwhelmed with regard to setting proper boundaries, especially if you grew up with unclear or inappropriate ones. But take heart; there is hope for repair. If you have been injured in your ability to set or respect boundaries, steps are available to repair this broken part of your soul. What follows is a suggested plan. Take a few minutes to fill in the blanks below with your personal responses.

1. *Make a personal inventory.* Begin by looking at the fruit, or symptoms, in your life. Here is a partial list of signs of boundary problems:

   - feelings of obligation
   - hidden anger/resentment toward others' demands
   - inability to be direct and honest
   - people-pleasing
   - life out of control
   - no sense of identity or "who I am"
   - inability to fulfill work demands
   - blaming others or circumstances too much
   - excusing/denying failure
   - depression
   - anxiety
   - compulsive behavior (eating, substance abuse, sex, money)
   - chronic conflictual relationships

   _____

   _____

   _____

2. *Categorize underlying problems.* Refer to table 8.2, and ask yourself: Which blocks identify my struggles? Do I say no to

good things and yes to bad things? Do I have difficulty respecting others' boundaries and/or hearing their needs?

_____

_____

_____

3. *Research causes.* Think about your family of origin. It will tend to contain the roots of the problem. Go over the items listed in the subsection titled "What Goes Wrong?" Ask yourself: Did I come from a family where I was responsible for my parents' happiness? Was I not given enough limits or responsibility for my life? Was my family so close that no one could set limits? As you identify the roots of the problem, begin to trace the line between patterns in your family of origin and your present struggles.

_____

_____

_____

4. *Link past to present.* Answer yourself: How am I repeating in my present relationships the boundary problems of my family of origin? In answering, look at your present family, work, social, and church relationships. Be specific.

_____

_____

_____

5. *Determine goals for repair.* Ask yourself these questions as you refer to table 8.2:

Block 1: Do I need to learn to set boundaries for myself with others? Do I need a "no muscle"?

Block 2: Do I need to be open to others' needs, after I've been a good steward of myself?

Block 3: Do I need to learn to respect others' boundaries? Do I need to hear no better?

Block 4: Do I need to learn to ask for what I need directly? Do I need to learn the difference between stewardship and selfishness?

_____

_____

_____

_____

6. *Evaluate your resources.* You will need the following to repair boundary deficits:

(a) *A willingness to understand God's boundaries as a model.* Study God's dealing with Paul in 2 Corinthians 12:7-9. Paul repeatedly asked God to deliver him from an affliction. The affliction was obviously painful, either physically or emotionally, for Paul called it a "thorn in the flesh." Yet God held His boundaries with Paul by refusing to deliver him, because He had something else in mind (a lesson in humility for Paul).

Not only is God able to say no, He also has boundaries against running over the wills of others. The story of the rich young ruler in Matthew 19:16-26 offers a good place to meditate on this point. After observing that the ruler worshiped money, Jesus challenged him to give up his god and follow Him. But when the ruler went away grieved (because he was unwilling to part with his worship), Jesus allowed him to leave. He didn't negotiate with him or say, "How about 90 percent?" God allows non-Christians to leave Him; He gives believers choices. He knows that we will grow only if we can make sound choices for which we are responsible.

(b) *A relationship with one or more people who will help you to set healthy boundaries.* Those relationships should incorporate accountability and unconditional acceptance of your being "unfinished."

Find out if your church has support groups or small group Bible studies where the emphasis is on "truthing and loving." Ask the leaders, "Is this a group where people give loving feedback to each other?" That's the sort of group you'll need, as opposed to an intellectual study or a "critical parenting" style of group. If an appropriate support group is not available, find a Christian counselor who understands boundary problems; if you need to, ask the counselor if he or she knows of Christian groups in your area where people work on repairing their boundaries.

(c) *Time.* Allow yourself time to repair your boundaries. Developing appropriate boundaries is a skill involving much practice with relationships. You won't accomplish it overnight.

_____

_____

_____

7. *Practice setting your boundaries.*

- *List the areas of your life over which you are a steward.* Which areas do you handle well? Which poorly?

- *Practice saying or hearing no in your safe relationships.* For example, when your best friend or spouse asks you, "Where do you want to eat dinner?" don't just shrug your shoulders and say, "Doesn't matter to me." Take a risk and say (if that is how you feel), "I really don't want to go to the restaurant you picked. How about this one?"

- *Notice when you tend to be dishonest about your needs or those of others.*

- *Practice setting small boundaries before you tackle large ones.* If you have never said no before, start out with something less crucial than putting your job on the line. Say no, for example, to picking up after your son or daughter (or someone else you tend to pick up after).

- *Expect resentment from those who are not accustomed to your newly set boundaries.* Jesus warned, "Woe to you when all men speak well of you, for in the same way their fathers used to treat the false prophets" (Luke 6:26). Why were the false prophets tolerated by their hearers? Because they said what others wanted to hear. The true prophets of God of the Old Testament rarely won popularity awards. Why? Because they were truth-tellers. Their truth sometimes rocked the boat.

  There may be people in your life who "love" you simply because you don't disagree with them. If so, when you decide to begin "truthing" in your expression of opinions, values, and emotions, and in your behavior, these people may resent the fact that they are suddenly in relationship with another will besides their own. If that occurs, you may need to rely on your support group while you work on establishing appropriate boundaries in the problem relationship.

BE ENCOURAGED: YOU CAN MEND BROKEN BOUNDARIES

Working through these steps in the power of the Holy Spirit, given the right relationships, wisdom, practice, and time, will help you repair boundary problems caused by a dysfunctional family. God is interested in your being able to protect yourself from evil and to choose good things for yourself. He knows that when you have developed this capacity you will have developed also the capacity to be a "good and faithful" servant (Matthew 25:21), taking care of the life and the self He has entrusted to you.

Questions for Reflection

Ask yourself the following questions, and make personal notes in the space provided.

1. How do boundary problems relate to the symptoms I listed in the Personal Inventory given in this chapter?

_____

_____

_____

2. As I identify how my family of origin contributed to my boundary deficits, can I commit to enter the process of forgiving them?

_____

_____

_____

3. What myths keep me from resolving boundary confusions?

_____

_____

_____

4. What is my greatest fear about setting limits with others?

_____

_____

_____

5. How am I not taking care of my knapsack? How am I trying to take care of someone else's knapsack?

_____

_____

_____

6. In which of my relationships (other than my relationship to God) would it be the safest to begin discussing my problems with boundaries? Can I talk to this person this week about the subject?

_____

_____

_____

9

Learning About Goodness/Badness

By Henry Cloud, Ph.D.

The Whitneys had "the ideal Christian family." They were an intact family unit: two nondivorced parents and three children. Mr. Whitney, a deacon in his church, earned a respectable living as a professional. The family lived in a nice neighborhood and had a lovely home, the modern version of the "white picket fence."

The children were doing well, also. They excelled in school and in extra-curricular activities. They had accomplished everything their parents and the community expected of them, with the exception of fourteen-year-old Derrick, the "black sheep" of the family. But all in all, the Whitneys were the perfect Christian family; at least they thought so. And everyone on the outside thought so, too.

But inside the walls of the house and inside the "walls" of each person, things were not so perfect, although no one in the family ever talked about it.

Though he was relatively placid at work and in other settings outside the home, in the family setting Mr. Whitney was given to outbursts of rage when things did not go just the way he expected them to. Likewise, Mrs. Whitney was sullen and disappointed when her children did not live up to her expectations. The children keenly felt her hurt over their failures.

The children were beset by a fear of failure and a constant drive to do better. They knew enough not to reveal their imperfections

For further treatment of the material in this chapter, see Henry Cloud, *When Your World Makes No Sense* (Nashville: Oliver Nelson, 1990).

and negative feelings to their parents or to family friends. Shameful things like imperfections and negative emotions were never to be shown outside the home. After all, what would people think? So went the Whitney family code.

For many years the Whitneys kept the praises of church and community coming, even if they lived behind a facade. And for a long time it worked. Then Susan, the sixteen-year-old, came down with anorexia nervosa, a severe eating disorder. She tried to hide it and so did the family, but one day she collapsed in church from sheer weakness.

The Whitneys could no longer hide their secret. The whole church now knew, and word began to spread outside the assembly to the community. Mr. Whitney began to get inquiries at his workplace, and Mrs. Whitney began to sense unspoken questions from her acquaintances. Their family doctor told them that anorexia nervosa was a life-threatening condition and that they had better get Susan to a psychiatrist at once, or risk her life. Mr. and Mrs. Whitney realized that they now had a serious and inescapable problem on their hands.

What went wrong? After all, hadn't they built the ideal Christian home?

IDEAL?

When we look at the basic needs a person has that should be met in the family, a foundational principle often gets overlooked: *the family is the place where we learn how to deal with failure, where we learn about being less-than-perfect beings in a less-than-perfect world.* There is no ideal person, no ideal world (short of heaven), and therefore no ideal family. When a family pretends it is ideal, or when it believes that it must be ideal, serious problems ensue. That is what this chapter is about.

When God created the first family, Adam and Eve, this problem did not exist. Adam and Eve lived in a perfect world and were perfect beings. They lived out the ideal. They were not even to know anything different: "But from the tree of the knowledge of good and evil you shall not eat" (Genesis 2:17). Their task was simply to go on being ideal. But as we all know, they ate the forbidden fruit, and we have been aware of good and evil ever since.

It is hard enough to live in a world of good and evil. But it is even harder to live in such a world without any way of dealing with it. Yet that is precisely what the "ideal" family tries to do. It tries to insist that good and evil are not both present in the home. As a result, it has no provisions for dealing with reality.

The Bible tells us that if we call ourselves ideal, we are liars (1 John 1:8). It recognizes our desire for the ideal, however, and says that we even long for it (Romans 8:22-23). It also provides us with ways of dealing with the coexistence of good and evil, and that is what every healthy family does. It gives the members of the family a safe place where they can learn what is ideal, realize their ineffectiveness at being ideal, learn how to deal with those disappointments, practice becoming better, and still be "real" throughout the process.

In this chapter we will look at ways a family can make itself a safe place for less-than-perfect people to learn the skills that will help them live in a less-than-perfect world. If you came from a dysfunctional family, you probably did not feel safety where badness, failure, and evil were concerned, and as an ACDF you are probably still a bit shaky on the matter. The goal of this chapter is to help you acquire the understanding and skills you did not develop at home.

THE "LESS-THAN-PERFECT" PARTS

We know that after Eden, our nature acquired less-than-perfect parts to it, but what does that mean? Let's look at some of those less-than-perfect parts.

FEELINGS

As real people living in a real world, we are going to have some negative feelings, such as sadness, anger, and fear. In addition, we are going to have some "fallen" sorts of feelings as well: jealousy, envy, pride, rage, lust, and so on. Every person has all of these feelings at some time in his life (Mark 7:21-22). That's a given. The family needs to be a place where its members are given the skills they need to deal with the less-than-perfect parts of their personalities and to find safe solutions for these deficiencies. We need to learn that it's OK to have less-than-perfect emotions.

ATTITUDES

We do not always have godly attitudes. The Bible says that our hearts are often out of line with reality and the ways of God (Ecclesiastes 9:3; Romans 3:23). Children do not come into the world with godly attitudes. They need to be taught how to face squarely the ungodly attitudes they do have, and how to grow out of them. If the family is a place where children must deny their bad attitudes and always look good on the outside, they will never learn to deal with those attitudes. They will become "whitewashed tombs," to use Jesus' words (Matthew 23:27). If such a stance is reinforced, the children will become hardened and emotionally impenetrable, hardly godly personality traits.

BEHAVIORS

The Bible tells us we are less than perfect in our behavior. It is amazing how often the Bible tells us that we can be expected to sin (Romans 3:23). That is our nature, but parents often act surprised when they have children who are sinners. We all fail in our behavior, and if we did not learn in our family of origin how to face our bad behavior honestly and to respond to the natural consequences of that behavior, we are in real trouble. We will either have to deny our behavior or stay stuck in it, neither of which is God's wish for us (Romans 6:1-2).

Dysfunctional Ways of Dealing with Badness

Now that we know that the ideal family is a fantasy and that the ideal world has been lost (as has the ideal person), what are some of the ways dysfunctional families deal with badness?

PRETEND THE BAD ISN'T THERE

An old illustration in the family therapy community illustrates this strategy. A family has an elephant living full-time in the house. It has become part of the family. But no one in the family says anything about it. They watch TV between the elephant's legs, they vacuum around its massive body, they silently pick up the mess when he rummages through the leftovers on the dinner table. They ignore the eight-ton elephant and go on being a family as if there were nothing wrong.

But after a while the elephant begins to smell, and his natural habits cause other problems. Pretty soon it can be denied no more. He *lives* there.

The family has realized the problem too late, though. The carpeting is ruined, flies and maggots have infested the house, the city is about to serve a condemnation notice, and myriad other problems are snowballing. They have a first-class crisis on their hands.

Comical as this story may be, it illustrates the way many problems are treated in a dysfunctional family. They are simply denied. An unspoken rule about badness seems to be in operation: *We will pretend it just isn't there.* As with the elephant, badness is stepped around, ignored, not talked about. And, also like the elephant, it begins to smell and cause serious problems.

Maybe the elephant is Dad's drinking problem, or Mom's pouting, or Derrick's behavior problems, or Susan's depression and isolation. Possibly it is Dad's verbal or physical abuse of the children, which can't be faced because he is "such a good Christian man." Maybe it is Derrick's inability to make friends, which is difficult to see because Mom and Dad want to believe that he really is popular at school. Perhaps it is Susie's inability in academics, which is denied because Mother has a master's degree in education and all of her children surely ought to be high achievers.

Or maybe it is the regular sort of negative feelings everyone has. When anyone feels sad or angry it is pushed under the rug. Negative feelings are smaller elephants and more easily hidden than big elephants like alcoholism.

Whatever the "bad" thing is that is denied, it will cause problems if it is not dealt with. The family may think that there shouldn't be negative things in their house, but the Bible affirms that negatives do exist in this fallen world. Like the elephant, these negatives must be dealt with honestly and correctly. Sell the elephant to the circus, but deal with badness or sin according to God's plan.

PRETEND THE GOOD ISN'T THERE

Some families deal with badness by denial of the good. They may do this in two ways: deny the ideal standard or deny the genuine good in an individual. Both strategies lead to serious problems.

When a family denies the ideal standard, it makes no attempt to achieve God's ideals. We have said before that it is a fantasy to believe that we can achieve all of God's ideals in this life, but that does not mean it is wrong for a family to try to uphold those standards or for family members to try to reach their potential (Philippians 3:14-16). God's standards are what gives us direction in our feelings, attitudes, and behavior, and if a family denies that those standards exist, it will drift rudderless and plagued by chaos. The children will have to find their way alone, and the parents will not be effective models.

In such families there is little teaching and correction when badness appears. Badness is allowed to be present as if there were no better way to be. Standards are not upheld. Maybe Dad's drinking is seen, but it is not called sin. Maybe Mom's extreme moodiness is accepted, but no one ever mentions that moodiness is not the best way to get one's needs met. Maybe the children's failures are never measured against the norms of other kids their age. They are allowed continually to make the same mistakes and not press on to anything better, even though they might be capable of very good work. Or perhaps the parents do not strive to be the best they can be in various areas, and sloppy work is what they model to the children, with no value placed on excellence. They do not show the stewardship value the Bible exhorts: to make the most of whatever talent we have (Matthew 25:14-27). God's good standard is not there, and consequently there is nothing against which anything can be measured.

What about the second way of denying the good: denying the genuine good in an individual and seeing him as all bad? All of us have heard the saying "being on somebody's bad side," and that occurs in a lot of families. The child is on the parent's "bad side" and is unable to get around the corner. He is labeled "bad," whether the thought is spoken or unspoken. His strengths and good points are never seen.

When this sort of labeling occurs, the child can grow up with extreme self-image problems, seeing himself as "all bad" whenever he fails or is less than perfect in his performance. He will call himself "stupid" and write himself off. He is unable to realize that even when he fails, he still has good points. Labeling of this kind often takes place in overly rigid, legalistic theological systems, whether a family system or a denominational system. In such settings, the inherent value of persons created in the image of God is ignored.

Children raised in such settings carry another disability: they cannot work out natural conflicts with others. For when "all bad" thinking is modeled, the child grows up seeing others' failures the same way. Whenever anyone fails him in any way, he sees that person as all bad and writes him off the same way his dysfunctional family wrote him off. He grows up leaving friends, jobs, and spouses whenever he finds any degree of badness present, for all he can see is the bad. He has learned to deny the good, so in his mind there is no reason to continue in the relationship, job, or marriage. This sort of all-or-nothing thinking causes many broken relationships and prevents the development of conflict-resolution skills, an ability that is sorely needed in today's society.

CONDEMNATION AND JUDGMENT

A third way of dealing with the elephant is to shoot it. Attack and condemn the less-than-ideal whenever it appears! In this mode badness is not denied but is simply condemned, along with the person doing the bad things. There is a complete lack of grace. No forgiveness is available to the transgressor. The strategy of condemnation and judgment has the sense of the Old Testament law, which is described in the New Testament as being merciless: "For whoever keeps the whole law and yet stumbles in one point, he has become guilty of all" (James 2:10).

Many people as adults struggle with the effects of growing up in a family with this attitude toward badness. Their parents followed the motto "If you can't join 'em, beat 'em!" They would not allow themselves to reveal that they, too, were struggling, imperfect beings like their kids, so they beat the children (physically or emotionally) whenever their imperfections showed up.

If the parents heard feelings that were not perfect, they condemned the child. If they heard a bad attitude, they attacked and judged the child. If there was a failure in the child's behavior, they screamed at the child and angrily disciplined him. They lived out the unmerciful law, which is a far cry from the way the Bible talks about dealing with badness. Condemnation is not the way of the cross (Romans 3:20-24).

When people come from a family in which there was a good deal of condemnation, they struggle with guilt and shame. They feel as if their failures can never be accepted and forgiven. Grace is a foreign concept to them, and it is difficult and sometimes impossible for them to feel and experience it. No amount of Bible study or encouragement to get their sins forgiven will sink into their damaged emotions.

These individuals are caught in what I call the guilt-sin cycle. They fail in some area, face all sorts of internal condemnation for the failure, and then feel unable to resolve the conflict. As their sense of guilt increases, they feel still worse and repeat the failure that started the process in the first place. That only increases their sense of guilt, and the cycle of compulsive behavior continues. "Who will set me free from the body of this death?" (Romans 7:24).

THE BIBLE'S VIEW OF DEALING WITH
THE LESS-THAN-PERFECT PARTS:
GRACE: NO CONDEMNATION

The Bible's way of handling our less-than-perfect parts is grace, or lack of condemnation (Romans 8:1). Our less-than-godly feelings, attitudes, and behavior are measured in the light of the grace of God. The believer is totally accepted and forgiven in Christ while he is still in an imperfect state. He has what the Bible calls a "standing" in grace (Romans 5:2).

Many people do not know how this standing in grace feels because their family of origin has not modeled it. Thus they have not experienced it in a real-life setting. The Bible speaks of two ways of "knowing." One is through learned information; the other is through experience. Many Christians "know" about grace intellectually, but their key learning experiences in their formative years were very different from the grace they read about in the Bible. Therefore, it is hard for their hearts to "experience" something they only "know" in their heads.

I recall a minister we'll call Carl, who participated in group therapy. Carl was struggling with a sexual addiction. Even though his training had prepared him to "know" in his head that God had forgiven him in Christ, his family-of-origin experience had him always "feeling" condemned. When his feeling of being a "bad" person reached its peak, he would succumb to pornography or prostitutes. Then he would feel worse! The cycle seemed impossible to break.

In the group we continued to express our unconditional love and acceptance of Carl, even when he slipped into such behavior. It dumbfounded him to have the group members express such unconditional love, and one day he blurted out, "I don't deserve your love. I don't deserve God's love."

To which we replied, "You're right. You don't. But you've got it anyway."

At that point in his recovery he began to make real progress. The simple experience of unconditional love began to change his life. He found that no matter what he did, he couldn't escape our love for him. That's grace—unmerited favor—for you. It can change anyone's life.

It is important to see how the grace approach is different from other ways of dealing with badness. First, it does not deny our sin. The book of Romans, which is all about our standing in grace and our justification from our badness, begins with three entire chapters on sin. There is no realization of grace if our sin is not seen. Thus denial of the elephant is not present in this strategy. The truth of the failures, the bad feelings, the ungodly attitudes, and so on, are all identified for what they are. They are seen realistically and not denied; the difference is that the person is still accepted with love. He is shown kindness (Romans 2:4; Ephesians 4:32).

Second, in addition to not denying the presence of badness, the grace answer affirms our value, for we are created in the likeness of God. It does not say that we are "all bad" and worthless. It just says that our attempts at perfection are worthless. The Bible continually affirms the worth of man (Psalm 8:4-6; Matthew 6:26), and in a healthy family the worth of each individual is continually affirmed, even in failure. No one should ever be seen as worthless and/or all bad.

Finally, the grace solution never condemns or uses anger as a way to point out failure. The entire New Testament conveys the thought that God is free from anger and condemnation toward us when we are cleansed by the blood of Jesus (Romans 5:1). The biblically based family deals with imperfection the same way and communicates safety and acceptance to its members. It creates an atmosphere in which badness, worth, and acceptance are not denied. Badness is called what it is, but the worth of the person is affirmed. Loving arms are put around him in the midst of his failure. Many ACDFs would give anything to have grown up in such an atmosphere!

"FAILURE" IS NOT ALWAYS FAILURE

Many times in Christian circles and families, there is even further confusion about the nature of failure. As we have seen, many families lack a realistic or balanced view of failure in that they expect perfection. But there is another element that parents must take into account in monitoring their children's progress: immaturity.

Immaturity occurs when someone has not had the time or resources to achieve a level of growth that would enable him to perform in a certain way. God has established a path of growth for children in which they become adults as part of a process. There are specific stages and steps in the process of gaining adulthood. If someone has not attained a certain stage, he will be unable to perform what is required at that level (1 Corinthians 13:11; Hebrews 5:12-14). Time is required for growth (Ecclesiastes 3:1-8), but many parents seem blind to this reality.

In many dysfunctional families, children are required to be more mature than they are, and their age-appropriate immaturity is not accepted. They grow up always expecting themselves to be further along than they are, with the result that they always interpret their present state as failure. Think about it: living with the constant thought that your present condition is always unacceptable, no matter what age you are. What a prison! Yet it's a reality for millions of ACDFs.

Unable is an unfamiliar word to these children. They live in a world of *shoulds.* They "should" be able to do this and that, even though they are not yet "big" enough. Imagine a little girl learning some new skill, such as cleaning up after painting. With all good intentions, she may put a dripping wet paintbrush into the silverware drawer. She may get a response from her parent, "You stupid idiot! Don't put that in that drawer!" But how was she supposed to know for the first time that the brushes didn't go there? She was just learning!

This happens frequently to baby Christians when others do not understand the stages of faith development the Bible speaks of (1 John 2:12-14) and expect too much spiritually of them. Older believers sometimes expect new believers, who have not yet been rooted and grounded in love, to display more fruit than they are able. This is common with addicts who begin to recover and then slip back into old habits. One slip does not a recovery invalidate! To a certain extent, we should expect a three-steps-forward/two-steps-back pattern from baby Christians.

When ACDFs become Christians, they carry with them into their new family, the family of God, this inability to allow for immaturity. They constantly feel like spiritual failures and compare themselves to other believers with different gifts and backgrounds, instead of accepting themselves where they are at a particular moment, however immature (Galatians 6:4; 1 Corinthians 12:29-30). It is easy to forget the "author and perfecter" of our faith, who has promised to bring us to maturity (Hebrews 12:2).

It is important for adult children of dysfunctional families to realize that a strategy of not allowing for immaturity was probably present in their upbringing and to fight against it. They need to work on accepting immaturity as a part of the growth process and to accept themselves where they are at any given stage.

That does not rule out pressing on toward maturity, for they are sure to do that. It does mean that ACDFs need to realize that growth is a process and that there will always be areas in which they will need to be stronger before they are *able* to do what they *want* to do. They will have to remind themselves constantly that an occasional spiritual failure does not mean that they are bad, but rather means they are still immature and "in process." Continually condemning themselves is like someone's scolding a toddler for spilling his milk. He's just learning; give him a break!

THE FAMILY AND BADNESS

We saw in chapter 8 how tricky it is to establish healthy boundaries in the family. Dealing with badness is not easy, either. But it can help everyone to grow into adulthood and to reach their potential as Christians and as people. We all need to learn how to deal with our imperfections and failures and at the same time hold on to ideals.

What goes wrong?

As we have seen, dysfunctional families deal with badness in hurtful ways. Let's look at a list of typical responses:

- the family acts as if someone is perfect and ignores that individual's badness
- the family idealizes one child, thus making him feel inappropriately important and the other children inadequate
- the family labels one child the "bad sheep"; that child becomes the "container" for all the badness in the family
- when someone fails, the family ridicules him, making him feel ashamed of who he is
- when someone fails, the family condemns him and responds angrily to his failure
- the family emphasizes how it looks to others outside the family, thus creating the belief that image is more important than being honest and real
- there is a hush-hush attitude toward failure, weakness, or immaturity; imperfection is thus ignored and implied to be worse than it is; consequently, fear develops
- the family holds up impossible standards and does not value where a person really is in his or her process of maturity
- the family compares members to one another and to other people outside the home in a futile search for the ideal; no one is good enough as he is

- there is no understanding that everyone has strengths and weaknesses and that having strengths and weaknesses is OK
- the idealized member acts as though he is too good for the rest of the family; he may complain about being "stuck with such a bunch of losers"

PROBLEMS

People who grow up in families that deal with failure and badness in dysfunctional ways exhibit a host of symptoms. Let's look at some of them:

"THE ALL GOOD ME"

This person cannot admit that she fails, is immature, or is sinful in her feelings, attitudes, and behavior. She sees herself as ideal and cannot own anything negative. She drives other people crazy, for obvious reasons.

"THE ALL BAD ME"

Some people reach this state when they fail, have a negative feeling, or realize some immaturity and cannot tolerate it. They have no grace inside to stand the failure, and so immediately go into a state of all badness.

DEPRESSION

People who cannot feel OK when they discover negative aspects of themselves are prone to feelings of depression. They also are depressed because they cannot deal with the negative emotions of anger and sadness, both of which cause depression.

ANXIETY

People who feel they have to be perfect are likely to feel a good deal of anxiety. They are always afraid they are going to fail or be discovered for who they really are: fallible human beings.

PERFECTIONISM

Perfectionism obviously has a lot to do with an inability to deal with badness. A perfectionist cannot stand to find that any aspect of himself, others, or the world around him is not perfect. He can make life for himself and those around him miserable by his compulsive insistence on perfection in everything.

ENABLING OR CODEPENDENCY

Many codependent people are codependent because they have never had permission to face and confront bad things about people they love. They feel they must help to hide the bad parts in themselves and others. The codependent helps others to cover up their problems by making excuses for them, taking responsibility from them, and carrying loads the other should carry. In short, they excuse sinful behavior and enable it to continue.

DISSATISFACTION

Many people have not been able to find satisfaction in a less-than-perfect world. They are always seeking for the elusive ideal, and as a result, nothing is ever good enough. This strategy practically guarantees unhappiness in life.

FEAR OF FAILURE AND RISK

Because their families did not teach them to tolerate and work with failure, many people are afraid to take new risks and therefore miss out on important opportunities to learn. They are stuck where they are in life, because change is too scary.

WHY DO WE DO IT THIS WAY?

If all of these dysfunctional ways of coping with life are not helpful, why don't we just do it right? Oh, if it were that easy! The truth is that we learned a great many confusing things in our families of origin, and those confusions block our ability to work with our failures. Those confusions are in the same three categories as they were in chapters 7 and 8:

Confusion about God:

- God thinks I am all bad
- God hates me for my failures and will punish me angrily; His grace does not apply to me
- God expects me to be further along than I am able to be at this time; He forgets that sanctification is a process
- God doesn't care much about my getting better

Confusion about others:

- If I show my failures to others, they will reject me as my family did
- If I show my sinfulness to others, they will think I am horrible
- If I ask others for help with my shortcomings, they will think something is wrong with me
- Others have it "all together"

Confusion about ourselves:

- If I am not perfect, I am worse than everyone else
- If I am immature, something is wrong with me
- If I fail, I am defective
- If I am unable, there is no hope for me

A FUNDAMENTAL MISUNDERSTANDING

Fundamental to all these confusions is a misunderstanding about the true nature of man and the true nature of God. The Bible teaches that all humans have strengths and weaknesses and that all people will, at times, fail. In addition, it teaches that God is a God of grace and truth; He is one who will face our imperfections squarely, forgive us, and help us to do better. His Word says that we all sin, that we will be forgiven freely if we seek it, and that He will cleanse us totally (1 John 1:8-9).

The problem is that in the dysfunctional family, we learn to hide. This hiding began with Adam and Eve in the Garden when they first became aware that they were no longer perfect. They hid (Genesis 3:7-10), and we have been doing it ever since.

The problem with hiding is this: nothing grows in the dark. The apostle John talks about walking in the light and says that through a confessional process the broken parts in our lives can be restored to righteousness (1 John 1:1-9). James says the same thing: "Confess your sins to one another, and pray for one another, so that you may be healed" (James 5:16). This is basically what happens in any good support group or therapy group, or in a good small group in a church setting: there is real confession.

FIGHTING BACK: ATTITUDES AND
ACTIVITIES TO DEAL WITH IMPERFECTION

Let's look at some specific things a family can do to help its members accept their badness, failure, and immaturity, while at the same time promoting growth:

- Creating a grace-giving atmosphere where confession of any failure is accepted

- When a member fails, loving him in his failure and not withholding love from him

- Parents' modeling an acceptance of their imperfections instead of acting as though they are perfect

- Parents' helping to make failures something to be learned from instead of condemning the child

- Not being afraid to point out badness when it appears; calling it what it is and not participating in the denial game

- Creating an atmosphere where everyone can talk about his negative feelings, attitudes, and behaviors and can find help for those negative areas without being scolded

- Allowing family members to express negative emotions appropriately

- Identifying as unacceptable considering any member of the family as perfect

- Affirming the value and worth of each person in whatever state of maturity he is

- Making confession a life-style instead of a legal, punitive thing that only criminals do

- Pointing out the strengths of each member and helping each member to overcome his weaknesses, instead of idealizing some family members and tearing others down

Above all, don't give up hope. Just as other issues we have discussed can be resolved, so, too, can this one. But it will take the learning of certain tasks and a renewed focus on healthy ways of dealing with badness. We learn poor ways of dealing with imperfections in a dysfunctional family; the only way to learn to deal with them effectively is in a functional one.

Jesus hinted at this truth when He asked a rhetorical question in reply to the news that His mother and brothers were seeking to speak to Him. "Who is My mother and who are My brothers?" Those who "[do] the will of God" (Matthew 12:48-50). We have to find new relationships in the Body of Christ that will help us resolve the dysfunctional areas in our lives.

David said it this way, "My eyes shall be on the faithful of the land, that they may dwell with me; He who walks in a blameless way is the one who will minister to me" (Psalm 101:6). David chose his company carefully.

In like manner, if you need to reform your attitudes regarding badness, failure, or imperfection, it is imperative that you find a support group, safe friend, or counselor. Then you need to put into practice the following steps:

1. Start working on counteracting your belief that perfection is a possibility and/or a demand. It may seem self-evident, but you need also to look at the ways you consciously or unconsciously expect perfection. Ask others to help you. That is real humility—confessing your proud self instead of perpetuating the false humility of denying strengths (James 4:6, 10).

2. List your strengths and weaknesses as honestly as you can, and become comfortable with the existence of those strengths and weaknesses. Until you fully appreciate that you are composed of the good and the bad, and accept that fact, growth will be difficult (Psalm 139:23-24). Get help from your group.

3. List the strengths and weaknesses of those whom you love. It will be helpful to you to see that they are real people and to

accept the whole package (Ephesians 4:32). Not judging others is part of learning self-acceptance. That way, the imperfections of others will not creep up and surprise you, even though you have seen them hundreds of times before. If we tend to deny things, it doesn't matter how many times we have seen an imperfection. It always seems like the first, and our reaction reflects our surprise: "How could you have . . . ?" The fact is, we should have expected it; that is their particular weakness. We can never become truly forgiving until we are comfortable with confronting the reality of others' imperfections (Luke 17:3-4).

4. Begin to talk more openly about your negative feelings, and become more accepting of those feelings in others. That will help you get get rid of the "all good," Eden way of looking at the world. It will also build intimacy with others, which in turn will lessen your fear of their imperfections. Growth produces growth. Be real (Ephesians 4:25).

5. Work diligently on joining or establishing a support group that will encourage the sort of thinking we are talking about in this chapter. When it comes to confessing your weaknesses and pains, stay away from perfectionists. They will only judge you and demand more perfection. Align yourself with people who understand the grace of God and practice it (Psalm 101:6-7).

6. Put a serious value on working through conflict with others and resolving it. That will help you greatly in learning to deal with badness. As you begin to work through conflicts, you will be reinforcing in your own mind the truth that badness does not have to destroy relationships but can actually enhance them (Luke 17:3-4; Proverbs 19:25).

7. Look at whatever area in which you are afraid to risk because of fear of failure or badness. Realize that this fear is a denial of the grace of God and of His willingness to let you fail in order to grow. Begin to step out, and get support from Him and others to learn new ways and skills (Matthew 25:24-28).

8. Research causes, and understand them. As seen in chapter 3 and throughout this book, we will repeat generational patterns if we do not acknowledge and repent of them. Left untreated, dysfunctional traditions of the past will bind our future, and the future of our children. Look at the history of dysfunction in the area of facing badness in your family and turn from it.

These steps will start you on the path of overcoming the family dysfunction over imperfections you grew up with. It is a liberating thing to find out that you do not need to be perfect and that you have the freedom to grow and gain support in those areas you might still be failing in.

But remember, as with the other developmental needs, you were made for a family. Even though you came from a dysfunctional one, God wants you to be a part of a functional one now, and you cannot grow apart from that sort of support. Work on getting into a safe setting, and then try the things we have been talking about in this book. Millions of recovering ACDFs will testify that they really work.

Questions for Reflection

Ask yourself the following questions, and make personal notes in the space provided.

1. How is the quest for the "ideal me" affecting me and the way I spend my resources (time, energy, money, and so on)?

_____

_____

_____

2. What do I see as the root of the problem?

_____

_____

_____

3. What do I need to change to turn it around?

_____

_____

_____

4. How will I do that?

_____

_____

_____

5. Who will I enlist to help me?

_____

_____

_____

6. When will I do the things listed just above?

_____

_____

_____

10

Learning to Achieve Adulthood

By Henry Cloud, Ph.D.

Phil entered his boss's office with an awful feeling in the pit of his stomach. He didn't know why, since he had been through performance reviews many times before. Rationally, he understood that his boss liked him, but he nevertheless felt afraid.

In the midst of his runaway thoughts, he found himself imagining ways in which his performance wouldn't be good enough or in which he himself would somehow be disapproved. The inner turmoil was almost unbearable, yet no matter how he tried to get rid of those feelings, he couldn't. He had tried memorizing verses on fear during the preceding week, but even that didn't seem to help.

Phil got more discouraged as he thought of other situations where similar feelings overtook him. When he went to the elder board meetings at church, he would almost break out in a sweat. He would sit at the table and have all sorts of good ideas, but he was afraid to say them, fearing that someone would disagree and think his ideas were stupid.

As he sat in the board meetings, he would look at the individual members and try to figure out why they seemed so powerful to him, but it made no sense. He was as accomplished as they, at least on the outside, and he should have felt as though he had a right to be there. But inside, his feelings of inferiority persisted. He had a recog-

---

For further treatment of the material in this chapter, refer to Henry Cloud, *When Your World Makes No Sense* (Nashville: Oliver Nelson, 1990).

nizable fear of being "one-down" to the rest of the men. Secretly, he was afraid they might find out.

The same fears would overtake him in social situations as well. When he played golf with his buddies, he would start to think that they were in some way better than he. Some of his friends would occasionally express strong opinions with which he disagreed, but he found himself afraid to express that disagreement. He'd just nod and go along with them. Sometimes that made him feel ashamed, even wimpy. He just didn't feel like a man around other men. He felt more like a little boy.

If you can identify with Phil, then you know what it is to feel like a "little person in a big person's world." The scenario Phil experienced is a predictable one for people who grew up in dysfunctional families, even for outwardly successful ACDFs. In a word, they haven't grown up.

God has outlined a system for development, one we have been exploring in these last few chapters. In chapter 7, we looked at how to attach to (bond with) others; in chapter 8, we learned how to be a separate person (set boundaries); and in chapter 9, we learned how to deal with issues of goodness/badness in ourselves and others. In this chapter we are going to look at the next critical link in the chain of recovery: becoming an equal with other adults. I call it achieving adulthood.

The Path

When we look at normal development, we find that it is a process. In a home, authority is vested in the parents. They are the authorities, the experts in living. Children naturally look to their parents for teaching in all areas of living, from finding food to driving a car. It is a long and painful process, but when it is over, a young adult should feel reasonably comfortable in assuming an adult role and exercising authority over his or her life. He should also have reached the point where he feels equal to other adults as siblings under God (Matthew 23:8-10).

There are advantages to assuming an adult position in life. A fully adult person comes out from under a "one-down" position in relation to other adults. He or she can think and reason for himself. He can choose what to believe and what values to adopt. He can decide which job or career he likes or is best suited for.

As he matures sexually, he can choose appropriate sexual expression and a mate. He can pursue, develop, practice, and hone his talents. He can establish mutual friendships with other adults, and he can experience the joy of establishing a community of his choice that reflects his preferences. He can choose hobbies and vacations that are to his own liking.

Adulthood is the phase in life characterized by independence of choice and expression. Paul gives us insight into this important developmental passage when he describes the bondage of childhood as compared to human adulthood and becoming a child of God:

> Now I say, as long as the heir is a child, he does not differ at all from a slave although he is owner of everything, but is under guardians and managers until the date set by the father. So also we, while we were children, were in bondage under the elemental things of the world. (Galatians 4:1-3)

A child is not free. He or she is under the authority or expertise of parents and is, in a real sense, practicing for adulthood. But when the child becomes an adult, he can truly "own" his own life and be his own boss. Ultimately, that is what gives him the freedom to surrender to the authority of God. An adult is the master of whom he will serve, because he decides things for himself.

Compare this freedom to the feeling of being under someone else's rule. You must gain "permission" to have an opinion, make choices, hold beliefs, choose your church—and on and on. It is not a pretty picture, but it is the world in which ACDFs often live.

PROBLEMS

It would be nice if everyone grew up in a family that allowed for the kind of development I have just described, a family that supported one's effort toward growth. But not everyone grows up in such a family. Some people grow up in dysfunctional families that do the opposite: they keep the children always in a childish position and send them out into adulthood still feeling "one-down" to other adults. That sort of treatment is a foundation for failure to achieve equality with the adult world, and it is the subject of this chapter.

Let's look at some of the symptoms of feeling "one-down" to other adults:

EXTREME NEED FOR APPROVAL

When an adult constantly needs the approval of other adults, that usually means he is stuck in some childish stage of development. He is always looking up to the people around him as though they were parents who held judicial power to certify him as acceptable. But no matter what level of approval he attains, it never is enough. As soon as one person approves of something he does, he feels a need to gain additional approval from someone else. His appetite for approval is insatiable. In one sense it is similar to drug addiction, for the individual caught up in the syndrome is on a merry-go-round of misery that no amount of approval can relieve.

EXTREME FEAR OF DISAPPROVAL

An extreme thirst for approval is the motivator of the one-down person's performance. The Bible teaches that we are to be motivated by the grace and acceptance of God and others. But if we feel as if we are constantly one-down to all of the parent figures around us, then we will constantly fear their disapproval and condemnation. That pattern will yield paralysis life-wide and stunt growth.

CONSTANT AND UNRELENTING ANXIETY

The one-down person experiences constant and unrelenting anxiety. This symptom is not surprising when one considers that the person living in the one-down position sees himself as always subject to criticism and disapproval. And that in turn means that from the one-down person's perspective, every other adult has the power to judge him unacceptable. What a scary way to live!

AVOIDANCE OF RISK AND FEAR OF FAILURE

If we feel one-down to others, we will avoid taking the risks necessary for growth. We can only learn by taking risks and practicing (Hebrews 5:13-14; Matthew 25:26-27), and Jesus commands us to use our talents. But if we are afraid of the opinions and criticisms of others, we have given them parental power in our lives and have to avoid their judgment at all costs. Judgment would be too much for us to bear.

INFERIORITY AND SUPERIORITY FEELINGS

If we are stuck in a one-down position in relation to other adults, instead of feeling like equal siblings under God with differing talents (Romans 12:3-8), we will always be comparing ourselves with others to see if we measure up. Invariably this system fails to give us the confidence we need, and we end up feeling inferior to our imagined picture of perfection in others.

On the other hand, if we are particularly aggressive, we may have a tendency to look at others as inferior and try to become a parental authority over them, constantly judging and criticizing. Neither extreme is what God has in mind for maturity.

EXTREME FEELINGS OF COMPETITION

Some try to overcome the feeling of being one-down by constantly competing with others. Their goal is to overcome everyone and end up king of the hill. They may win the battle, but they will lose the war, for all their relationships are characterized by power struggles. People don't feel close to them and maintain their distance, because they don't trust them.

POWERLESSNESS

Children are by nature "under" the power of adults. That's OK for a child, but as developmental processes take over, this attitude needs to be shed. If a person fails to get rid of it as he grows older, as an adult he will tend to resist expressing assertiveness with other adults. He will be passive in relationships and conflicts and often will feel like a victim in relation to his peers. He will have little sense of direction in his life.

What's more, it will likely be difficult for him to be assertive against evil, even though the Bible commands us to take that position. A verse such as 2 Timothy 1:7 will be emotionally mystifying to him: "For God has not given us a spirit of timidity, but of power and love and discipline." He will truly be handicapped.

"DIFFERENT IS WRONG" THINKING

Adults naturally differ on many things, such as opinions, tastes, and thoughts. People who still think of themselves in the childish position believe that their thoughts, opinions, and tastes are subject to being judged by the parent figures around them. If their opinions differ from those parent figures, they see themselves as automatically "wrong." They fear going to the "wrong" church, wearing the "wrong" clothes, practicing the "wrong" hobbies, and so on. They experience little sense of freedom to choose their life-style and are subject to a lot of rules. They experience drabness and bondage as they deny their true selves in the name of this type of thinking.

RULES-DOMINATED THINKING

People who think of themselves as children do not experience the freedom to be governed by principles. Jesus was slow to give rules about anything, but He gave a great many principles. He even provided a principle to govern all other rules: "Love the Lord your God with all your heart, and . . . love your neighbor as yourself" (Matthew 22:37-39).

Paul says the same thing in many places, observing that we as children of God have been freed from parental-type rules (Colossians 2:20-23). He says that we should not subject ourselves to such rules, for they reduce us to legalism and take away the freedom that a child of God who is led by the Spirit should have. But of course if one is afraid of parental or legalistic disapproval, rules will dominate one's thinking.

IMPULSIVENESS

A child is kept in check by parental structures, or what the Bible speaks of as the law. But the problem with the law is that it actually has the effect of leading to greater lawlessness. It produces more rather than less passion, more rather than fewer sinful impulses (Romans 5:20; 7:5). The person under the parental commandment of the condemnation of the law ends up sinning more. He is subject to powerful, almost compulsive behaviors such as overspending ("I just couldn't help myself"), overeating, and the like. He feels the "should" of the law and rebels against it. This is the sin-guilt cycle, which we identified in chapter 9.

HATRED OF AUTHORITY

Many who have been crushed by strict authority figures during childhood have not been able personally to identify with the expertise of adulthood. Being an adult means having a certain amount of expertise in various areas; you aren't perfect, but you certainly have adult-level talents and strengths. Instead of acquiring this attitude as they grow up, some ACDFs resent all authority and rebel against it, always trying to find freedom through rebellion.

The problem is that the rebellious child is just as controlled by the parent (even as an adult child) as the compliant child is, only in another direction. The rebellious child may look at first glance as though he is not being controlled by authority, but in reality he is, since his every action is ruled by his reaction to that authority. Rebellion and hatred of authority is a child-like stance, in that one vests all power in authority figures.

DEPRESSION

It should be clear by now why this is a depressing way to live. If one constantly feels inferior, guilty, and put down, it is difficult to be happy. In addition, feeling one-down naturally brings with it a good deal of unresolved hurt and anger, which in turn sets a person up for depression in adulthood.

PASSIVE-AGGRESSIVE BEHAVIOR

Passive-aggressive behavior is asserting one's will in an indirect way. Instead of being honest about our aggressive urges, we cloak them in actions that are superficially neutral. We are conveniently late to an appointment with a person with whom we're upset. Perhaps we resent our supervisor on the job, so we struggle with procrastination, never seeming to get to the tasks at hand. Or we might exert an overabundant amount of control in relationships.

Passive-aggressive behavior is a frequent symptom resulting from feeling one-down. The loss of power felt in the one-down position leads to covert attempts at restoration to power through resistance. We see this in the parable of the two sons whose father asked them to work in the vineyard (Matthew 21:28-31). The first son passively obeyed on the outside but resisted on the inside. In the end, he "did not go" (v. 29). He had not yet reached the place where he could openly say no to his parent. But his brother had reached such a point. His more healthy pattern of saying what he really felt resulted in his being able to change his mind and actually do the work, whereas the first son was stuck in resistance and resentment.

PERSON WORSHIP

When someone is still looking at other people as parent figures, he tends to inappropriately idealize them. He will follow them as though they were mini-gods and forget who the real God is. He has failed to make the transition from being under man (his parents) to being under God, as seen in Matthew 23:8-10:

> But do not be called Rabbi; for One is your Teacher, and you are all brothers. And do not call anyone on earth your father; for One is your Father, He who is in Heaven. And do not be called leaders; for One is your Leader, that is, Christ.

Some people caught in this syndrome may worship a pastor or other spiritual leader instead of God, in the name of honoring their leaders. In reality, such a practice is a modern-day form of idolatry.

How Does It Happen?

If it is God's plan that we all grow up into functioning adults, what goes wrong in a dysfunctional family to prevent that? Let's explore some of the patterns that keep people from achieving adulthood:

LACK OF PROPER DEVELOPMENT IN PREVIOUS STAGES

As we have seen in previous chapters, there are stages to normal development, and there are prerequisites that must be fulfilled before a new level of maturity can be approached.

Take the bonding discussed in chapter 7. If a child does not know how to attach emotionally to others, he cannot form the peer support groups that allow him to separate from his family at the age-appropriate level and thus achieve adulthood.

It is important in adolescence for a teen to develop deep attachments to friends and other people outside his home in order to prepare for leaving home. If a teenager does not have skills to form these close and supportive relationships, leaving home and becoming an adult will be impossible for him. He will be like a jet airplane without fuel. He can't fly to new destinations. Appropriate relationships provide the resources for growth through the entire process, and this stage is no different.

Boundaries (chapter 8) are important elements of adulthood, for they teach us a basic sense of responsibility and ownership of our lives. We need to be able to be separate people and become our own people apart from others, thus having our own identity. Boundaries are the cornerstone of this identity formation. Without them, it is impossible to become an adult.

Boundaries define what we think, feel, want, do, choose, and value. The ability to stake out positions in these areas is part of the transition to adulthood and must be well-developed if an individual is to keep on moving toward adulthood. If he does not have this capacity, he will not come out from under a one-down opinion of himself, for he will not be able to distinguish his thoughts and feelings from someone else's. He will not be able to overcome parental disapproval of his feelings (and therefore "own" them as an adult) if he is not separate enough from his parents even to know what his own feelings are.

Well-established boundaries provide a sense of limits. If someone is unable to set limits on another's abuse, he is too frightened to go out into the world as an adult. He is still assuming that he is to remain forever a child, protected by parent figures from "all the mean people in the world." We need to be able to have good limits to stand as adults.

We need also to be able to set limits on our own behavior and to have ample self-control. Having a good sense of boundaries will do this for us, and well-developed self-control is a prerequisite for achieving adulthood. When people lack self-control, they are likely to subject themselves to parent figures to keep themselves in check. That is an ineffective strategy long-term, but it is usually one of the first-line attempts an impulsive person will make as a means of staying in control.

Similarly, persons with this bent will often gravitate toward rigid, legalistic churches and/or dominant spiritual leaders who will "whip them into shape" and "keep them in line." They know they lack self-control and are seeking external vehicles to provide it. But God's ideal is for a person to develop internal self-control as he submits to and is guided by the Holy Spirit. Self-control is specifically listed in Galatians 5:16-25 as one of the nine elements of the fruit of the Spirit.

With regard to the good/bad struggle discussed in chapter 9, we must be able to handle failure in order to assume the adult position. The extreme need for idealism and perfection in all things is childish. If we are to be adults we must be able to shift into reality. The real world is imperfect. We must be able to deal with imperfections in ourselves, in others, and in the world around us. People who demand perfection of themselves and others are unable to deal effectively with reality because reality is not perfect. To become the best adults that we can be requires the ability to learn, and perfectionists learn very little, while demanding a lot.

AUTHORITARIANISM

The Bible teaches that parents are to be authorities in the home who "grow up a child in the way he should go," to paraphrase Proverbs 22:6 (see also Deuteronomy 6:6-9). The goal is for parents to impart God's ways to the children and get them ready for independence. Developing such independence in a child will require the parent gradually to shift power from himself to the maturing child.

The principle of exercising authority through empowering subjects is seen in many places in the Bible. God the Father gave Jesus all authority and power to accomplish the goals He wanted Jesus to accomplish (Matthew 28:18). When God made Adam, He empowered him by giving him important responsibilities. Adam was to be responsible for the whole earth, to rule and subdue it (Genesis 1:28). There was a real delegation of power from God to Adam.

The earthly family is to be the same way. The parents, as authority figures, are to teach the children how to gain expertise in living and then to become authorities over their own lives. Parents build this expertise in their children through gradually giving over responsibilities to them.

There is a difference between an *authoritative* style of parenting and an *authoritarian* one. In the authoritarian home we do not see a biblical view of authority. The authority figure is dogmatic, dominated by black-and-white thinking, and rigid, domineering, and controlling. These characteristics of his behavior keep his children powerless, prohibit learning, and stunt meaningful growth.

In contrast, when a maturing child is learning to deal with, for example, money, the wise (authoritative) parent should allow the child to exercise an appropriate degree of authority over his or her own "assets." Even when the child is anticipating what the parent feels is a dumb buy, the smart parent offers counsel only, and lets the child live with the consequences of his purchase decision. Perhaps the child impulsively spends money on inconsequential things and then later lacks the funds to buy something much more important to him; the next time around, saving (self-control) will be more important personally to the child. An important lesson has been learned through the parent's staying out of the process, apart from giving advice. Learning experiences of this kind are the ones that form solid stepping-stones to adulthood.

Authoritarian parenting has been linked in research to many behavioral problems and all sorts of immaturity in children. The New Testament warns the father to avoid provoking his children to anger, causing them to lose heart (Ephesians 6:4; Colossians 3:21). The authoritarian ruling style does not empower the child whatsoever. Rather, it keeps the child powerless, stifling his maturity and setting the stage for later episodes of aggressive rebellion or for a passive death of the spirit. In contrast to this authoritarian style, the authoritative parenting style positions the parent as an expert in living who passes his expertise on to his children, preparing them for adulthood.

LACK OF PRACTICE

Hebrews 5:14 tells us that we mature as we practice. That means that there must be the freedom to fail. Homes that are critical of failure do not produce learning in the child, yet achieving adulthood is practically impossible without learning. Children growing up in a hypercritical atmosphere tend to avoid risk-taking for fear of the consequences.

One young adult told me that as a ten-year-old boy he built a tree house he was very proud of, but his father came home and chewed him out because the angles in the roof weren't "architecturally correct." Every time he tried something new, his father berated him over the particular way in which he did not do it perfectly. Eventually, he gave up trying. As an adult he was horribly afraid of trying to learn new skills on the job or in his personal life because the threat of failure was too great.

Parenting that does not allow for mistakes sets up a fear dynamic in the child that inhibits learning, for it is difficult to learn when one is dominated by fear. What a contrast to our heavenly Father, who "knows our frame" (Psalm 103:14) and is "slow to anger" (Psalm 103:8). As parents we ought to follow His practice, patiently watching our children grow toward adulthood.

LACK OF RESOURCES

Some parents do not look for emerging talents in their children and fail to provide them with the resources they need to develop their talents. God has given everyone talents and abilities, and parents need to provide their children with the resources for developing them.

There are parents who withhold resources even when they are available. Being too poor to provide resources is one thing, but withholding support that is possible financially is quite another. What is involved here are specific kinds of refusals: not allowing a child to attend workshops, clubs, or join sports teams; refusing to buy necessary sports equipment; refusing to help with the purchase of costumes for dramatic productions at school; and so on. In the healthy family, if a child shows some ability, the parent tries to provide the setting and tools needed to develop that skill.

Invariably the child will do some shopping around to find his niche or area of expertise and interest. Too many parents give up at this stage. When a child wants to try a new skill, they say, "No, I won't allow you to play baseball. Remember when you were going to learn to ski? I sent you on that church trip and spent all that money, and you haven't been skiing since." Now I'm not advocating reckless spending of money. Instead, I'm encouraging a bit of freedom for kids who are trying to find their niche. That will normally involve some false starts. That's OK. No one knows what he is going to wind up liking without trying it out first.

On the other hand, I'm not advocating indulgence. If a child wants to learn horseback riding, the parent need not rush out and buy a ranch. There needs to be a balance between providing resources where they are available (the parents' task) and the exercise of responsibility by the child.

PERMISSIVENESS

The extreme opposite of the authoritarian parent is the overly permissive parent who establishes insufficient authority in the home and provides little in the way of limits. Such a parent does not provide an adequate structure for the child to learn right from wrong or to learn to be an authority as an adult later in life (Proverbs 19:18). There is nothing wrong with parents being the boss. Indeed, that is necessary, for parents really do know more about life. What's more, God desires it. But He does not advocate dictatorship.

The problem comes with the extremes of too authoritarian or too permissive a style. The result is either lawlessness (in the latter case) or an identity confusion (in the former). We need a balance of structure and limits for a secure sense of who we are.

INCONSISTENCY

The inconsistent style vacillates between authoritarianism and permissiveness. It sets up a split in the child between impulsiveness that knows no limits and guilt that knows only limits.

Many parents are in conflict over their own sense of authority. As a result, they act out both sides with the child. When they do this, the child never develops a consistent authority structure within himself. He is either impulsive or guilty, just like the home structure. The result is chaos, both in the family and within each personality.

LACK OF RESPECT FOR PERSONAL DIFFERENCES

In the authoritarian home compliance is the norm. But in reality, people are different from one another. They have different tastes, opinions, and talents, to name but a few. In some homes this difference among individuals is punished, unnoticed, or in some way devalued. That keeps the child from developing an adult identity.

The child in such a home fears his difference from his parents' choices. He may not want to be a professional like Dad; he may not want to be a missionary like Grandfather; he may not like sports and instead prefers music. There may be many differences he will want to express. But he knows that expressing those differences will not be accepted in his home. Children like this sometimes have to become "black sheep" in order to avoid conformity and fusion with others. Their differences need to be accepted.

IMBALANCE OF LOVE AND LIMITS

Developing authority over one's adult life comes from an internalization of the style of parents who are balanced in love and limits. As children observe their parents, they take their balance into their own souls. Parents who balance love and limits, research tells us, have children who are independent, outgoing, and social.

On the other hand, when there is an imbalance of love and limits, problematic combinations develop in homes. A home atmosphere might be loving (good) but controlling (bad); or loving (good) but permissive (bad); or controlling (bad) and unloving (bad again). All of these parenting styles produce authority problems in children.

The Bible tells us that there should be standards and limits in a home but also grace and love. This combination is like God's very nature, which is sometimes described as being composed of justice (limits) and mercy (love). Whenever there is an imbalance of justice or mercy, we have left out one side of the nature of God, and all will suffer from that imbalance.

DENIAL OF SEXUALITY

Achieving adulthood includes learning about our God-given sexuality. Homes that exclude sexuality from normal existence prohibit development into healthy adulthood. Here, as elsewhere, balance is important. Homes that repress any sexual aspects of the personality do not allow the child to grow into adult sexuality, whereas permissive homes sometimes overwhelm a child with sexual impulses. Some homes are so Victorian that even mentioning sex is a mortal sin, whereas others have virtually no sense of decency or modesty.

Sexuality must be balanced in the home for a little person to incorporate that aspect of his or her personhood into existence, and thus become a "big person." Homes that avoid or repress sexuality cause teens to fear their sexuality and thus avoid adulthood. Permissive homes, on the other hand, force children into adulthood much too early, causing equally grievous problems.

Sexuality needs to be talked about and affirmed in its rightful place, given a high value, and placed within biblically appropriate boundaries. That will allow the child to grow up in touch with his sexuality and free of shame and guilt, while at the same time having self-control.

CONVICTIONS OF THE HEART
THAT PREVENT ACHIEVING ADULTHOOD

Let's look now at some of the attitudes of the heart that can stifle our move to adulthood. Consider whether any apply to you and/or to your upbringing. Though sometimes stated in this list in seemingly ridiculous, absolute form, these attitudes can often creep into our thinking in lesser degrees and still cause problems in achieving adulthood.

Distortions about God

- God is dogmatic about everything and does not like me to question things; such questions represent a lack of faith
- God is a rigid parent who will crush me if I disagree with Him

- God wants me to be a clone of my spiritual leaders and authority figures and to do everything their way
- God does not allow me freedom in the grey areas of Christian conduct, such as entertainment options; in fact, I doubt whether there even are grey areas in God's view
- God will punish me when I try to learn new things and don't execute them perfectly
- God does not like me to have my own opinions; having my own opinions would be rebellion

Distortions about others

- Everyone is always critical and disapproving of my actions and thoughts
- No one allows me to fail and thus learn to do better
- Others will hate me if I disagree with them
- Others will like me better if I am compliant to their wishes, demands, and plans
- Others never fail like I always seem to be doing; they seem to know everything
- My leaders are perfect; they have no weaknesses; their beliefs are better than mine; they know what I should do better than I do; they are always right

Distortions about ourselves

- I am worthless if others don't approve of me
- I should never have tried that; I really messed it up; I am a miserable failure
- I have no right to my opinions; they are usually wrong anyway
- My beliefs are the only right ones
- I know what is best for him or her
- I should always do what I am told
- My sexual feelings are bad
- I shouldn't feel angry/disappointed/sad/lonely (and so on)
- I will never measure up to him or her

NEW ATTITUDES AND ACTIVITIES THAT YIELD GROWTH

In order for us to achieve adulthood and grow past a dysfunctional background, we must challenge old ways and practices. That will require new skills.

Before we look at those skills, though, let us emphasize that there is no solid, long-term growth apart from the Body of Christ. You must get into supportive, Christian relationships that encourage your movement into adulthood. That is the way it should have happened the first time around. You were designed to begin to develop relationships outside the home when you were still a teenager that would help you join the family of adult brothers and sisters as a peer. It is just as crucial now for you to do so.

Let's look at some of those skills:

1. *Confess to God and to others your need to become an adult (Matthew 5:3; James 5:16).* God and His family (the church) feel OK about your inadequacies in this area; they do not expect you to be all grown up all at once. Find a family of believers who will accept your present state of maturity and encourage you into adulthood by gently pushing you back onto the playing field of life when you skin your knees.

2. *Develop a theology that allows for the concept of practice.* You are about to embark on a road of learning; there is no way for you to know already what you need to learn. Give up the need to be already there, and get onto the practice field. The only the way to gain expertise is through practice.

3. *Find your talents and pursue them.* God has given you certain talents and abilities, and He wants you to develop them. In fact, He will be displeased if you fail to try to develop and use them (Matthew 25:14-29). He is on your side in this endeavor (Romans 8:31-32).

4. *Become aware of your own opinions and thoughts.* Adults think for themselves. You should listen to counsel from teachers and experts (Proverbs 11:14), but it's OK to develop your own expertise in important areas so that you don't constantly need parent figures to make your decisions for you. This point applies to both husbands and wives as they relate to one another. Yes, the husband is the head of the home, but that does not mean that wives are to abrogate responsibility for thinking for themselves. (Husbands may also be in danger of failing to think for themselves; independence of thought, so long as it is genuine independence and not run-

ning roughshod over others or an exercise of arrogance, is necessary in all adults.) Pray for guidance and wisdom (Psalm 32:8). God wants to teach you in many areas, and He will guide you to the information you need. Gather lots of data from the experts, but then identify what you believe. That will keep you from being a groupie or a cult member.

5. *Respectfully disagree with authority figures when you have a different opinion.* This sort of assertiveness is the only way to get into dialogue, which is where we learn. The authority figures we are talking about here include God. If you disagree with Him about something, tell Him. Job and David did (Job 10:1-22; Psalm 22:2). That was the beginning of dialogue and learning for them. This capacity for dialogue needs to appear in a marriage, too; wives and husbands need to learn how to respectfully disagree with one another when their opinions differ. In terms of people in general, you may be surprised that even the authorities can learn something sometimes and change their position.

6. *Dethrone people whom you may have put on pedestals (1 John 5:21).* If you have set anyone up as perfect, you have set him up as an idol. Try to see him (or her) more realistically and as a brother or sister instead of a parent. Your goal in this is to achieve brotherhood with men and establish the Fatherhood of God (Matthew 23:8). Here again, wives who enthrone their husbands (or husbands who enthrone their wives) need to think through what it means for them as adults to place someone in such a position. The next chapter of this book, which shows how Jesus interacted with others as an adult and not a child, relates to the point being made here.

7. *Submit freely to those in roles of authority over you.* Acting like a rebellious child in relation to authority (e.g., government or church) is to be controlled by your compulsive reaction. Submission proves our freedom; rebellion against authority proves our childish state. The equality-minded adult is able to submit to the God-ordained role as to God and does not feel as though he is somehow giving in to a person (Romans 13:1). There is a delicate equality involved

in balancing the need to submit freely to those in authority and the need to dethrone people one has put on a pedestal. Wives, particularly, can find this process difficult. They need to remember that it *is* a process. When a laboratory assistant weighs out grains on a balance, he rarely hits the mark the first time. So, too, here. The process of finding the right balance is complicated. There will be some trial and error at first. And once a balance is struck it shouldn't be considered sacred. Seasons of life change, and individuals change; so, too, may the balance that "feels right" vary later on in the marriage.

8. *Treat others as equals.* Do not parent them; yet do not allow yourself to be controlled or judged by them either. To do the latter is to put yourself or them under the law. In the free/grey areas, make up your own mind, and allow others to do so also (Colossians 2:16-19). Here again, wives and husbands need to see their spouses as equals and not as parents or as children.

9. *Give up your rigid thinking and don't succumb to the black-and-white thinking of others.* Appreciate the things that we cannot know for sure (Romans 11:33-36). That is to allow God to be God and us to be human. Give up the need to have certainty and rules for everything. Worship God, not rules.

10. *Deal with sexuality.* If you are afraid of your sexual feelings, get in a setting where it is safe to talk about them, and accept them without shame. Remember, shame is a product of the Fall (Genesis 3:10). Marriage is a wonderful opportunity often ignored by Christian couples to talk about sexual feelings. Sexuality is something you talk about in marriage, not just do. Sexuality is good when it is practiced under God's guidelines; He made it.

11. *Take responsibility for your life.* When you were a child, you were under the rule of stewards and managers, typically parents (Galatians 4:1-3). But as an adult, you are no longer under their responsibility. You are now the steward of your life. This holds true for married people as well as for

singles. Marriage is a partnership, a yoking of two walking along together, but there comes a point when each of the partners must assume responsibility for his own life. In fact, it is a misunderstanding on this very point that leads to the enabling behavior exhibited by spouses married to persons caught up in compulsive disease. Accept responsibility, for with responsibility comes freedom and fulfillment.

12. *Look at every adult around you as an equal.* These adults —and they include your spouse—may have very different talents and experiences, but you are equal to them in terms of worth. Learn to cherish your differences instead of being judged by them or by being proud (Romans 12:3-8).

13. *Realize where you disagree with your parents.* The Bible tells us that we are to examine our actions and to avoid blindly doing things according to the "tradition of the elders" instead of God's ways (Matthew 15:1-3). Distinguish your plans and views from those of your parents.

14. *Pursue your dreams.* Share your dreams with God, and allow Him to shape them (Proverbs 16:3). Then go for it!

Questions for Reflection

Ask yourself the following questions, and make personal notes in the space provided.

1. How do I feel that I am one-down to others? In what areas do I most keenly feel this?

_____

_____

_____

2. What has caused such feelings?

_____

_____

_____

3. What attitudes do I need to change to gain equality with other adults in the human race?

_____

_____

_____

4. How do I still have my parents (or other authority figures) on a pedestal? How can I get them off it?

_____

_____

_____

5. With which of their thoughts do I disagree?

_____

_____

_____

6. What about my thoughts and opinions? Do I value them adequately? If not, how can I improve in this area?

_____

_____

_____

7. Who am I allowing to inappropriately parent me? How will I stop?

_____

_____

_____

8. Where will I go for mutual support? When?

_____

_____

_____

11

Jesus Models Healthy Relationships

By Earl Henslin, PsyD.

Theologians call it the mystery of the incarnation. We ordinary Christians call it both wonderful and puzzling. Wonderful in that Jesus shed His heavenly glory and came to earth to accomplish salvation; puzzling because it is hard to reconcile the homely details of Jesus' thirty-three years on earth with His majesty as holy God. Oh sure, we can glibly say that God dwelt on earth for a relatively short time in a human body, but when we actually think what that means, we realize that it is unfathomable.

What we can do is to state certain facts. We know that Jesus was both fully human and fully God during His years on earth. We know that He fully felt the whole range of human emotion and temptation yet never gave in to sin (Hebrews 4:15). We know that He had a divine Father and a human mother. And we know that He grew up into adulthood in a family that must have been very much like yours and mine.

What was that home like? The Scriptures say relatively little about it. We have only glimpses of His childhood and early adulthood. Some incidents are revealed, however. We know the story of the flight into Egypt and the subsequent return to Nazareth. We know the story of Jesus' five-day sojourn at the Temple as a young boy (Luke 2:41-49). We know that as He grew from childhood to adulthood He "kept increasing in wisdom and stature, and in favor with God and men" (v. 52).

What was Jesus' family of origin like? Again, the details are sketchy, since the overarching emphasis of the gospels is on Jesus' adult ministry, those three years before His crucifixion, resurrection, and ascension. Nevertheless, I believe that reasonable clues in the scriptural record give us some idea of what Jesus' human family was like. We will examine this evidence in this chapter.

Jesus' mother, Mary, had a unique role in history. She of all women was to give birth to the very Son of God. What can it have meant to her to give birth to her Savior, the very One through whom all things were created? In our attempt to keep her in perspective and remind ourselves that she was, after all, a mortal woman, we forget how awesome a role she was given. Or we take her presence in the Nativity scene for granted and forget what it cost her to be there. So although in this chapter we are going to look at Jesus' human family from the perspective of their humanity, nothing should be construed as denegrating Mary and Joseph's remarkable place in the gospel record and the awesome task for which they were selected by Almighty God.

In this chapter we will look into Mary's role in the first of Jesus' "sign" miracles, the turning of water into wine at the marriage at Cana; into the way Mary and Joseph responded to Jesus' sojourn at the Temple; and into the way Jesus' stepbrothers and stepsisters responded to His launching of what turned out to be a very controversial, and very public, ministry. I will point out that remarkable though she was, Mary was still human, still subject to the stresses all mothers and parents experience; we will see as well that strong though Jesus' stepbrothers' and stepsisters' faith in Him became (many scholars believe that two New Testament books, James and Jude, were written by two half-brothers of Jesus), during Jesus' public ministry on earth before the crucifixion they lacked faith in Him.

In short, in this chapter we are going to look at the sharp contrast between how the human members of Jesus' family of origin reacted to various events and how the perfect Son of God reacted to them. We will see how Jesus resisted the pull toward dysfunctional relationships and behavior, even while people around Him, in their humanity, succumbed at times. In Jesus' living example we have a clear-cut pattern to follow in relating to others in the most healthy and functional ways possible.

JESUS' FIRST MIRACLE

The wedding at Cana is a favorite story of many Christians. You've probably read it dozens of times and think you've analyzed it sufficiently. But I want to challenge you to read it again below and see what you may have been missing. There are some interesting family dynamics going on in the interaction between Jesus' human mother and her divine Son.

> And on the third day there was a wedding in Cana of Galilee; and the mother of Jesus was there; and Jesus also was invited, and His disciples, to the wedding. And when the wine gave out, the mother of Jesus said to Him, "They have no wine." And Jesus said to her, "Woman, what do I have to do with you? My hour has not yet come." His mother said to the servants, "Whatever He says to you, do it." Now there were six stone waterpots set there for the Jewish custom of purification, containing twenty or thirty gallons each. Jesus said to them, "Fill the waterpots with water." And they filled them up to the brim. And He said to them, "Draw some out now, and take it to the headwaiter. And they took it to him. And when the headwaiter tasted the water which had become wine . . . [he] called the bridegroom, and said to him, "Every man serves the good wine first, and when men have drunk freely, then that which is poorer; you have kept the good wine until now." This beginning of His attesting miracles Jesus did in Cana of Galilee, and manifested His glory, and His disciples believed in Him. (John 2:1-11)

"Woman, what do I have to do with you? My hour has not yet come."

Powerful words spoken by Jesus directly, honestly, and respectfully to His mother. What did Jesus mean when He said them? Observe again the context. Mary and Jesus and the disciples are at a wedding, and the wine is low. Mary recognizes the situation and wants to help. She knows her Son can take care of the problem, so she asks.

But note that she didn't really ask; instead, she sort of hinted: "They have no wine" (2:3). Instead of just being honest and asking if He could do them a favor, she used what may have been a form of guilt motivation (i.e., "they're out of wine, you *should* help them"). Instead of humbling herself and asking Him for help, she "suggested" what He really "ought" to do.

Do you know anyone who acts like that? Perhaps even you do. Yet it's much more healthy to flat-out ask a person to do you a favor instead of hinting around, expecting that person to pick up on what "obviously" is the "correct" response.

Jesus responds strongly, clearly, and directly. No, now would not be a convenient time for a miracle. He lets His mother know His true feelings about her suggestion, and He indicates part of the reason in His reference to time. The timing of the moment to "go public" with His minstry through the inauguration of public miracles—in effect, His declaration that He is the Son of God—is a delicate matter that ought to be between Him and His heavenly Father, not between Him and His mother.

But then, for some unexplained reason (very possibly He is just showing His characteristic graciousness), Jesus goes ahead and changes the water to wine. He would rather not, as expressed by His reply to Mary, but decides to comply, possibly for her sake. He doesn't do it out of obedience to His mother, for by now He is an adult (approximately thirty years old) and can decide for Himself. Rather, He deliberately decides to perform the miracle.

Too, He gets spiritual mileage out of the situation. The final verse of the passage (v. 11) indicates that Jesus used the miracle to build the faith of His disciples and to manifest His glory: "This beginning of His signs Jesus did in Cana of Galilee, and manifested His glory, and His disciples believed in Him." Jesus didn't let the pushiness of His mother get in the way of communicating a spiritual truth in the midst of an everyday, mundane setting. His parables would later follow that pattern: using whatever situation was at hand to communicate a spiritual lesson.

Mary didn't seem to care much about Jesus' desire for the right timing in unleashing His first miracle. Look what she does immediately after Jesus says, in effect, "Not now." I can almost see Mary turning on her heel, disregarding Jesus' objection as she addresses the servants: "Whatever He says to you, do it." She apparently didn't discuss Jesus' objection with Him at all; she simply turned and told the servants to follow her Son's instructions, assuming that such instructions would be forthcoming.

Let me say that in suggesting such an interpretation of this familiar and beloved passage I have no less respect for Jesus' mother, Mary. In fact, by viewing her as more human and less like a sinless, magical person, my respect for her grows. She becomes more of an everyday person, just like you and me, and her faith and obedience are magnified. In seeing how human Mary was, Jesus' divinity becomes even more sharply focused—even when He graciously gives in to what seems to have been a pushy and controlling interaction on the part of His mother.

Dysfunctional families have a way of operating like that: they tend to push their children too fast and fail to respect the natural growth cycles that are best for each child. Dysfunctional parents tend to force their own hidden agendas upon their children, even when those children have become adults. They tend to force adult children to continue to meet needs in their lives, the exact opposite of what God intends (i.e., God's ideal is that parents should meet children's needs, not the other way around). If ACDFs do not identify these hidden issues in their relationships with their parents, they can live a lifetime being governed by them.

Rod was such a person. He was married and had small children. He was a hard-working man and well liked by many people. Yet his wife was continually angry at him. It was hard for him to accept his share of the responsibility for the trouble in the relationship. As therapy progressed he discovered that he was more emotionally married to his parents than he was to his wife. He had failed to adequately "leave" his parents in order to sufficiently "cleave" to his wife. In an emotional sense, Rod was living the life of a bigamist.

When his dad was depressed, Rod was always there to listen. When his mom was upset with his dad, he was there to listen. If his brother called and was angry at their dad—you got it—he listened, sometimes for hours on end. The problem was that Rod would listen and then try to "fix" the problem. His custom was to always give his parents and brother advice and bail them out emotionally so that they felt relieved.

Of course, with this family system pattern in place, no one in his family of origin was forced to do anything to improve their relationships. They just used Rod as an emotional dumping ground. Rod had been fulfilling this role since he was a young boy, and the various family members knew their roles well. Theirs was a typical family systems-style arrangement within dysfunctional families. Without intervention, the emotional merry-go-round would have continued to spin.

After "fixing" whatever relative needed it, Rod "carried" the relative's feelings around with him and became depressed, sometimes for days, sometimes for weeks. He bore within himself the hurt and anger of his family.

Rod's wife found him useless during these periods. She could recognize him sinking downward, and that was her signal to withdraw and not share her feelings with him. Then he would gradually come out of his depression and want to be more involved with her.

That's when she got angry. After all, had he not emotionally abandoned her?

The solution was for Rod to emotionally "divorce" his parents so that he would not end up divorced from his wife. He could no longer pick up his parents' pain. He had to learn to let them carry their hurt themselves. It was their hurt to carry, not his. Or, in the language of knapsacks and boulders (see chapter 8), it was their knapsack to carry, not his.

It was hard for Rod to learn this lesson. He had learned to carry his parents' knapsacks at a young age, and he had lots of practice doing it. And, besides, it made him feel important. Stopping such behavior meant that he was losing a special position in the family. Now no one would lean on him, and he might have to share things about himself. And that would be frightening. He had been so busy "solving" everyone else's problems, he hadn't had time or energy to focus on his own.

After much struggle, Rod was finally able to say in a conversation with his dad, "I do not want to listen to you talk about your problems with Mom. You should talk to *her* about them. Let's you and I talk about you and me."

For Rod to say that to his father was just like Jesus saying to His mother, "Woman, what do I have to do with you? My hour has not yet come." Rod let the feeling be there; saying what he said didn't mean he did not love or respect his father. All it meant was that he was refusing to carry his father's knapsack. It was not his burden. With a simple communication, Rod liberated himself from what had become a very dysfunctional pattern. Moreover, by casting off the burden his father wrongly insisted on placing upon his son, Ron freed up his father to begin recovery himself by forcing him to realize that he needed to deal with his wife, not his son, on such a matter.

Carrie struggled with hidden agendas and expectations in a different way. Her parents' marriage was not a close one. It was rare that there was open conflict, yet there was a distinct emotional distance between them. Even though Carrie was now a single adult woman with her own career, she could not bring herself to move out of her parents' home and get her own place. She felt a pull to stay there and remain "available" for her mother and father. She filled a need in their lives; their world revolved around her.

The payoff cut both ways: Carrie received the warm feeling of being needed in her special role; focusing on their daughter gave purpose to the already dead relationship between Carrie's mother and father. As long as she met that need in them they would never have to face the emptiness in their marriage.

Yet Carrie, now in the prime of her life and quite eligible for dating and marriage, never had a consistent dating relationship. After two or three dates, the men never called her again. We discovered in therapy that Carrie was somehow telegraphing to the men she dated that she was already emotionally committed. Her bargain within her family system was to stabilize her parents' marriage; in return, their role was to make her feel special. So she did not need a relationship with a young man her age; she "had everything she needed" at home.

When Carrie became aware of this agenda in her family of origin, it frightened her. She was afraid to talk to her parents about it, for fear that they would divorce each other. That had been her job—to hold off dealing with their difficulties. It had been OK for her brothers and sisters to grow up and progress in life, but for her to do so was unthinkable.

In a family counseling session with her parents present, Carrie was finally able to talk with her parents about her feelings. At first her parents denied what she was saying; her father basically shamed her for having such thoughts about the family (see chapter 4 for a fuller discussion of shaming). Yet as the session progressed and Carrie was able to be firm and direct about her feelings, her mother began to cry uncontrollably.

Her mother did not want Carrie to move out. She wanted her to stay. Carrie's arrival home at the end of her workday was the only part of the day that the mother could look forward to. Carrie's mother desperately "needed" to have Carrie play her dysfunctional role. The pain of not having Carrie around—and of having to address issues with her husband—was terribly frightening to her mother.

Just as Jesus firmly and honestly addressed His mother at the wedding in Cana, Carrie needed to say strongly, directly, respectfully, and firmly to her parents, "Mom and Dad, I need to move out. Deep down in my heart, I'm afraid to do that because you depend so much on me. I'm afraid your marriage won't survive and that I'm the one who is keeping you together. But it's not right that I should continue to play this role. You two have got to deal with each other, and I've got to get on with becoming emotionally independent."

Carrie saw bringing those feelings out of the closet as a sign that she was somehow being disloyal to and disrespectful of her family. Yet hiding the truth was keeping her from becoming all that God had for her in adulthood. Slowly and painfully Carrie did reeducate herself on these and other topics. It was difficult for her to begin her new life on her own, as she had become codependent in her relationship with her parents. Codependence meant in her case that she had assumed that she was to take care of her parents and that her own needs did not matter. She had assumed that if she loved her parents fully enough and was good enough to them, they would give her love and approval. Her worth and value as a person rested on their response to her.

When she did move out, her parents' relationship did indeed deteriorate. Their arguments became more frequent and more heated. Her mother had several "crises" that were in reality attempts to pull Carrie back into a caretaking role again. But when Carrie gave her mother support from a distance and refused to move back in to take care of her, the message was clear: Carrie was not moving back in. Then the crisis would subside. Eventually Carrie learned not to feel guilty for the turmoil her parents managed to get themselves into, and to let them carry their burdens by themselves.

"Woman . . . my hour has not yet come." Amazing, isn't it, when we realize that there was potential tension and conflict in Jesus' human family? But we need not be surprised, for in Jesus' human family there was only one divine member. I think that we often let some of Jesus' divinity rub off on Mary and Joseph and let that color our reading of passages involving His parents. We know that the perfect Son never even got close to interacting with His parents or other family members in a dysfunctional way, yet there was occasionally a less-than-perfect response to events from among His human loved ones.

There was nothing bad or shameful in what happened at Cana between Jesus and His mother. It was a normal process that needed to occur between Jesus and His family; it was a normal clash that occurred largely because of (Mary's) humanity meeting the divine. The clash showed a growing, healthy independence in which Jesus did not always agree with His mother. In giving such a reply, Jesus moved right into one of the tough issues in the family; He did not avoid painful areas.

Jesus' response to Mary's "suggestion" that He provide additional wine was definitely not codependent. A codependent response would have been to ignore His true feelings and say, "Sure, Mom, I'll be glad to do it. You want a miracle right now? No problem." A good codependent gives the response other family members want to hear, not the response that is the truth they have within them. But Jesus responded in an honest and healthy way.

Jesus' healthy response to His mother is similar to a response He made to His parents years earlier, when He was twelve.

"Lost" in the Temple

The story is told in Luke 2:41-52. Joseph and Mary had made their regular pilgrimage to celebrate the Passover in Jerusalem and were journeying back to Nazareth. They were one day's journey back toward home when they realized that their twelve-year-old Son was not, as they had supposed, with another family or somewhere else in their traveling party. Panic struck, and they immediately headed back to Jerusalem to search for Him.

Imagine for a minute that you had driven to Los Angeles for some occasion, and that during your return trip to the East coast, you stopped overnight in New Mexico and realized that your son was missing. You thought he was in a friend's car. Your mind begins to race. *Where is that rascal? Didn't he know he was supposed to ride with the Jones family? What's happened to him by now?* Your feelings are a mixture of fear for his safety and anger that he has upset the normal pace of the return trip.

Joseph and Mary spend a day going back to Jerusalem, then another three days looking for Him in that huge city. By now Jesus has been on His own for five days. Those days of wandering about in the Holy City are interesting, for during that entire period Jesus' parents seem not to have made the link between Jesus' interests and His probable whereabouts.

Jesus comments on that very point, when they finally find Him: "Why is it that you were looking for Me? Did you not know that I had to be in My Father's house?" (Luke 2:49). He seems to be saying, in effect, "Why did you wander about Jerusalem for three days? Don't you know Me well enough to have guessed that I'd be here, discussing the things of God?" Mary and Joseph seem to have had the same difficulty we modern-day parents have in understanding our developing teenagers: they needed to tune into Christ's motivations and interests, needed to truly understand the unique Person in their midst and not let their own dreams and aspirations and needs smother who He was.

When Mary and Joseph find their Son, Mary uses a shame-based type of accusation in her first words with Him. The Living Bible puts

Mary's exclamation so well: "Why have you done this to us? Your father and I have been frantic, searching for you everywhere" (2:48).

Again, we do not see Jesus acting in a codependent way. He doesn't reply, "Oh, I'm sorry, I feel terrible that you have been so worried and hurt. I know that it's my responsibility that you are feeling panicked—your feelings and reactions are really not your responsibility. And it's probably my fault that you've not been trusting Jehovah to keep me safe over the last few days. Mom and Dad, would you please forgive me for treating you so badly?"

Rather, Jesus responds directly, clearly, and to the point. There is no guilt or shame in His response. He says that He is about His Father's business and that His Father's house would have been a logical place to look for Him three days before! In a sense, this event is Jesus' declaration of independence at the brink of adulthood, and it is very difficult for His parents to accept.

Was it hard for your parents to understand your interests and accept your growing independence when you were a teen? Or are you having trouble doing that now, as a parent of teenagers? Now I'm not saying that parents of teens need to exert zero control over their kids. I'm only saying that the degree of control during adolescence needs to be at an appropriate level. We need to stay considerably out of the way as our teens develop and be careful not to smother them with our lack of understanding and/or dependency needs.

To illustrate, let me share the case of Valerie, a fifteen-year-old Christian girl whose parents brought her in for counseling. The problem, explained the parents, was Valerie's "obsession with boys." As we explored the situation, I found that in reality Valerie was not showing an abnormal preoccupation with boys; in fact, she was not even pressuring her parents for permission to date, as many fifteen-year-olds naturally do.

Yet her parents were convinced that she was becoming sexually active, and they grilled her when she came home from school or church events. They were constantly seeing in their minds torrid love affairs, when in reality they were just innocent friendships. *They* were the ones obsessed with boys.

As we explored family-of-origin issues with Valerie's parents, we discovered that Valerie's father had watched his father treat his mother with constant disdain. His father had consistently cheated on his wife, communicating to his son, Valerie's father, that women were good for one thing only.

Valerie's mother grew up in an alcoholic family and had been sexually molested as a child. When Valerie's mother reached dating age, she became sexually active and wound up "having to" marry Valerie's father. Family secrets were coming out, and Valerie's parents' preoccupation with teenage sexual issues began to make sense. They were parenting out of fear. They had not dealt with their own issues, and this was putting a spin on their parenting of a young, healthy, vibrant Christian daughter like Valerie.

From Jesus' courageous example of facing up to shaming parents we can take heart to face our own family dysfunctions straight on. One such person who learned that it's OK to face crippling problems head-on was Jessica.

Jessica grew up as a person whose mission in life was to please and take care of everyone. It was as though she had neon signs on her forehead that blinked, "I'm codependent. I'll take care of you. I'll serve you. My feelings and needs are unimportant. Come and get it."

When she married Bill she was attracted to his strong Christian commitment and the strength that he projected as a man. She felt safe with him, which is something she had never felt growing up in her alcoholic family. As time progressed, she discovered that Bill did not just have a beer once in a while, but that every weekend she could count on him being drunk at least once and consistently "medicated" (semi-inebriated) the rest of the time. Periodically she found pornographic magazines in the garage. All of this scared her, and she didn't know how to react.

As a submissive wife, she felt her only recourse was to "love him into reform." Her Bible study group and pastor emphasized that if she changed her attitude and stayed in her submissive role he would be won back to the Lord "without a word." This type of response by her Christian friends, who were themselves codependent, made her feel that her husband's problem with alcohol and pornography was all a matter of her not being a good enough Christian.

Jessica didn't realize that she needed to take strong steps to begin her journey out of codependency. So she poured herself into Christian activity. If someone needed a thousand cookies for some church event, she would bake them. If someone needed her to "fill in" in the church nursery for twelve weeks in a row, she would do it.

As her husband's alcoholism and sexual addiction progressed, his sexual demands on her became more intense. She became a sex object to him, which grieved her. In time, she became cold toward him, though she felt great internal shame about it. It meant to her that she was not being a good, submissive, Christian wife. She couldn't see that her cold feelings were a normal response to an incredibly insane situation.

Jessica's children learned to hide their feelings and keep their hurt and anger to themselves. After all, didn't Mom always have a smile on her face? Wasn't she "trusting the Lord"? Sure, Mom got severe headaches often and seemed to be sick much of the time. But things were pretty much OK, weren't they?

Jessica's recovery began when she attended her first Al-Anon meeting (Al-Anon is a recovery group for relatives of alcoholics). One of the most difficult steps for her was to tell her Christian friends that she was finding help in Al-Anon. Most of them had encouraged her not to go. But it was in that Al-Anon group that Jessica learned how to stop covering up for her husband's addictions and let him begin to face the consequences of his actions. She learned how to "respond to" and not "react to" the insanity of his addictions.

These difficult steps of recovery were her first movements out of codependency and toward making her home emotionally safe for herself and her children. A strength began to build in her that eventually allowed her, in an intervention guided by a trained interventionist, to say to her husband: "Bill, either you go into treatment now for your addictions, or you leave this house." A strong statement, true. But her husband, who had been abusing Jessica and her kids, did enter treatment that very day. Jessica's direct approach to addressing problems—similar to the Savior's approach—ushered in an era of recovery for her family.

FAMILY SYSTEMS RESIST CHANGE

Another interaction of Jesus and His human family is recorded in Scripture. It is an amazing event, yet it is consistent with the interactions we have examined so far. It had to do with Jesus' relatives' reactions to the "publicness" of Jesus' ministry:

> Then Jesus entered a house, and again a crowd gathered, so that he and his disciples were not even able to eat. When his family heard about this, they went to take charge of him, for they said, "He is out of his mind." . . .
> Then Jesus' mother and brothers arrived. Standing outside, they sent someone in to call him. A crowd was sitting around him, and they told him, "Your mother and brothers are outside looking for you."

"Who are my mother and my brothers?" he asked. Then he looked at those seated in a circle around him and said, "Here are my mother and my brothers! Whoever does God's will is my brother and sister and mother." (Mark 3:20-21; 31-35, NIV)

This is a special time in our Savior's life. He has just selected His team of key men, and His ministry is starting to take shape and gather momentum. As He does this, He is further separating Himself from His family and marking out His chosen course in life. He is following God the Father's special call on His life—but the change is traumatic for His family members.

It is so traumatic, in fact, that in verse 21 they come to collect their kinsman, since He has "obviously" lost His mind! Can you imagine what this situation must have been like for Jesus' parents and siblings? Their brother and son had left Joseph's carpentry shop and was striking out on His own. Again. In their minds it must have been just like He did when He was twelve years old in the Temple incident. *There he goes again,* they must have thought. It must have worried and embarrassed them that He was causing such a public ruckus. They would take things in their own hands and bring Him home.

Often in families it is very hard for parents and siblings to accept a deviation from the family pattern, no matter how healthy the new course might be or how unhealthy the old course was. I remember finishing college and becoming aware that I was going on to graduate school and would not be going home to work with my dad on our family's farm. That was a sad time for my father. His dream was that all his sons would farm with him. Yet the direction God would have me to go was different.

I felt a sadness as well, since the work on the farm with my father was something I enjoyed. It was very difficult for me to share my personal vision with my father; those few months were a time of unspoken grief and loss. My father and I did not know how to discuss it, yet it was something that we felt between us. It was a difficult but necessary step of change in my life, and a challenging transition within our family.

For many families any significant transition is a difficult step to take. Dysfunction in the family may be so strong that normal stages of growth and independence pose a threat. When the son chooses a different path from the father, that choice is often met with guilt and shame. When he brings the attention of the community upon the family, the family system often resists the new course. In the case of Jesus' human kinsmen, it was no different.

JESUS' FAMILY ATTEMPTS TO REIN HIM IN

In biology, it's known as homeostasis. It means that a system tends toward sameness. An example is our body's maintaining, when possible, a constant temperature of 98.6 degrees Fahrenheit. In family systems, when growth or change of any kind presents its threatening head, it is often interpreted as an unconscious threat to the family, and the family system will try to encourage that family member to stop the steps of change. Ironically, this principle holds true regardless of whether the anticipated change is going to lead to health or dysfunction.

Unless it can see a good reason to accept the change, the family will attempt to go back to the old balance (homeostasis) it had before change entered the picture. I can tell you from experience that families do not like too much change.

Jesus' relatives were no different. Jesus had begun His ministry, had appointed the disciples, and now was so busy there were times that He didn't even have the opportunity to eat. Crowds gathered wherever He went. His family heard of this and decided to collect their "loony" relative before further embarrassment could happen (3:21).

JESUS' FAMILY ATTEMPTS TO "FIX" HIM

In verses 31-35 we see Mary and Jesus' brothers coming to take custody of Him. When they arrive, they send word to Him to stop whatever He is doing and come with them. Incredible, isn't it? Jesus was in the middle of ministry to hundreds of needy people, and His family comes to "rescue" Him from what they interpret as overactivity and even lunacy. They have decided that they know what He needs better than He does.

Dysfunctional families often struggle with this issue. They believe that they (and only they) know what's best for the unconforming family member. It's like the middle-aged mother having "thermostat problems" due to menopause who says curtly to her teenager, "Will you please put on a sweater! I'm really cold." She assesses what's best for the other person out of her own need, not out of informed concern for the other.

At this point in the story, Jesus is right in the middle of setting the foundation for His three-year public ministry. Now is a time for Him to press forward in a special way, but pressing forward does not match up with what the family perceives as being best for Him.

How does Jesus respond? He doesn't say, "Yes, Mom, I'm coming. I'll be right there." He doesn't turn to everyone around Him and say, "It's time for me to go home. Come back again tomorrow, and maybe Mom will let me talk with you then."

Instead, He strongly, directly, and firmly asks the rhetorical question, "Who are My mother and My brothers?" (v. 33, NIV). Then He answers His own question, motioning to those sitting around Him and saying, "Behold, My mother and My brothers! For whoever does the will of God, he is my brother and sister and mother" (vv. 33-35, NIV).

It's a strong statement, first to His family and then to the people around Him. In just a couple of sentences He fully responds to the issues underlying His family's attempt to "take custody" of Him. He does not argue, does not become defensive, does not give in and say, "OK, Mom."

Instead, He clearly, firmly, directly, and respectfully says, in effect, "This is my new life. These people understand who I really am, and if you want to see Me as I really am, then you are My mother, brother, and sister."

Powerful words that come from deep down within our Savior. Then He puts His words into action, and in the next verse (4:1) He begins to teach by the sea. So many people are crowded on the shore that He has to get into a boat and drift out a little way from the shore to teach from the boat.

What if Jesus had chosen to go back to Nazareth, back into His family's care, as they were urging Him to do? God the Father had a different plan in mind for Jesus, and He was determined to follow it.

Jesus acted authentically, in honest accord with Who He really is, and took the bold steps necessary to fulfill God's call on His life. We should follow His example, regardless of how shrill are the cries of dysfunctional family members who would want to hinder our growth and pull us back into old patterns of behavior and thinking. We can honestly tell them, just like Jesus did here, what we think the best path for us is.

Questions for Reflection

Ask yourself the following questions, and make personal notes in the space provided.

1. What was life like as a teenager for you? Did your family have difficulty with either the direction you took in life or the strengths you showed as you developed?

_____

_____

_____

2. When Jesus was asked by His mother to make the wine, He replied, in effect, "The timing is not right." Were there times when you felt pushed by your family of origin to do something or to behave a certain way before you were inwardly ready?

_____

_____

_____

3. In Mark 3:20-35 Jesus' family thinks He has lost His senses when He begins His ministry. They are concerned that He is not taking care of Himself. When you first began your recovery program or first began to face the issues dominating your family of origin, did your family think you were crazy or try to make you "come home" by returning to the old ways of doing things?

_____

_____

_____

12

Facing Life's "Unfair Assignments"

By Dave Carder, M.A.

Julie (see Introduction) put her journal on her lap and sighed during a review of her spiritual and emotional odyssey of the last eighteen months. She was gradually learning to bond with her children and her second husband. She was still experiencing the anxiety that accompanies change. It seemed as though she was always feeling vulnerable; she wanted so badly to start feeling normal. She wanted the normal experience of feeling close to those she loved to stop feeling so scary. Everthing seemed like such hard work. Why did God make relationships so difficult, anyway? Oh well, she thought, at least she was making progress.

Julie was also learning to say yes and no more appropriately. She was feeling more in control of herself and her personal environment. For that she was glad. However, she had to admit that at times even that area appeared to be going backward. Why did everything seem to take so much time?

She could admit to herself now (and even, on occasion, to others) that she had many good qualities. When she failed, she found herself picking up the pieces more quickly and getting back on track sooner than she ever had before. She remembered the days when failure led to one kind of out-of-control eating binge after another. Now, thankfully, all that seemed far away.

She also was feeling quite pleased with herself over her new-found ability to stand up to authority figures such as her parents or her boss. She would never forget the years she cowered in the presence of those more powerful than she and then later, after their abuse, acted out her rage at them with flagrant abandon.

Entire months, entire years, were still missing from her memory. Some memories were probably gone forever, due to the drugs and alcohol she had consumed during those periods. Other memories she would just as soon not think about anyway, though at times they seemed right on the verge of returning, much like an unwanted relative. There had been such inner turmoil during those periods that she couldn't sleep and food had no taste. It even didn't satisfy temporarily, as it used to. She felt so many panic feelings during those episodes that she often worried about whether she would either fall apart or fly into uncontrollable rage.

As Julie continued to reflect on the transition that had occurred in her life, she recalled a conversation she and her counselor had had about her "Gethsemane," as she called it. She could feel the process at work. The focus of her recovery was shifting from what she could rebuild to what she had to accept as unchangeable.

It seemed so unfair—and it *was.* If a loving God created children and put them in families, why had He given her to such angry parents? She still couldn't understand that. She was so fragile, and they had been so brutal. It didn't make sense.

Jesus called the little children to Him when He taught, yet Julie had felt somehow abandoned by Jesus as a child. She could feel the pain welling up within her as she allowed herself to think about the reality of her experience. On many occasions she had curled up on the sofa in a fetal curl, convulsed by uncontrollable sobs. Her pillow was frequently soaked with tears.

In retrospect, she realized that through it all, Jesus really had been there with her. His presence in her pain had been her only resource. He was as real as her desperation required. At times she felt Him sitting on the bed beside her. Other times He had seemed simply to hold her hand and say, "I know."

GETHSEMANE: JESUS UNDERSTANDS

I have found in my many years of ministry to others in recovery, and indeed, in working through my own recovery, that it is a supreme comfort to realize that our Savior has been there before us. In addition to feeling massive physical pain as He hung on the cross, Jesus felt excruciating emotional pain. Nowhere is this fact more evident than in the account of Jesus in the Garden of Gethsemane (Matthew 26:36-46; Mark 14:32-42; Luke 22:39-46). Julie, whose story we examined at the outset of this book and again this chapter, is in the midst of a process that has numerous parallels to Jesus' experience there.

This fact should encourage us to come boldly to the Lord for help in times of trouble because He understands what it is like to go through suffering (Hebrews 2:14-15; 4:14-16).

Some of the parallels between Jesus' work in the Garden and the recovery of an ACDF are discussed in this chapter. This material is offered as an encouragement to those in the midst of agony. It does not represent a series of steps or stages that everyone in recovery *must* pass through, nor does it represent the *only* way to "work through" an issue. It is simply an account of Jesus' personal pattern.

One further caveat before we get into the material: by examining the parallels between Jesus' Gethsemane experience and our own recovery, I am in no way implying that Jesus was dysfunctional. He simply did some very healthy things in dealing with His emotions that night in the Garden, and we can benefit from His practice. He was fully God and man during His years on earth, and in His humanity we can see health-giving patterns.

You will develop a recovery style that fits you, your personality, and your situation as you go through your own pilgrimage. It might be somewhat different from the one examined here, but it will probably have many parallels to Jesus' Gethsemane experience of coming to terms with something so painful every cell in your body wants to avoid it. Jesus was able to walk *through,* instead of *around,* His Gethsemane; in studying His experience, we can glean ways of handling our most difficult life assignments.

JESUS WAS VULNERABLE TO PAIN BECAUSE HE LOVED

Jesus was in Gethsemane because He loved us, you and me. If He had not loved us so much, the experience of the cross and the process of preparation in Gethsemane would not have been so painful. He was torn because He fully felt the emotional agony of the experience. Unlike many ACDFs and their parents, He didn't practice emotional stifling. He didn't say, as many parents of ACDFs have said, "Suck it up, stop crying, it's going to be all right," or, "Don't be so emotional—just hurry up and make a decision," or, "You can't change it, so just go on and forget it."

The hurt and memories of a child from an alcoholic or dysfunctional family linger and are almost overwhelming because of the love the child has for his parents. Sure, he cannot change the past. Sure, he is a Christian now. But he still wants intensely to change the experience he had. Jesus, the omnipotent Son of God, wanted just as intensely, at the outset, to change His experience: "Everything is possible for you. Take this cup from me" (Mark 14:36, NIV).

Jesus eventually gave His life for the ones He loved (and He could do so without being dysfunctional, for He alone had the right to give His life in this way); so also the child from a dysfunctional family becomes willing to "give his life" for his family. Julie bore all her family's pain in order to keep her family together. She truly sacrificed a large part of herself. Other children might similarly keep quiet about wrongs done to them so as not to hurt a parent, or, more importantly, so as not to injure what they perceive as a very fragile relationship.

JESUS STRUGGLED WITH FEELINGS OF ABANDONMENT

Though the moment of total abandonment was to come later at the cross, there in Gethsemane a growing sense of aloneness welled up inside of Jesus. Accompanied perhaps by the feeling that no one really understood what it was like to carry His pain, He felt more and more isolated as He came to grips with its agony. He was consumed with the struggle. He even cut Himself off, to some degree, from His three closest disciples by going a little farther into the Garden to pray alone (Matthew 26:39). His other close friends, supposedly there to comfort Him, were sleeping. He felt as though He would explode from the internal pressure. You know how it is if you have ever struggled emotionally: sweat, tears, runny nose. You feel flushed, intensely tight on the inside. Jesus was experiencing that same distress.

JESUS WENT TO A SPECIAL PLACE TO DO THE "WORK" (MATTHEW 26:36)

When the moment finally came to face the pain and the Last Supper was over, Jesus went to His special place, Gethsemane. He had possibly visited it many times. There, in that familiar place, He had in the past repeatedly experienced a sense of comfort and relief.

Every child in a dysfunctional family has a Gethsemane, a place where she can pour out her heart, a place where she feels understood and from which she leaves with a sense of relief. It might be a hideout in the back yard or an empty lot next door where she can cuddle with the dog. It might be a closet where she can cry for extended periods, alone and unheard. Maybe it is only her bed and a stuffed animal to hug there, but it is a refuge in the midst of a painful world. When there are few quality relationships in a child's family of origin, that special place takes preeminence. It becomes the point of attachment where a sense of belonging, a sense of being "at home," warms the little heart. Like Jesus' refuge the night before the cross, that place becomes a Gethsemane.

As a recovering ACDF, you will often come upon a second Gethsemane experience, a transition period that occurs between the phase of learning all about what happened to you as a child and the phase of actually having to do something about it. In counseling terms, you are at the stage where you must face tough "work," the task of working through difficult personal issues.

When the time has come to work through a painful experience, make sure you have found a new "familiar place" to go. This is where a long-term relationship with the Lord can be very important. Many ACDFs have been on the run from family, God, and most other relationships. They have cut themselves off from painful experiences, preferring to journey through life emotionally numb and alone. Survival has been their all-consuming goal.

Eventually, though, the pain returns, simply because life is cyclical. Then that new haven becomes important. It will provide you a safe place where you can talk, feel listened to while you unload, and from which you can walk away, leaving your burden behind you. That safe place might be a support group.

Simply Knowing About the Cross Did Not "Fix" Jesus' Feelings

Information is usually helpful and facts are always necessary, but knowledge alone is not sufficient when emotions are involved. Jesus knew He would go to the cross, He even *chose* to go, but He still needed to work through the feelings involved. Thus the agonized prayer to His heavenly Father.

Obtaining knowledge about forgiveness and choosing to forgive are not the same as struggling through the feelings of unfairness that usually surround the circumstances requiring forgiveness. It was in Gethsemane that Jesus truly came to grips with the cost of forgiveness. If anyone was capable of "just deciding" to do something (without processing the emotions), as many well-meaning friends often advise those struggling with forgiveness to do, Jesus certainly was. He could have toughed it out, sucked it up, let it go. But He didn't.

Gethsemane says to us that feelings are real and valid, and that they need to be worked through. That is one of the purposes of Gethsemane: Jesus wanted to show us how to work through the difficult, unfair, and usually unasked-for assignments in life. The pilgrim walking through a painful family-of-origin recovery process will have to follow his Master's path: right through the middle of the pain. Avoiding such a difficult process is not sufficient. Otherwise Jesus' journey would have led straight from the Last Supper to the cross. Similarly, we can learn from Gethsemane that feelings are not necessarily to be trusted to dictate a course of action. If that were true, Jesus would have never gone to the cross!

JESUS SAID IT BEFORE HE BELIEVED IT

One of the wonderful encouragements of the great struggle in Gethsemane is that Jesus had to pray the same prayer three times (Matthew 26:36-44). Can you imagine that? The Son of God having to repeat Himself! You and I tend to do so, and even the apostle Paul prayed multiple times about his thorn in the flesh (2 Corinthians 12:8), but we usually do not think that Jesus would ever have to do that.

Why do we think that? In part because we tend to equate repeating prayers with inefficiency or ineffectiveness, which for us is bad. Our first thought is that if one time through didn't "work," it must represent a failure. *One time should do it,* we think, and then we feel guilty when we bring a certain matter up in prayer again. Jesus in Gethsemane shows us that it is OK to struggle.

For those of us who are compulsive about scratching things off of our "to do" list and pronouncing them "done" with an air of satisfaction at how much work we are accomplishing, this picture of Jesus is alarming. How many times have you decided to forgive others during times of prayer, got up off your knees, and thought, *I'm glad I'm through with that,* only to have to repeat the process the next day or the next week? Sound familiar? Repeating difficult prayers over a period of time is not only OK, it is downright helpful. And, I might add, it is good to say prayers out loud, too, even when you are by yourself.

JESUS DID THE WORK IN STAGES

Jesus did His work at Gethsemane in separate distinct periods (His three prayer sessions), each ending with a conversation with

His support group, the disciples. Here we see that time is important to the process. Jesus worked on the issue at hand with all the time He had, but He did not work on it all of the time. ACDFs typically want to cram a childhood of tough experiences into one prayer session or one week of nonstop reading if possible.

But recovery doesn't work that way. It takes time to recover from childhood hurts. Jesus' pattern allowed for intense times of struggle followed by relief. In between normal conversations with His friends He returned to the struggle, as it welled up within.

Recovery work often parallels the original creative work of God in Genesis. Each new day brought progress toward the goal of a perfect and complete environment. But each day was also complete in itself. For example, each day after Day 2 received the same benediction, "it was good," as did Day 6, when the project was complete: "behold it was very good" (for these benedictions see Genesis 1:10, 12, 18, 21, 25, 31). In contrast to God's way, many of us would have pronounced only Day 6 "good," because that was when the project was finished. We fail to see each step of the journey as good, and impatiently await the final outcome before we can feel satisfaction about the project.

One of the twelve themes of the A.A. (Alcoholics Anonymous) movement is summarized in the phrase "one day at a time." That is exactly the process God used in creation when He recognized each day as complete in itself, even though the entire project was unfinished. That is also the same process used in sanctification: we will never be perfect in the recovery and growth God brings about in our lives, short of heaven. But the daily progress we make as we walk with Him can be reassuring, if we'll view it that way as we take life day by day, one step at a time.

There is another application of this idea to parenting and recovery: if we as parents would accept the fact that the *product* of our parenting (our children) lies in God's hands, whereas He has only placed the *process* in ours, we would do much better. God wants us to focus on the process, not the outcome. Remember, most of us left home "half-baked," and God has brought us through it all; He will bring your children through it, too.

Jesus Stayed Close to His "Support Group"

Now it is time for the Master to be ministered to. Going into His greatest trial, He wants His support group close at hand. He's invested three years with them; they know Him well. They have been through the good and the bad together. He motions to the eight where He wants them to stay and takes His three closest friends a little farther on. He wants to know exactly where everybody is as He prepares to go through His struggle.

One reason Gethsemane experiences are so tough on some people is that the individuals going through them lack a support group. They don't have the multilayered network Jesus established over the last three years of His life on earth.

As the pressure builds, Jesus chooses to be with friends instead of family in this crisis experience. Many commentators say the disciples let Him down, that His support group failed Him at the moment of their greatest opportunity. Luke (22:46) suggests otherwise, when he reports that when Jesus finds them sleeping, it is a sleep brought about by exhaustion from sorrow. They have grieved to their limit.

Similarly, it is critical for us to remember that recovery can be supported only so far by others. A support group can sustain one through just so much and for only so long. Because the one in grief hurts so badly, he often has unreasonable expectations of his friends. It was true here as well. Jesus did not let His disappointment deter Him from the task at hand. Back He goes, to work on it some more alone in prayer.

Jesus Did the Hard Work Himself—Alone

Recovery is a personal assignment that only you can do. No one else can do it for you. No one else can feel as deeply as you do about the issues affecting you. No pastor, no counselor, no support group can wrap it up for you. They can stand with you for a while, but the hard work you will often do by yourself in the middle of the night without a lot of support, except for the Son of Man who has gone through it before you (Hebrews 2:14-18; 4:14-16).

Jesus Recognizes Our Vulnerability to Temptation

Jesus in the garden urged His disciples to pray for strength in resisting temptation (Matthew 26:41).

The pain encountered while doing work in recovery is often so intense that we crave relief in any form. We each have our own vulnerability, or ways we seek relief, and they will become almost irresistible as we approach the apex of the pain. For some it will be a craving to eat, for others it will be a craving for drink, and for still others it will be the impetus to work ourselves to death or to exercise until we injure ourselves. Whatever your vulnerability, be especially alert in times of turmoil.

It is often during times like this that the temptation for illicit sexual activity flourishes. If the spouse is not nurturing to the sufferer, or if an individual is single and dating, this vulnerability can be intense. He feels a need for someone to care, someone to hold, someone to understand and reassure. What often starts as a simple, caring, platonic relationship can escalate into a flaming infatuation overnight.

This is one of the dangers of a support group. Many times a simple nod of the head, word of affirmation, or "brotherly hug" is so refreshing to a barren soul that it is misinterpreted as meaning more than was originally intended. But relationships developed in the midst of pain cannot last. The pain won't always be there, and once it diminishes, so does the need for the relationship.

That is exactly why second marriages have higher divorce rates than first marriages. Those relationships are often formed in the midst of one (or both) individual's pain, and that temporary need overshadows all other components of a healthy marriage. As was pointed out in chapter 2, this is probably why Isaac and Rebecca had such a tough time. He had never worked through his separation from his mother prior to marrying Rebecca. Instead, he used his marriage to attempt to heal his extended grief over her death.

GETHSEMANE OCCURRED IN MID-LIFE

In a culture where the life span was somewhat shorter than today, Jesus was in mid-life at Gethsemane. During this time many of us reach the point where we need to go back before we know we can go on. Our own children have provoked feelings requiring evaluation. Our aging parents remind us that time is running out. There is a growing sense that the clock is working against us.

All of this is to be expected, because very shortly in a person's life cycle at mid-life, a major role reversal will indeed take place: aging parents will become like the children, and the children will become like the parents. Often long-buried secrets from the family of origin surface at mid-life. That is one reason we have so much "elder abuse" in the land today. Children who were abused when they were young are growing older, changing roles in relationship to their own parents, and treating those parents exactly how they were once treated as children. Having never been able to talk about the earlier abuse, they now act out their rage against those who practiced it against them. It's an explosive situation.

Even if one's family of origin was not abusive, the original family pattern has a tendency to be repeated when the roles reverse at mid-life. If a parent was absent, the adult child will not want to visit much. If a parent was controlling, the adult child will respond the same way. If the parent was always irritated, the adult child is often angry beyond what the circumstances warrant. The roles of parent and child may change, but the pattern between the parent and child won't, unless the adult child works through unresolved issues.

Once the ACDF has resolved some of the unfinished business of her family of origin, she is more accepting toward her parents and can even achieve the ultimate sign of recovery: caring for the parents who wounded her while in the midst of her own pain. Though Jesus had no unfinished business to clear up personally, we see Him demonstrating the ideal of caring for aging parents. As He hung from the cross, one of His last statements (John 19:25-27) was directed toward the care of His mother, who, by that time many suppose was a widow.

JESUS DEFERRED THE OPTION OF CONFRONTING HIS ATTACKERS

Gethsemane closes, as does all recovery, with the task of confronting the people who helped to cause the pain. Peter initiated the effort by cutting off a man's ear with his sword. But Jesus, knowing the right action to take at this critical juncture, said in effect, "Now is not the time" (see Matthew 26:45-57; John 18:10-11). He could have blasted that mob in the garden, and all humanity with it, but instead He chose to defer confrontation until a more appropriate time. Then, at His second coming, He will confront those who hurt Him; His scars will condemn them (Revelation 1:7).

Similarly, in recovery, though confrontation is utterly necessary, it must sometimes be deferred. It needs to be delayed until the anger and rage can be channeled into constructive, as opposed to destructive, action. The timing varies with each case: sometimes confrontation can occur early, other times late. And, though it is often best to receive some coaching from a Christian counselor or other confidante in how the confrontation should proceed, the timing of that confrontation is best left up to the individual. He will know when it is time.

Before confrontation, you need to work through the anger and hurt you feel. Otherwise confrontation will become retaliation that leaves you resentful because it brings no relief. Confrontation is different from revenge. That is why the Lord urges, "Never take your own revenge, beloved, but leave room for the wrath of God, for it is written, 'Vengeance is Mine, I will repay,' says the Lord" (Romans 12:19).

Jesus' future confrontation at His second coming invalidates the all-too-common advice given ACDFs who are processing anger against parents or others: "Well, that's water under the bridge. It's in the past. It won't do any good to go back and to confront them. Just leave it alone. What's done is done. You can't change it." Such advice is usually based on fear of confrontation in general. It merely perpetuates anger and prevents the ACDF from experiencing a healthy resolution to the recovery process.

Jesus will confront the people who wronged Him in His past, and it is OK for you, as His child, to do the same. The difference is that He, as Lord of the universe, will give those who wronged Him just recompense and cast into hell those who are not washed by the blood (Romans 2:5-6).

Sometimes the individuals who helped to cause the pain are no longer living by the time an ACDF reaches the confrontation stage. That does not erase the need for accomplishing confrontation and forgiveness. Many ACDFs have found it helpful to write a letter to their deceased parent(s), outlining their lifetime of pain and subsequent recovery. Sometimes it is helpful in the letter to reflect on the kind of parenting your parents received from their parents, and to see the factors that predisposed them toward the relationship styles they practiced with you. Complete the process by closing with a clear statement of your final forgiveness.

Often writing the letter provides enough relief in itself, but you may find it necessary to visit the gravesite and actually read the letter aloud to the parents who are now gone. This exercise is simply for your sake. The goal is to bring you to the point of being able to verbalize what has been left unspoken for so long.

Confrontation never changes what has been done, but it can stop the repetition of the pattern. It also allows the perpetrator an opportunity to gain some sense of relief from the guilt he feels, if he is able to acknowledge and repent of his actions. Finally, the injured one can feel affirmed and invested with new-found dignity. He has managed to stand up against his attacker (before whom he formerly cowered emotionally). The self-respect he thus gains will speed the recovery process.

JULIE, JESUS, AND YOU: LETTING GO

During the recovery process, Julie received word from her parents that her father had become ill. Since returning home required a substantial drive and since she hadn't been back in several years, she decided that this might be the time to confront her father about his abuse and her mother about the incident of sexual molestation. She hoped that their acknowledgment and brokenness over the experiences would provide additional relief for her and for them.

Unfortunately, neither happened. Her dad justified his rage, and her mom denied her behavior. Initially, Julie was devastated, but gradually her depression lifted, and she came to accept the fact that she would have to work on her forgiveness of her parents without an acknowledgment from them that they needed to be forgiven.

This is the pain of the cross, the pain Jesus must have felt as He hung dying on a cross for millions of people who would never acknowledge their need for His death. As Julie struggled with forgiveness, she more than once thought in anguish, *Why go through this forgiveness when they don't even want it?* Truly "the fellowship of His sufferings" (Philippians 3:10) is often all that supports anyone going through this struggle.

One final element needs to be addressed: "letting go." To let go of something is the essence of The Serenity Prayer, which has ministered to millions of recovering ACDFs and other sufferers:

The Serenity Prayer

> God, grant me the serenity
> to accept the things I cannot change,
> the courage to change the things I can,
> and the wisdom to know the difference.
> Living one day at a time,
> enjoying one moment at a time,
> accepting hardship as a pathway to peace;
> taking, as Jesus did,
> this sinful world as it is,
> not as I would have it,
> trusting that You will make all things right
> if I surrender to Your will;
> so that I may be reasonably happy in this life
> and supremely happy with You forever in the next. Amen.
> (Reinhold Niebuhr)

Letting go is a part of the idea that Jesus would die for those millions who would never care that He did so. And note that Jesus truly let go: He did not force everyone in the world to become a believer. God gives free will to all of His human creation. That is the ultimate letting go. He chose to let the first pair go against Him in the Garden of Eden, and He sees fit to let millions continue to do so. It is sad to see people forsake the Lord and His provision of salvation, but it is true that He allows it.

We, too, need to let go of the outcome of the process of recovery. We cannot force other people to forgive, to change their minds, to apologize. And, of course, they cannot live their lives over. We cannot make another pay for the past, though we may often wish we could. God will repay evildoers for their deeds in the final judgment unless they repent and receive Christ. We can only be responsible for our own responses in the present and for our future choices. In our walk of accountability before the Lord, we need to work through the process of recovery so we can reach the ultimate stage of forgiveness. The bottom line is that there are no excuses for not working through life's unfair assignments.

Recovery from a dysfunctional family is never easy, but it is always good. And though it may seem at times to be impossibly difficult, God is there for those who want to do it right, in His strength, in His power, and under His care, guidance, and healing hand.

Questions for Reflection

Ask yourself the following questions, and make personal notes in the space provided.

1. After reading this chapter, how do you feel about:

   - the concept of Gethsemane experiences as a whole?
   - the process that you might have to go through?
   - the area of confrontation: how, why, and when?
   - the idea expressed at the chapter's conclusion: that there is no excuse for not addressing forgiveness?

_____

_____

_____

2. Have you ever been through a Gethsemane experience? If so, have you ever told anyone else about that experience? What do you wish had happened differently in your Gethsemane experience?

_____

_____

_____

3. Who is your support group? What kinds of experiences have you had together that make you think those persons would see themselves as a support group for you?

_____

_____

_____

4. To whom do you offer support? For what? How often? What kind? What could you do differently?

_____

_____

_____

5. What responses are you going through in relation to this book? Which chapter or section

- has been the most/least helpful? Why or why not?
- has been the hardest to understand? The easiest?
- has matched your own experience the best?
- has been the most unsettling for you?

_____

_____

_____

6. What are some action steps you might take now in relation to what you have read in this book?

_____

_____

_____

13

How the Local Church Can Help

By Earl Henslin, Psy.D.

A revival of sorts is taking place within the church today. It is a silent, ever-increasing revival just starting to gain a foothold, an anonymous revival of thousands of Christians who are tired of hiding their hurt behind the veil of shame that prevented them from bringing the tough issues of life out into the open.

This revival involves thousands of Christians who have been struggling secretly with a myriad of problems: alcoholism, drug addiction, sexual addiction, eating disorders, workaholism, gambling compulsions, codependence, domestic violence (including physical, sexual, or emotional abuse), the silent living with the guilt and shame of having had an abortion, the secret life of homosexual behavior, or the complex package of problems inherent in being an adult child of an alcoholic (ACA).

All this is happening against the backdrop of a Christian community that historically, if unintentionally, made it emotionally unsafe for people to have serious problems. Christians have lumped all serious problems right alongside those "unsaved people" who dwell "out there." They have proposed a one-size-fits-all prescription: personal salvation will automatically fix all personal problems. Rather than seeing the Holy Spirit (and His people) as a source of healing for people with problems, the Christian community has either dismissed the existence of problems altogether or has associated serious problems with non-Christians. In doing so, it has missed the opportunity to make the local church into a truly healing community. But, thankfully, it seems that the tide is beginning to turn.

What I think we are now experiencing is God opening a door for change to occur—lasting change, change that is deep and meaningful to hurting people, hurting *Christians,* who up until now have been shackled by their pain. We are at a special time and place in the history of the Christian community, and an opportunity is opening up before us. That is what motivates me and the other authors who have written this book and it is why I am writing this chapter on support group ministry for those in recovery.

REACH OUT—NOT DOWN

What has created the need for support groups is that within the Christian community we have lost the realization that we are human. We have come to believe that Christians must be literally perfect rather than simply people who are truly "growing in the Lord." We have forgotten that we cannot get through this life alone. Indeed, "doing it on our own" has become so customary for us that we have come to think it is normal to stay alone in our hurt. And besides, hurting alone is one way of hiding the fact that we aren't perfect, that we don't have it all together.

In American evangelical culture, needing help of any kind is considered shameful and humiliating. Yet acknowledging that we need help is often the most effective way to begin the process of healing. In a history of the Alcoholics Anonymous movement, Dr. Earnest Kurtz says that the first thing Alcoholics Anonymous did was to decide that it would help people by "reaching out, without reaching down," and he further asserts that this distinction has been a key element of the success and widespread acceptance of Alcoholics Anonymous.[1]

Dr. Kurtz is right. It is sad that the Christian community somehow missed it. We Christians have tended to reach down to people rather than reaching out to them. In 12-step groups, people reach out through acceptance.[2] No one makes the judgmental assumption, "I am better than you." No, it is "one drunk helping another." Or, in Christian language, "one sinner helping another." It is understanding that I, too, am broken, and that in helping you I help myself. It is understanding that in sharing my brokenness with you, I receive in turn the support and understanding that will help me face another part of me that isn't so pretty; that when I share my brokenness with a person who has already "been there," healing can take place.

As that healing occurs I can genuinely feel what Romans 8:28 means: "And we know that God causes all things to work together for good to those who love God, to those who are called according to His purpose." I can feel what it means to say that purpose arises out of hurt. Injury then becomes a resource, a way I can identify with and help others who are in the midst of deep pain.

THE DIFFERENCE BETWEEN THINKING (KNOWLEDGE) AND FEELING (EMOTIONS)

For centuries there has been a strong emphasis in Christianity on "right thinking" or "knowing." And, surely, right thinking is important. We need to know the facts of our faith, need to memorize Scripture and make it part of our thinking and conscious life, need to apply to our lives the disciplines of the Christian faith—prayer, meditation on God's Word, Bible study, fasting, discipleship. But that isn't all there is to Christianity.

There is also a feelings side to the Christian faith. Contemporary research points to the left side of the brain as being the more analytical and fact-oriented, whereas the right side is the more creative, intuitive, and feelings-oriented. If our Christianity leaves out the right side of the brain, we will end up knowing a good deal about our faith but feeling none of it inside. And when we cannot feel inside our own hearts, we cannot feel the hurts of others, either. All of us suffer, including our spouses and our children. When our kids don't see us modeling in our lives the truth that feelings are OK, they will have trouble experiencing their own feelings, and a downward cycle will have begun.

We need sermons and books that address the right-brain side of Christianity, books that show the scriptural basis for our emotional lives. We need a theology of feeling.

John was a successful professional, highly respected by everyone who knew him. He looked like he had it all together. No one could see from the outside that he had experienced years of physical and emotional abuse at home as he was growing up. That was a secret his family kept well hidden from the small Bible church they attended.

As a teenager and young adult, John was a faithful student of the Bible and was committed to the disciplines of the Christian faith. But as he grew older he became more depressed and reclusive. The depression became so strong he entered therapy and began to attend a support group for ACDFs.

The support group was an overpowering experience for John. He had never before been with Christians who openly shared their hurt and anger. Some in the group told of the struggles they were going through in their marriages; others shared how they thought of suicide. After John had been attending the group for about eight months, he began to sob uncontrollably during one of the sessions. Tears flowed down his cheeks as he truly felt what he had always known to be true about his childhood. The hurt of the abuse began to surface.

The fact that he could express hurt and anger in the presence of other Christians was overwhelming to John. He kept waiting for someone to tell him he was being sinful in expressing the hurt he felt. But, thankfully, that never happened. Instead, he received words of support, feelings of acceptance, and hugs that let him know that there were others who had "been there" and who had similar stories to tell. Amazed, he actually began to experience the sense of being supported and encouraged. For him, that group experience was a minor miracle; it was his first step on the road to emotional recovery.

For the first time in his life John could *feel* God's love, grace, and acceptance. He had always *known* that those things were available, but he had never experienced them emotionally, for the emotional, feelings side of his personality was almost completely out of touch with the intellectual side of his nature. Now his *knowing* parts and his *feeling* parts were connected.

Jesus was made real to John through the hugs and words of acceptance of his support group. What is so hard for us "big adults" to acknowledge is that inside we are just a bunch of kids who, in times of trouble, have difficulty openly admitting our pain or experiencing Jesus as real at that moment. But Jesus will become real to us in our pain when we share openly and honestly with others who accept us as we are and who do not judge us or shame us for having problems.

When we can share with other understanding Christians the fact that we are that very day fighting the desire for a drink, Jesus becomes real to us. When we can share the fact that we have slipped back into an eating disorder and have been bringing home ice cream and cookies every night, Jesus becomes real to us. If a pornographic bookstore has begun again to call our name and we can take that admission to another person, then the temptation will begin to lose its power, and we can take a step toward becoming liberated from a sinful pattern. That's what Christian support groups and 12-step programs are all about. They are places where rigorous honesty is valued and accepted, where what we know to be true about the Christian faith can also become what we feel is true.

WHO NEEDS SUPPORT GROUPS?

It is almost easier to ask, Who does *not* need support groups? At one time in America, the adult Sunday school was a kind of support group. Yet today's emphasis on the "school" in Sunday school has made the weekly experience more of an academic encounter than one of sharing and full-orbed fellowship. What sharing does occur, happens in an indirect, almost cloaked way through prayer requests. These prayer requests serve as a signal that someone in the group is hurting.

Unfortunately, the prayer request usually comes at a time when *crisis* is a better description of the situation. Often by then it is too late to take effective corrective action, or at least very late. A young woman who has been married three years will almost whisper in an uncomfortable tone, "Please pray for me . . . uh . . . my husband is having an affair and has decided to leave me." At that stage it will be extremely tough to pull the marriage out of a nose-dive. More than likely one or both of the partners has already made usually irreversible decisions and has taken action on those decisions.

Now don't get me wrong. It's OK to bring the crisis to the attention of the brethren, but it would have been much better to have started praying for the marriage maybe two years earlier. Then the young woman's request, if she had felt free to make it, would have been simply, "Please pray for us. We're not very close anymore . . . our marriage is dry . . ." If she had been able to go on to share what the first year of her marriage had been like, the process of change and healing could have begun, often with effective results.

So who needs a support group? We *all* do at different times in our lives. When someone close to us dies, we need someone with whom to grieve. When a new child is born, we need someone with whom to rejoice. When a job or our finances go down the tubes, we need someone with whom to share our fear. When memories of childhood abuse come back, we need someone with whom to share our anguish.

Support groups are particularly needed in the case of compulsive disease. It is virtually impossible to overcome this kind of illness alone. True, you may be able to overcome a particular manifestation of the disease all by yourself, but you are likely to drive everyone around you nuts as you do it, for you will not have changed the way you live life. You may indeed be sober in that you are not using drugs or alcohol, but apart from the deep healing a support group can give, you will still be driven by compulsions, will be a "dry drunk," as we put it in chapter 3.

A support group is important for people who have tried to obtain healing and have not been able to. Possibly long-term anger or resentment has been eating away inside you, with no relief. Perhaps you are an ACDF and have no sense of what "normal" behavior or feelings might be. It is helpful to be in a group that will help you to develop an inner sense of what to do in certain situations.

When something within you or within your relationships makes you feel stuck or overwhelmed, it's time to seek out a support network that will allow you to share your life with others. After all, who does not have some struggle or turmoil in his life? If you are breathing, you are struggling to some degree with good things and painful things. It will not work to stay alone with them.

WHAT ARE SOME TYPES OF SUPPORT GROUPS?

A vast array of support groups is springing up across America. It seems, sometimes, there are about as many support groups as there are problems!

Support groups are usually thought of as applying to adults only, but many specialty groups are proving to be helpful to kids, both elementary school age and teenagers. Just as in the case of physical disease, where early detection and treatment makes for a more favorable outcome, so treatment for dysfunctional families works best when it is started early. Hence, the ministry to kids.

Children are born with feeling and spontaneity. Dysfunctional families destroy that sense of aliveness and send feelings and spontaneity underground in the child. Support group ministry can help a child from such a family hold onto the life inside himself even though his family is going through painful times.

Overcomers Outreach (O.O.) is developing a support group for children called "OK Kids." In this group, children from four to eleven years of age are beginning to learn what a "feeling" is, and what to do with it. The group uses art, songs, and other media to help children rediscover their emotions, such as hurt or anger. Another goal is to help children learn that the alcohol, drug, or marital problems of their parents are not theirs to be responsible for. The adults in their lives must carry their own responsibilities.

Overcomers Outreach has also developed groups for teens. There an environment is created in which it is safe for teens to share. The groups seem to work best for teens who are either themselves recovering from a compulsive disease or who are members of an alcoholic/dysfunctional family. At one such gathering a teenage girl told how she found herself at the brink of suicide and decided to share her anguish with a girlfriend. The girlfriend invited her to the O.O. meeting at her church. This young teenager later told us what a relief it was to have a group with whom she could share her pain at a deeper level, without pretending that everything was OK. Both of her parents were alcoholic/addicts, she said, and home was not a safe place to share her feelings.

The mainstream application for support groups is with adults, however. An organization in southern California called Virtues helps churches set up support groups for women who have been victims of incest. Another support group, Desert Streams, helps Christian homosexuals find a heterosexual life-style through Christ's love and power. The First Evangelical Free Church of Fullerton, where my co-author Dave Carder serves, has a single parents' program that regularly draws more than seven hundred people a week, both from within and without the church body. Among other purposes, this program helps the newly divorced, single parent work through the trauma of divorce. There she can work through her grief at the loss of her marriage and can begin the intense work of dealing with being a single parent and living with her singleness. With the divorce rate continuing at around 50 percent, there are significant numbers of people who need to find their way through this painful season. Thankfully, many churches across our nation are responding. But the need is still far greater than the supply of programs.

Support groups are not just for people who have been through severe trauma or who are struggling with a compulsive disorder. They can be helpful for couples struggling with infertility, for the parents of an infant child who has suddenly died, or for adult children who are experiencing the pressure of dealing with aging parents. Patients (and their families) who are struggling with a chronic illness such as cancer can find help in a support group, as can parents whose teens are in crisis, or husbands or wives whose spouses have had affairs.

THE BEGINNING OF A MOVEMENT

OVERCOMERS OUTREACH

One of the groups mentioned above, Overcomers Outreach, Inc. (or as we affectionately call it, Overcomers) is a Christian 12-step program designed to help churches set up support groups for adults, teens, and children who struggle with compulsive disease or who have grown up in alcoholic or dysfunctional families. I have worked closely with O.O. for many years and am now chairman of the board of directors; I can vouch for the Christ-centered, effective way they help ACDFs along the road to recovery. I greatly value my relationship with the founders of Overcomers Outreach, Bob and Pauline Bartosch.

Bob took his first drink of beer at the age of twenty-four and found that he liked the rush it gave him. For a while, his social drinking didn't interfere too much with the way he ran his business or served in leadership positions in his church. But gradually, even limited use of alcohol led to loss of control. He puts it this way: "Then I crossed a line into the disease of alcoholism, where my body, mind, and spirit were governed by alcohol. I was lost in my addiction, which nearly destroyed my wife and my relationships with my three sons. One out of three Christians who drink develops a problem." In fact, some 15 million Americans are entwined in addictive behaviors such as alcoholism.[3]

Through the efforts of Bob and Pauline Bartosch, and others like them, at press time more than 800 Overcomers Outreach support groups meet weekly in churches in forty-five states throughout America. In addition, groups are springing up in Canada and Europe, and interest in Overcomers Outreach has even been expressed in the Soviet Union, where alcoholism is rampant.

NEW HOPE

The First Evangelical Free Church of Fullerton has begun an effective and fast-growing support group for ACDFs called New Hope. It started small, but after six years it has grown beyond the church's wildest expectations.

Katherine is one of the persons who has benefited from New Hope. She grew up in an alcoholic home and had a traumatic childhood. When she became a Christian she had trouble believing she'd fit anywhere in the church. The adult fellowship she attended was unsatisfactory to her because she felt no one there could relate to the pain she carried. The people in the class always gave the impression that everything in their lives was perfect and OK. No one talked about anything deeper than how the kids were doing, the new purchases they had made, or the trips they were planning.

When Katherine began attending the New Hope group, she found other Christians who carried the same deep hurt and shame she felt. As they spoke of the pain they had experienced, she began to expresss emotions she had never before shared, emotions that had been trapped inside because there was no safety to share them in her family of origin.

In Katherine's words, "My ACA [Adult Children of Alcoholics] group gave me a road back to the church. I was at a point where I could not go to Sunday school or church anymore because of the hurt and shame I carried. I had always looked at those feelings as being there because I was not a good enough Christian. At New Hope I found for the first time in my life that I could share my feelings and still be accepted. Once I could feel that acceptance in a small group, I was then able to feel more comfortable in larger groups in the church. The more I brought my hurt and shame out in the open, the more they began to lose their power over me."

WHERE TO GO FROM HERE

"OK," you may be saying, "I believe in the value of support groups. But what if my church doesn't have any? Are they going to enthusiastically embrace my suggestion that we start one?"

Good question. Change of any kind is hard for most people to handle. It is threatening and unfamiliar and basically makes people uncomfortable. Just as your family of origin may not initially welcome with open arms the changes in you brought about by recovery, so, too, organizations initially may respond hostilely to change.

Most resistance is due to a lack of information. The leaders who make the decisions have not had the opportunity to learn about or to experience what you are talking about. They might not be aware of the problems you are trying to address, or the support group you are suggesting might strike all too close to home. They may themselves be dealing with ACDF issues (see chapters 5 and 6) and may not be ready to discuss such issues comfortably.

I suggest that you begin by sharing with the leaders in the church the story of your own recovery, and if there are others in the church who are also in recovery programs, encourage them to do the same. Or suggest that your pastor or other board member attend a seminar devoted to ACDF issues. There are many of these available on a host of issues related to recovery (for information, contact some of the organizations listed in Appendix A of this book). You might ask your pastor to attend a seminar with you or offer to pay his way. You might share this book with your pastor and other leaders in your church. First Evangelical Free Church in Fullerton has a video that highlights their New Hope program and discusses recovery for people from dysfunctional families (again, see Appendix A). Talk to your pastor about sponsoring educational seminars at your church to begin to heighten the congregation's awareness of these issues. Donate books on recovery issues to the church library.

Now I'm not naive regarding this process of education. I know that often it is not easy to convince those who are not in recovery that such a program is desirable. You may try to open the subject and get rebuffed. What do you do then?

What speaks loudest is a changed life. Working on your own recovery responsibly and as God leads you is probably the most important thing you can do. And besides, if the support group you someday are able to start is to succeed, the people at its core—and that includes you—must already be in recovery. You will know when the time is right to approach your church about starting a support group.

Early in this book we discussed family systems, a way of thinking about families that forms the basis for much of what we examine in this book. The church is also a family system. Just as families have trouble handling feelings and change and conflict, so, too, do churches and other Christian organizations.

One church I know of has had steadily declining membership over the past ten years. It is solidly locked into the belief that the people who remain are the only really spiritually committed ones; the ones who have left were the carnal ones. As an organization, the church is in denial about its condition, very much like a prerecovery individual. If the people who have left the church were interviewed about their reasons for leaving, a common thread would run through their remarks: their feelings and hurts were not important to anybody. Yet this is a church where worshipers are met at the door with a smile and a warm handshake.

Unfortunately, that is about as deep as relationships in that church get. It is largely a shame-based organization (for a discussion of shame, see chapter 4) whose members have learned to take their deeper hurts elsewhere. Eventually they have found Bible studies and/or other churches where they have felt more accepted and understood as people, rather than always having to pretend that everything is OK. The church's situation is truly saddening to me. I wish it were atypical, but unfortunately it is not. The only encouragement I can see in the church is the flip side of the equation: those churches today that do validate feelings and hurts are among the fastest-growing.

It is very difficult to start a support group in a church that is still in denial. The people trying to start such a group are made to feel as though they are the only ones around who have problems. The reality is that everyone in the church has learned to be silent about his troubles and to keep his hurts outside the church. That usually results in their feeling increasingly more crazy on the inside. Soon numbness and denial become their strategies for handling life.

WHAT IF NOTHING "WORKS" TO GET THINGS ROLLING?

In churches and Christian organizations that are more open to new ways of meeting human needs, once the leaders have an opportunity to learn about the problem and its solution, they will be interested in finding effective ways to address those issues. So when you are working to get a support group started, be patient, persistent, and, above all, don't get discouraged! I have worked with some churches and organizations for up to three years before getting a program under way. God will lead you in the right way to approach your church.

If education, patient persistence, and the other methods mentioned above do not help in getting your church to start investigating support group ministries, then you might be better off finding a fellowship that is more open to and supportive of this need. After all, it is not necessary for you to try to change an entire organization just to get the help you need. Often an organization will not change unless its leaders begin to experience their own pain. Sad to say, that is how many positive changes occur. A key person's life falls apart, and then adjustments are made within the organization that should have been made years before.

Many times the root of a church split is the inability of the core families in the church to face their own issues of dysfunction. So someone needs to be sacrificed or blamed. One church I know of went through such a process. The pastor had made the transition from an almost exclusively evangelistic emphasis to more of a teaching ministry aimed at helping the people in the church grow as Christians. Part of his new program involved dealing with recovery issues. The core families of the church were bothered by this. It was more comfortable to have the focus shifted from them and their neediness to the unsaved! The church's becoming more discipleship-focused placed more accountability on them than they were comfortable with.

So the core families declared the pastor "all bad" (see the discussion of "badness" in chapter 9) and tried to shame him for not preaching more evangelistic messages. The pressure they brought to bear on him and his family was so great he had to leave the church. He went to another church and there pioneered a highly successful ministry, one of support and caring in a church that was open enough to want to address the needs of the people inside the church, as well as the needs of those people who had yet to be saved.

But the story doesn't end there. Over the next few years the issues in the lives of the core families of the first church became more acute, and the dysfunction in the church got worse before it got better. The church finally turned the corner and began to look at its responsibility for growth rather than seeing problems as being entirely the responsibility of the pastor. Yet in the meantime several pastors and their families had been sacrificed because of the dysfunction in the church. Sad, isn't it, that such pain has to occur for change to happen?

Change in any organization may be scary and threatening, but in healthy organizations, there will be a willingness to evaluate new options and take the risk of trying them, where possible benefits are seen as outweighing the risks. Unfortunately, many religious organizations often equate any kind of change with an alteration in the fundamentals of the gospel.

For example, although a particular format for a Bible study or growth group is not actually sacred, the members of a church may confuse the inspired Bible with their (noninspired) method of its study. God's Word is of critical importance to our lives, but the way the Bible is studied, experienced, and made real to people can take many forms. For some people, Bible studies and prayer groups are the best way of truly grasping what the Bible has to say; for others, the caring arms of a support group is the means of seeing God as real. In my opinion, a fully developed local church program should include *all* elements—both the "thinking" side (as discussed at the outset of this chapter) and the "feelings" side.

Do you believe that your church is too small to sponsor a support group, or too inexperienced? No problem. Many support groups have been developed by churches or a group of churches working together, so that resources, both human and financial, can be shared.

Have you concluded that you cannot find any such group among your community's churches? No problem. Seek them out in the community at large. Alcoholics Anonymous (A.A.) is listed in most phone books in America, and often the folks involved in A.A. can refer you to another type of group if that is what you need. If no explicitly Christian group is available, it is better to join another, similar group than to struggle by yourself!

Or perhaps you could start a support group by yourself or work with others to form one. See Appendix A of this book for the means of getting more information about O.O. and other, similar groups. There are, I am sure, other support groups we are not aware of, but the groups listed in that appendix are all lay-led movements and are trustworthy.

CHECKLIST FOR CHANGE

What churches are likely to be more open than others to starting support group and recovery-related ministries? The checklist below is not exhaustive, but it will help you assess where your church stands in its capacity for starting a support group. It will come in handy as you contemplate starting a dialogue with your church leadership or with a fellow-recoverer.

1. The leadership is open to reading books and attending seminars on support groups, or to visiting other churches who have support group ministries in operation.
2. The leadership is not overly fearful of change and does not equate change in method of ministry with change in the fundamentals of the faith.
3. The leadership is responsibly dealing with issues in their own lives; the church as a whole is an open and growing organization. The leaders of the church do not project an image of perfection but are honest and real in their walk with God.
4. The leaders of the church are responsive to peoples' hurts and are not judgmental or shaming.

Conversely, the characteristics below may be true of churches that would find it very difficult to start support group or recovery-related ministries. Again, this is not an exhaustive list, but may serve as a starting point. Also, keep in mind that God may do a miracle and change the hearts of those you would not expect to pursue the development of such ministries.

1. The leadership is not open to new ways of dealing with peoples' problems.
2. The church spiritualizes all problems to the point of excluding emotional and physical factors.
3. The church has a pattern of handling conflict by removing the person who does not follow exactly the unwritten rules of the church. There is no attempt at working conflicts through.
4. The church is evangelistic in the extreme, to the exclusion of discipleship or other avenues of growth or recovery for the Christians already there.

HOW DOES A PERSON ACTUALLY START A SUPPORT GROUP?

Bob Bartosch says that it is important for a support group not to be run by a pastor or therapist. If a pastor runs a group, it will probably turn into a Bible study; if a therapist runs a group it will probably turn into group therapy. The best initiators and leaders of this particular type of ministry are lay Christians who have already been involved in a 12-step program. In Overcomers we strongly encourage the participants in the support group to be also involved in a traditional 12-step program.

It is important that the people starting a support group are well into their own recovery. Unfortunately, many Christians are drawn to this type of ministry out of their own codependency, which is to say that they are in the group to "fix" or "help" others, rather than being there for their own recovery. That is why it is so important to have people at the core of the group who are actively involved in one of the 12-step groups, such as Alcoholics Anonymous, Al-Anon, Adult Children of Alcoholics, Overeaters Anonymous, or Sexaholics Anonymous.

One day I was talking to a therapist who was frustrated that no more than two or three people would show up for an O.O. meeting. He described how he had been there night after night for the past six months. As we talked, it turned out that he would lead the group but not share any of his own issues; he was there to help the "poor" alcoholics and drug addicts. He did not see himself as needing to recover himself. His attitude was one of self-righteousness and condescension toward those who were hurting. Consequently, anyone coming to the group sensed his attitude and was immediately turned off.

At Oceans Hills Community Church in San Juan Capistrano, California, Christian education staff woman Beth Funk started a 12-step study group at her church. There was such a positive response to that support group that the senior pastor asked her to be in charge of all the church's small group ministries. Ten months later they had developed fifteen 12-step study groups! The support groups have now become a significant part of her church's adult ministries, and have fast become a new way of reaching people in the community. Many people find it is easier to invite a friend or relative to a support group for, say, codependency, than to invite that same person to a church service. The guest then begins to experience God's love through the other group members, and many times he also finds Christ as his personal Savior or becomes recommitted in his Christian walk.

WHO LEADS THE GROUP?

At O.O. we have attempted to follow the format used in traditional 12-step meetings. Consequently, the group is lay-led. People who are themselves in recovery are the ones sharing with those who seek recovery. Given that this format is "grass-roots" and not dependent on staff or professionals, some churches and their pastoral staff have found it difficult to handle, because there is so little formal structure and control. Yet this method has worked successfully in 12-step groups for fifty-five years, for millions of people.

Leaders come from within the group; we use the rotating leadership format. Each member takes his or her turn leading the meeting. It's a scary step to lead the meeting for the first time, yet that seems to be an important step in recovery. Another benefit of rotating leadership is that the group does not become dependent upon one person; the entire group develops its leadership skills.

One leader in New York City put it this way: "Group members tend to dump their problems on the so-called expert" in conventional professional-led treatment programs. "Their attitude becomes: 'Here I am—fix me.' But in a support group . . . the members know they can't be lazy. The responsibility for getting better is in each member's hands."[4]

WHAT ROLES DO PROFESSIONALS PLAY IN RECOVERY?

Twelve-step programs and other support groups are not intended to be cure-alls. The main emphasis is that laypeople minister to other laypeople. But there are times when additional help by a physician, pastor, or therapist is needed. A depression may become overwhelming, and the person may need to be evaluated for a physical cause. Or painful memories from a childhood trauma may need attention from a professional therapist.

It is important that the core group members know of resource people to whom referrals can be made. In addition, if psychological help is needed, the therapist should be knowledgeable about ACDFs, dysfunctional families, codependence, and compulsive disease. If the therapist is not knowledgeable in those areas, he may at best unintentionally prolong recovery or at worst not help at all. There may be a need for pastoral counseling during the recovery process. The same requirement is true of the pastor as of the therapist: expertise in recovery issues is essential.

Physicians, too, are becoming more knowledgeable about these issues. Dr. Willard Hawkins, a Christian family practice doctor with whom I am associated, is one such physician. At the history-taking and physical examination portion of his time with the patient, he begins to find out if the patient is from a dysfunctional family, or if he has been the victim of physical, sexual, or emotional abuse. Once he identifies those issues he begins to encourage the patient to get to the appropriate support group and to psychotherapy if needed. A physician who understands recovery issues can be vital to the recovery process.

Pastors who are knowledgeable about recovery issues are an indispensable part of the recovery process. A pastor is often the first person contacted by someone who is hurting. At O.O. we have a network of pastors who we know will help support people in their recovery process and not shame or judge them. There are times that a pastor will pick up the threads of an unconfessed sin that is holding a person back in the recovery process, or the pastor will help that newly sober person get into a discipling or supportive prayer relationship in addition to encouraging the individual to continue his or her 12-step work.

It is not easy to find a physician, pastor, or therapist who understands these issues. When seeking such a helper, feel free to ask plenty of questions regarding his training and experience. And ask him if he is working through his own recovery program. After all, the best help comes from those who have "been there." If the professional becomes defensive or cannot answer your questions, look elsewhere. Many times the best place to find a solid referral is to talk to people whose recovery program you respect. Support groups play a role, physicians play a role, pastors play a role. A team approach often works best. That is why it is important to seek out churches and key people who understand the issues.

A MATTER OF LIFE AND DEATH

After reading this chapter you might think I'm making too big a deal about our need for support groups. "You're overdoing it, Henslin," you might say. "You're making it sound like a matter of life and death."

Well, it *is* a matter of life and death. A recent study at Stanford University showed that terminally ill cancer patients who attended weekly support group meetings in addition to receiving medication lived *twice* as long as a control group who only received medication.[5]

And it's a matter of life and death in a figurative sense, too. True life includes full emotional health, and support groups are a key element in achieving that. We in the Christian community have only begun to tap the potential of what God intended the church to be. As I said at the chapter's outset, I believe that we are right in the middle of an incredible change period—a revival of sorts—in the Christian community. During this time of change there is tremendous opportunity.

Can you imagine being able to attend a Sunday school class or adult fellowship that is working through a series of Sunday school lessons on dysfunctional families by using this (or another) book, along with discussion questions? Can you imagine being able to open a church-sponsored class with the words "Hi, my name is William. I'm an alcoholic (or sex addict, compulsive overeater, adult child of an alcoholic, ACDF, codependent, workaholic, and so on)," and then sharing with the class in a confidential and anonymous manner? It would be marvelous! Millions of people from around the world benefit from such a format in Alcoholics Anonymous (which began as an overtly Christian program). There's no reason God's people can't have similar blessings.

Can you imagine using material right out of Scripture (as we do in this book) to teach about and give permission to experience feelings? To teach junior high and senior high students about codependency? To teach adults and children alike that it is OK to bring issues out into the open? Then, when the issues are in the open and in the light, change can happen. When we can do that, we will be living out John 8:32: "You shall know the truth and the truth shall make you free."

The Power of a Healing Community

At the beginning of *The Different Drum: Community Making and Peace* M. Scott Peck tells the story of a little monastery "in the deep woods" that had "fallen upon hard times."[6] It and the great order of which it was a part were in danger of extinction. The monastery and the order were revived as its members pondered the meaning of a statement made by a rabbi sought out by the abbot for advice. "The only thing I can tell you," the rabbi had said, "is that the Messiah is one of you." As the following "days and weeks and months" went by, "the old monks began to treat each other with extraordinary respect on the off chance that one among them might be the Messiah. And on the off, off chance that each monk himself might be the Messiah, they began to treat themselves with extraordinary respect." In time, an "aura of extraordinary respect . . . began to surround the five old monks and seemed to radiate out from them and permeate the atmosphere of the place." Visitors were drawn to the monastery, and new men joined the ranks. "Within a few years the monastery had once again become a thriving order and, thanks to the rabbi's gift, a vibrant center of light and spirituality."

The monastery is, of course, mythical, and the true Messiah is, of course, the one Lord Jesus Christ, our Savior. But the point of the story, that respect for oneself and one's neighbors creates an atmosphere of peace that leads to "light and spirituality," is highly relevant to this book. As a Christian community the opportunity is before us to become a healing community, one that gives genuine support and acceptance to the broken and hurting, no matter what the issue. We need to become a place where the shattered can share their pain with a community of believers, a place where caring people handle that which is broken in us in a delicate, accepting way. This will happen as we see each person, and ourselves, as someone very, very special.

Questions for Reflection

Ask yourself the following questions, and make personal notes in the space provided.

1. Who are the key people in your church who would be involved in making the decision to start a support group ministry? Write down their names, and begin to pray for them, that God would give them an open mind to investigate starting a group that would give people a safe place to share their hurts.

_____

_____

_____

2. It is dangerous and even destructive to begin a recovery support group ministry in your church without first having worked your own program of recovery. Where do you need to begin? What support group or 12-step program would be best for you?

_____

_____

_____

Notes

1. "Historian Ernest Kurtz Discusses A.A. and the Challenges It Faces," *Sober Times,* January, 1990, p. 6.
2. For a bibliography of Christian materials related to the 12-step method, see Appendix A: "Where ACDFs (Adult Children from Dysfunctional Families) Can Find Help."
3. " 'Overcomers' Group Reaches Out to Those in Need," *Focus on the Family,* June 1990, p. 15.
4. Charles Leerhsen et al., "Unite and Conquer," *Newsweek* (February 5, 1990), p. 51.
5. Ibid., p. 52.
6. M. Scott Peck, M.D., *The Different Drum: Community Making and Peace* (New York: Simon & Schuster, 1987), pp. 13-15.

Appendix A

Where ACDFs Can Find Help

SUPPORT GROUPS

New Hope Recovery Group
First Evangelical Free Church
2801 North Brea Boulevard
Fullerton, CA 92635-2799

The materials below can be ordered by writing to the address above.

1. Directory

   National Directory of more than six hundred groups that submitted their names in response to a 1989 Focus on the Family questionnaire

2. Training materials

   (a) Worksheets for rules, roles, and birth order relationships
   (b) *Facilitator's Training Manual* (Self-Study)
   (c) *Facilitator's Training Manual* (Leader's Guide)
   (d) A 16-characteristic study guide

3. Videos

    (a) *New Hope Video* (VHS only; 60 minutes total length)
       Part 1: Rules and Roles of the Dysfunctional Family
       Part 2: New Hope: Its Structure, How and Why It works
       Part 3: Gethsemane: Handling Life's Unfair Assignments

    (b) *Facilitator's Training Video* (available early 1991)

Overcomers Outreach
2290 West Whittier Boulevard, Suite A/D
La Habra, CA 90631
(213) 697-3994

Overcomers Outreach, Inc., is a nonprofit ministry to chemically dependent/compulsive people and affected family members through Christ-centered 12-step support groups. It is financed by tax-deductible contributions from individuals who believe in the work. Overcomers groups are not intended to replace Alcoholics Anonymous, Al-Anon, and so on, but are designed to be a supplement from the Christian perspective in which A.A.'s "12 Steps" to recovery are directly related to their corresponding Scriptures. Overcomers groups refer freely to the "higher power" as Jesus Christ. We seek to be a "bridge" between A.A. and churches of all denominations.

If you are interested in starting a Christian 12-step group in your church, contact O.O. at the address listed above. These groups are initiated and maintained with the use of the *Freed* guidelines booklet. Contained therein are a meeting format, the 12 steps with Scriptures, additional topics with scriptural references, and guidelines for starting a group. If an Overcomers group gets started where you are, we ask that you will share the good news with the home office (above) so that we may add the information to the directory of meetings, enabling us to refer people to groups nationwide.

Materials available from Overcomers Outreach:

    Group Starter Kit
    Audio Tape of Bartosch's Story
    Freed booklet
    Freed booklet (Spanish Edition)
    TNT Teen

Circus of Codependency
Alcoholism: Sin or Sickness?
The Big Cover Up (Bartosch story)
Food: Friend or Foe
12 Steps and Corresponding Scriptures
Working the Steps
Don't Just Say No (youth brochure)
Better Choices for Teens
The 5 R's of ACA (Adult Child of an Alcoholic)
Chemically Dependent Christians
Cocaine Isn't Cool
Does Someone You Love Drink Too Much?
Intervention
Disease Chart of Alcoholism/Family
Alcoholism/Drug Dependency in Church
O.O. National Meeting Directory
O.O. California Meeting Directory

Adult Children of Alcoholics, Central Service Board
P.O. Box 35623
Los Angeles, CA 90035
(213) 464-4423

Alcoholics Anonymous
P.O. Box 459 Grand Central Station
New York, NY 10163
(212) 686-1100

Al-Anon/Alateen Family Group Headquarters
P.O. Box 182 Madison Square Station
New York, NY 10159
(800) 344-2666
(212) 302-7240

Debtors Anonymous
314 West 53rd Street
New York, NY 10018
(212) 969-0710

Emotions Anonymous
P.O. Box 4245
St. Paul, MN 55104
(612) 647-9712

Gamblers Anonymous
P.O. Box 17173
Los Angeles, CA 90017
(213) 386-8769

Incest Survivors Anonymous
P.O. Box 5613
Long Beach, CA 90800

Narcotics Anonymous, World Service Office
16155 Wyandotte Street
Van Nuys, CA 91406
(818) 780-3951

National Association for Children of Alcoholics
31582 Coast Highway, Suite B
South Laguna, CA 92677
(714) 499-3889

National Clearinghouse for Alcohol Information
P.O. Box 1908
Rockville, MD 20850

Overeaters Anonymous, World Service Office
2190 190th Street
Torrance, CA 90504
(213) 542-8363

CLINICS

The Minirth-Meier Clinic West
1-800-545-1819

The Minirth-Meier Clinic, the recognized leader in Christian mental health services since 1975, has assembled a comprehensive network of therapists, educational services, and treatment programs which comprise the Minirth-Meier Clinic West.

1. Inpatient hospital program

   The inpatient hospital program specializes in helping Christians recover from such problems as depression, anxiety,
   panic attacks, issues of victimization, and chemical and sexual addictions.

2. Partial hospitalization program

   The day hospital program is designed to provide the same
   treatment benefits as the inpatient hospital program with the
   difference being that the patients live at home and attend the
   program during the day.

3. Free referral network of Christian counselors

   The clinic has developed a comprehensive list of Christian
   counselors throughout the United States. Staff members can
   use this list to match counselors with patients based on the
   individual needs of the patient along with the strengths and
   specialties of the counselor.

4. Speakers' bureau

   Churches, schools, businesses and other Christian organizations can make arrangements through the clinic's speakers'
   bureau for presentations on a number of topics.

5. Weekly "Monday Night Solutions"

   Various topics concerning mental health issues are presented to the public each Monday. Call the clinic for the location
   and time.

6. Monthly seminars

   Monthly seminars are presented on a variety of topics focusing on improving life-styles.

7. Book and tape catalog

A catalog of Christian books and tapes written and produced by Minirth-Meier Clinic West staff is available.

Henslin and Associates
2720 North Harbor Boulevard, Suite 200
Fullerton, CA 92635
(714) 992-6660

Christian family medicine and family psychology are the focus of Harbor Family Practice, Inc. and Henslin and Associates. Willard Hawkins, M.D., is the director of the family medicine program, and Earl R. Henslin, Psy.D., MFCC, is the director of the counseling program. Dr. Hawkins and Dr. Henslin specialize in the treatment of adult children of alcoholic/dysfunctional families, codependency, and the compulsive diseases of alcoholism, drug addiction, eating disorders, workaholism, and sexual addiction.

Persons who would like help with any of the problems mentioned above or who would be interested in arranging for a workshop presentation on issues related to marital problems, family problems, and addictive disease should contact Dr. Hawkins or Dr. Henslin at the address given above.

BOOK AND VIDEO RESOURCES

CHRISTIAN MATERIALS RELATED TO THE 12-STEP METHOD

Dr. Bob and the Good Oldtimers: A Biography with Recollections of Early A.A. in the Midwest. New York: Alcoholics Anonymous World Services, Inc., 1980.

Fish, Melinda. *When Addiction Comes to the Church: Helping Yourself and Others Move into Recovery.* Old Tappan, N.J.: Revell, 1990.

Minirth, Frank, Paul Meier, Robert Hemfelt, and Sharon Sneed. *Love Hunger: Recovery from Food Addiction.* Nashville: Nelson, 1990.

Spickard, Anderson, and Barbara Thompson. *Dying for a Drink: What You Should Know About Alcoholism.* Dallas: Word, 1985.

The Twelve Steps: A Spiritual Journey by Friends in Recovery. San Diego: Recovery Publications, 1988.

W., Claire. *God, Help Me Stop! A Twelve-step Bible Workbook for Recovery from Compulsive Behavior.* 3d ed. San Diego: Books West, 1988. (Workbook may be obtained by writing Books West; P.O. Box 27364; San Diego, CA 92128.)

GENERAL BOOK LIST

Beattie, Melody. *Co-Dependent No More: How to Stop Controlling Others and Start Caring for Yourself* (Center City, Minn.: Hazelden, 1987; Harper & Row, 1988).

———. *Beyond Codependency.* New York: Harper & Row, 1989.

Black, Claudia. *It Will Never Happen to Me.* Denver: M.A.C. Printing, 1982.

———. *Repeat After Me.* Denver: M.A.C. Printing, 1985.

Buhler, Rich. *Pain and Pretending: You Can Be Set Free from the Hurts of the Past.* Nashville: Thomas Nelson, 1988.

Cloud, Henry. *When Your World Makes No Sense—Four Critical Decisions that Can Bring Hope and Direction into Your Life.* Nashville: Oliver-Nelson, 1990.

Dickinson, Richard. *The Child in Each of Us.* Wheaton, Ill.: Victor, 1989.

Feldmeth, Joanne, and Midge Finley. *We Weep for Ourselves and Our Children.* San Francisco: Harper, Fall 1990.

Frank, Jan. *A Door of Hope.* San Bernardino, Calif.: Here's Life, 1987.

———. *When Victims Marry.* San Bernardino, Calif.: Here's Life, 1990.

Halverson, Ron. *12 Steps: A Spiritual Journey* (workbook). San Diego: Recovery, 1988.

———. *When I Grow Up I Want to Be an Adult* (workbook). San Diego: Recovery, 1990.

Heitritter, Lynn, and Jeanette Vought. *Helping Victims of Sexual Abuse.* Minneapolis: Bethany House, 1989.

Hemfelt, Robert, Frank Minirth, and Paul Meier. *Love Is a Choice: Recovery from Co-Dependent Relationships.* Nashville: Thomas Nelson, 1989.

Ripped Down the Middle (video). Downers Grove, Ill.: InterVarsity, 1988.

Leman, Kevin. *The Birth Order Book.* Old Tappan, N.J.: Revell, 1985.

Rinck, Margaret. *Can Christians Love Too Much?* Grand Rapids: Zondervan, 1989.

———. *Christian Men Who Hate Women.* Grand Rapids: Zondervan, 1990.

Rowland, Cynthia. *The Monster Within: Overcoming Bulimia-Anorexia.* Grand Rapids.: Baker, 1985.

Seamands, David. *Healing for Damaged Emotions.* Wheaton, Ill.: Victor, 1981.

————. *Putting Away Childish Things.* Wheaton, Ill.: Victor, 1982.

Sell, Charles. *Unfinished Business.* Portland, Oreg.: Multnomah, 1989.

Sullivan, Barbara. *First Born/Second Born.*

W., Claire. *God, I'm Still Hurting.* San Diego: Books West, 1988. (This book may be obtained by writing to Books West at P.O. Box 27364; San Diego, CA 92128.)

————. *God, Where Is Love?* Books West, P.O. Box 27364, San Diego, CA 92128.

Woititz, Janet. *Adult Children of Alcoholics.* Deerfield Beach, Fla.: Health Comm., 1983.

————. *Guidelines for Support Groups.* Deerfield Beach, Fla.: Health Comm., n.d.

————. *Struggle for Intimacy.* Deerfield Beach, Fla.: Health Commission, 1985.

Appendix B

Patterns Predicting Pastoral Infidelity

by Dave Carder

One of the secrets long known in Christian circles but rarely examined openly is the tendency for some of its leaders to get involved in immorality. Recently, the cloak of secrecy has been removed to a great extent, as some of the scandalous sexual behavior has made the national news. That coverage has in turn resulted in a flurry of articles in the religious press addressing the issues of morality and spirituality.

Most of the discussion has centered upon preventing affairs through developing spiritual piety. Some of the discussion has addressed the emotional components involved in infidelity. But to my knowledge, none of the commentary has addressed the personality factors involved in sexual temptation, even though those personality factors are of major importance. In this appendix I hope to set aright that omission, specifically making the following points:

1. The inclination to have an affair is at least as much a question of personality as it is a question of spirituality.
2. The "unfinished business" in a family history is the single most powerful influence in predisposing an individual toward marital infidelity.
3. The affairs under discussion are triggered by a fairly predictable pattern at their onset (in other words, there are times when the risk is greater).
4. The affairs under discussion can be placed into one of three categories, and consequently, because not all affairs are the

same, recovery and counseling work need to take an affair-specific approach.

INFLUENCE OF THE FAMILY OF ORIGIN

In my work with pastors who have engaged in marital infidelity, and as a result of other research, I have found that the six factors most important in predisposing an individual toward marital infidelity are all part of the family of origin history. Post-affair interviews substantiate the point that the greater the number of these factors in an individual's history, the more at risk he is for marital infidelity.

Although one's family history can never force an individual to behave in a specific way since he has freedom of choice, it can predispose him toward an affair-prone life-style and place him at high risk for infidelity.

LIFE-STYLE THEMES

The high risk individual's life-style choices initially appear to be well thought out, and the individual himself appears to be well balanced. But in post-affair interviews five life-style themes occur repeatedly. Although this general topic was discussed in chapter 6, those five themes bear brief mention again here:

1. *Compulsivity.* These individuals are hard working, driven, unable to relax easily, achievement-oriented, and addictive-prone.
2. *Propensity toward risk-taking.* These individuals enjoy living on the edge and dislike routine, safety, and predictability.
3. *Rejection of authority.* These individuals often practice fiscal irresponsibility and credit card abuse, and they maintain high income-to-debt ratio. They are prone to accumulating tickets for speeding and parking violations, and they dislike being told what to do.
4. *Emotional isolation.* These individuals are not genuinely close to the significant others in their lives. They do not express feelings well. They have superficial relationships and are rarely vulnerable. They are starved for affection and an unmanipulative, "no strings attached" type of nurturance.
5. *Managed anger.* These individuals do not blow up easily, but one senses a great amount of anger just below the surface. They appear to be working always at controlling irritation

and frustration. They often get the angriest at those to whom they are the most closely related, their wives and children.

PSYCHO-SOCIAL STRESSORS

The family of origin and life-style themes discussed above are shared with many individuals who will never have affairs. But when these themes occur in the presence of specific psycho-social stressors (examined below in the evaluation form titled "Patterns Predicting Pastoral Infidelity"), high-risk males may very likely slip over the line into inappropriate emotional and sexual relationships.

TYPES OF AFFAIRS

Not all affairs are alike. When an affair occurs, it needs to be evaluated as to its kind, for affairs have different underlying dynamics. This evaluation only helps identify a high risk group for Type I and Type II affairs. Type III is considered an addiction pattern and, as such, operates on a different set of emotional dynamics.

TYPE I: THE ONE-NIGHT STAND

Type I is truly a temptation for any individual in the high risk category, given the right combination of hormones, circumstances, secrecy, and partner. Only this type of affair, which is essentially a one-time experience, can be repented of through a single confrontation of the kind brought on by Nathan when he exclaimed against David, "Thou art the man" (2 Samuel 12:7, KJV). One of the identifying differences between Type I and Type II affairs is that the initial lust, and its resulting sexual activity, is present at the onset of Type I, whereas it might not be present in Type II for months.

TYPE II: LONG-TERM FRIENDSHIP

This kind of relationship is genuine friendship initially and only becomes sexual at a later date. It is built on mutual attraction and has many emotional components. Even if this type of affair is only platonic and never consummated sexually, it is often inappropriate because it robs the marital relationship of energy needed for intimacy between spouses.

Type II affairs are often maintained through secrecy, lies, and deceit. The breakup of a Type II affair requires a time of grieving much like that after a divorce. When such a relationship becomes sexual, the bonding is so intense that the individuals involved will risk everything they have—families, fortunes, careers, even their life and health—in order to maintain it.

Probably the best biblical example of this type of affair and its risks is the affair of Samson and Delilah. Repentance following a Type II affair is necessary but *not sufficient* for recovery. Time is required here for healing.

In actuality a Type II affair is prone to repetition: statistically speaking, the chances are very good that it will indeed occur again. Therapy is often needed to explore why the appeal and attraction occurred in the first place. If a husband and wife are able to reconcile after such an affair has occurred, they will need to explore together what contributed to the affair and what benefits the affair provided that were unavailable in the marriage.

Again, the Type II affair affects the psyche to the extent that an individual once involved in such an affair is at high risk to have another one. If a second affair follows, its duration will usually be shorter, and the individual will have begun the journey toward sexual addiction (Type III affairs).

TYPE III: SEXUAL ADDICTION

Though sexual addiction has many forms of sexual expression, these affairs (involving heterosexual partners) become less and less fulfilling emotionally. The individual literally runs from partner to partner looking for more and more fulfillment. There is no emotional attachment in these affairs, and the risk to the individual continues to escalate, partly because his sexual behavior is out of control and partly because his behavior puts him in serious danger of contracting a life-threatening sexually transmitted disease (STD). A biblical example of this type of sexual behavior occurs in the description of Eli's sons sleeping with women involved in Temple ministry (1 Samuel 2:12-25, especially verses 22-25).

The recovery process involved in Type III affairs has many parallels to recovery from any addiction: acknowledgment, sobriety, undertaking a 12-step recovery process, help from a sponsor, addressing ACDF issues as discussed in this book, and so on. Public confession and repentance is *only the start* of what will be a very time-consuming journey.

Only recently has the medical and psychological community even begun to come to terms with this type of behavior. The individual involved in this type of extramarital affair can never again be placed in a position of ministry. To do so would be much like forcing the alcoholic to tend bar, just to prove that he is truly sober. A return to ministry would, in my opinion, be a set-up for continued failure.

PATTERNS PREDICTING PASTORAL INFIDELITY
Copyright © by David M. Carder

This survey is a nonscientific instrument highlighting patterns that appear regularly in the lives of pastors who have been involved in infidelity. It is not intended to predict who will definitely become sexually immoral, and it should not be interpreted as a necessarily reliable or valid indicator of those who are struggling with sexual temptation. Furthermore, it does not claim to discriminate between those who have committed adultery and those who might do so in the future. Its usefulness as a screening device is also, as yet, undetermined. This survey is designed to help you evaluate your personal history and life-style for parallels with those who have been involved in adultery.

This evaluation form only applies to men. No effort has been made to include information from interviews of females who have had affairs. This evaluation only helps to identify a high-risk group of males who, given the right combination of unfinished business in their lives, life-style pattern, and current psycho-social stressors, would be prone to having an affair.

PERSONAL AND FAMILY HISTORY

1. Did you grow up in a family that used a substantial amount of alcohol?

    _____ Yes   _____ No

2. Were your parents strict disciplinarians, possibly even abusive at times?

    _____ Yes   _____ No

3. Were you sexually molested as a child?
    _____ Yes   _____ No

4. Did you experience early adolescent heterosexual activity with an older partner (babysitter, older sister's friend, and so on)?
    _____ Yes   _____ No

5. Were you involved in pornography prior to puberty (magazines, video)?

_____ Yes   _____ No

6. While you were living at home, were either of your parents involved in an extramarital affair?

_____ Yes   _____ No

LIFE-STYLE PATTERNS

Please use the following criteria to answer questions 7-24: "The higher the score, the truer the statement."

7. As an adolescent I did not get along with authority figures, and I continue to have conflict with the law and/or my supervisors.

1   2   3   4   5

8. I feel driven, unable to relax and/or to have fun.

1   2   3   4   5

9. My self-control and anger management skills are strengths in my life.

1   2   3   4   5

10. I like testing the limits that surround me, e.g., the speed limits, tax and banking laws, church policies, and so on.

1   2   3   4   5

11. I enjoy getting through a project so that I can get on with the next one. It is important to me to have a number of projects "waiting in line" for my attention.

1   2   3   4   5

12. I feel alone even in my marriage and am unable to share my fears, deepest feelings, and the longings of my heart with my spouse.

1   2   3   4   5

13. I recognize in myself the tendency toward compulsive behavior with different things at different times (e.g., food, ex-

ercise, work, saving money or spending money, fast driving, and so on).

1   2   3   4   5

14. I have lots of acquaintances and appear to be close to my family members, but I don't have an intimate friend.

1   2   3   4   5

15. I like to win and would be described as a fierce competitor in whatever I do.

1   2   3   4   5

16. My dating life was marked by a series of broken relationships that were ended by me.

1   2   3   4   5

17. I feel stressed out, almost numb, from all the demands of the ministry upon my life.

1   2   3   4   5

18. I like to be around important people and find myself playing up to relationships with those types of people.

1   2   3   4   5

19. A review of my financial history contains a series of bounced checks, a large debt-to-income ratio, poor credit, regular use of credit cards to support my life-style, and possibly even bankruptcy.

1   2   3   4   5

20. I have trouble expressing my anger in ways that provide me with relief without wounding others emotionally.

1   2   3   4   5

21. I don't mind conflict and find that it actually helps me feel better and more in control.

1   2   3   4   5

22. I like to see what I can get away with by living "close to the edge."

    1   2   3   4   5

23. An area that the Lord has to help me with is a tendency to harbor grudges and a desire for revenge.

    1   2   3   4   5

24. Most of those who know me would say that I am intense, easily irritated, and have high standards of excellence.

    1   2   3   4   5

CIRCUMSTANTIAL FACTORS

Give yourself five points for each of the numbered items you have experienced within the past year.

25. Loss of a close loved one (e.g., child, parent, spouse).

    ____

26. Suffered a major stressor (e.g., job loss/change, divorce, medical diagnosis/hospitalization, cross-country move).

    ____

27. Approached a major life transition (e.g., the birth of a child, mid-life crisis, retirement).

    ____

TEST-WIDE SCORING

Questions 1-6: "Yes" answers count 10 points each. If all six questions are answered "yes," give yourself an additional 40 points.

Total score for questions 1-6:   ____

Questions 7-14: Total the numbers that you circled.

Total score for questions 7-24:   ____

Questions 25-27: Give yourself 5 points for each category experienced.

Total score for questions 25-27: ——

Total score: ——

EVALUATION OF SCORE

Questions 1-6:   A score over 50 for this section places you in the high risk group.

Questions 7-24: A score over 70 for this section places you in the high risk group.

Total score: A score over 100 is cause for concern. A score of 175 indicates extreme vulnerability to an affair.

A final word. If you find yourself to be in the high risk category, start working on your family of origin issues. If you are married, focus on developing emotional intimacy with your spouse. There are a number of materials available, and the suggestions herein are just a start.

A final warning. High risk individuals are more vulnerable than they realize. Whatever you do, do not discount your initial score —talk it over with your spouse and get started!

ONGOING SUPPORT FOR MARITAL ENRICHMENT

These materials are designed to support and deepen intimacy. Some take more time than others, but you can do them in any order. The only step-by-step process is the area of prayer assignments, and that will have an explanatory note.

BOOKS AND PROJECTS

Try Marriage Before Divorce by David Kilgore

This is an excellent book with a 30-day project for couples. Guaranteed you'll find out a lot about yourself and the other individual as you work through it.

Ten Dates for Mates by Claudia and Dave Arp

This book contains ten structured dates that have homework assignments prior to the meeting you have together. This project will preferably last a year, with one date a month.

The Secret of Staying in Love by John Powell

John has approximately fifty paragraphs in the back of his book, plus a number of questions and a list of emotions that are very helpful. If there were one book that a couple could use in marriage, this would be my first choice.

The Mystery of Marriage by Mike Mason

As the couple grows, both will find this book very reassuring. It is more meditative in style—quite different from the self-help outline of the previous materials. Excellent.

Building Your Mate's Self-Esteem by Dennis Rainey

A good book again for both husband and wife to read and on which to work. Projects are good, and both of you will receive a boost from each other.

ASSIGNMENTS TO BUILD INTIMACY

Talking/Self-disclosure. One night a week for four straight weeks one of you talks about yourself for a full half hour. Each of you chooses different nights to talk. The word *you* cannot be used—you must talk about yourself. No questions can be asked, and no comments can be made until the end of the half hour. Once a partner has finished the thirty-minute presentation, separate and go your various ways. It works best if you plan what you want to say or at least have a central theme as you begin to teach your partner about yourself.

Couples' Brain Map. This is the title of a self-contained exploration guide built around the recent research on left brain/right brain hemispheres. It is available from Interpersonal Communications Programs, Inc., 7201 South Broadway, Suite 6, Littleton, Colorado 80122 (303-794-1764). Lots of fun and very helpful. The guided exploration is excellent. If you will do the work that is suggested, this is worth the time and effort.

Meyer/Briggs Short Form. This is the name of an evaluation available from any counseling organization. It is a self-scoring, guided exploration about each others' basic personalities. Should the actual test be unavailable, a somewhat altered version is given in the book *Please Understand Me*, by Keirsey and Bates. This book is excellent in getting in touch with your own personality as well as the personality of your spouse. This group operates on the assumption that personality comes with birth. This particular assessment is the most widely used personality inventory in the world.

Understand How Others Misunderstand You (book and workbook; both Chicago: Moody, 1990). This book and workbook discuss personality styles and how an understanding of personality styles gives a person a handle on getting along with other people. The workbook contains a copy of the Performax assessment instrument, including extra assessment pages so that a couple can participate in the exercise together.

PRAYER

The following prayer assignments are done in a graded fashion. You should start with the least difficult first. Work on that assignment until you become comfortable with it, and then move on to the next step. A couples' prayer time can be extremely beneficial to you. Charles Shedd says that sixty days of doing this will revolutionize your marriage. I agree.

Level 1: Personal requests

Each of you fills out a 3 x 5 card with three requests about your person. Then you exchange cards. With that exchange you are committing to your spouse that you will pray for him (her) once a day at the time of your choosing, out loud or in silence, for each of his (her) three requests. The requests must be personal in nature, and the content cannot deal with anything except what is going on inside of you. The requests can also be changed at any time by the partner who has written them on the card; however, only three requests can appear on the card at any given time.

- The first week you pray alone.
- The second week you pray together silently.
- The third week you pray together out loud for each other's requests.

296 Secrets of Your Family Tree

Level 2: Personal praise

For the next three weeks you identify a special compliment that you would like to praise your spouse for to your heavenly Father. Out loud in prayer together, thank God for this special personal characteristic. This is done best at meals. You cannot thank Him for the same trait twice. That means an identification of twenty-one different areas concerning which you are thankful for your spouse. It is extremely reassuring to hear your partner tell God how grateful he is to have you in his life. It is a very special time. You will find yourself beginning to look forward to what you are going to find out next about you. The theme here is "bring out the best, build up the rest."

Level 3: Personal change request

For three weeks, ask your partner at the beginning of the week to answer this question, "If there were one thing that you could change about me, what would it be?" For the rest of that week, you pray out loud in front of your partner that God will help you bring about this change in your life. This is very intense, but at this point in time you've already been praying daily for each other for several weeks. You're ready for it. Take the risk.

Need I remind you? Human nature is fragile, and either of you can sabotage the best effort done by the other. The Bible reminds us to be tenderhearted, kind, and forgiving of each other.

Cut each other a little slack. You won't believe how much you'll grow in your feelings of love for each other and how much you'll begin to grow individually.

Appendix C

*The Twelve Steps of Alcoholics Anonymous**

1. We admitted we were powerless over our dependencies—that our lives had become unmanageable.

2. Came to believe that a Power greater than ourselves could restore us to sanity.

3. Made a decision to turn our will and our lives over to the care of God *as we understood Him.*

4. Made a searching and fearless moral inventory of ourselves.

5. Admitted to God, to ourselves, and to another human being the exact nature of our wrongs.

6. Were entirely ready to have God remove all these defects of character.

7. Humbly asked Him to remove our shortcomings.

* The Twelve Steps are reprinted with permission of Alcoholics Anonymous World Services, Incorporated. Permission to reprint and adapt the Twelve Steps does not mean that A.A. has reviewed or approved the contents of any publication that reprints the Twelve Steps, nor that A.A. agrees with the views expressed therein. A.A. is a program of recovery from alcoholism. Use of the Twelve Steps in connection with programs which are patterned after A.A. but which address other problems does not imply otherwise.

8. Made a list of all persons we had harmed, and became willing to make amends to them all.

9. Made direct amends to such people wherever possible, except when to do so would injure them or others.

10. Continued to take personal inventory and when we were wrong promptly admitted it.

11. Sought through prayer and meditation to improve our conscious contact with God *as we understood Him,* praying only for knowledge of His will for us and the power to carry that out.

12. Having had a spiritual awakening as the result of these steps, we tried to carry this message to alcoholics, and to practice these principles in all our affairs.